Customize and burn music, video, and data CDs

CD RECORDABLE
SOLUTIONS

Martin C. Brown

CD Recordable Solutions

Credits: Martin Sterpka, Copy Editor; Michelle Frey, Cathie Tibbetts, and John Windhorst, DOV Grapics; Molly Flynn, Editorial Services Manager; and Rima S. Regas, Technical Editor.

Library of Congress Catalog Number: 00-106700
ISBN: 1-929685-11-4

5   4   3   2   1

Educational facilities, companies, and organizations interested in multiple copies or licensing of this book should contact the publisher for quantity discount information. Training manuals, CD-ROMs, and portions of this book are also available individually or can be tailored for specific needs.

MUSKA&LIPMAN

Muska & Lipman Publishing
2645 Erie Avenue, Suite 41
Cincinnati, Ohio 45208
www.muskalipman.com
publisher@muskalipman.com

This book is composed in Melior, Columbia, Helvetica, and Courier typefaces using QuarkXpress 4.1, Adobe PhotoShop 5.0.2, and Adobe Illustrator 8.0. Created in Cincinnati, Ohio, in the United States of America.

Foreword

The compact disc has revolutionized two entire industries in less than two decades: consumer electronics and computing. When was the last time you bought software on floppy disk? Or music on vinyl or tape?

But for too long, the two fields remained distinct, with one set of CDs (CD-ROMs) for computer users, and another for audio CD players. With the advent of consumer-friendly recording software like Roxio's Easy CD Creator, plus built-in operating system support for CD recording, the promise of computer/consumer electronics convergence is finally being fulfilled.

Today you can create top-quality audio CD mixes in minutes on your computer, just by dragging and dropping. You can even create VideoCDs from your home movies that can be played back on most DVD players. The popularity of digital cameras and camcorders is further facilitating convergence by making it simple to get family photos and video into your computer—no scanning necessary.

And CD recording makes it possible to store the resulting mountains of digital data quickly, easily, and safely. That's what this book is all about. We at Roxio are pleased to see such a comprehensive guide to recording all types of discs, from simple audio CDs to CD-ROMs/RWs, and even DVDs.

You'll learn all about the different disc formats, and which to choose for different purposes, as well as what media to buy. There are even some cool tips and tricks, such as using Roxio's Spin Doctor to clean up your audio files prior to burning. Martin even covers all three major platforms, Windows, Mac, and Linux; making it easy for a Windows user to create a disc that a Mac user can read, and vice versa.

Read on for the inside scoop on CD recording, as well as tips on using Roxio's Easy CD Creator and Toast software, long the standard-setters for both Windows and Mac CD burning. This book and Roxio software make an unbeatable combination. Start enjoying the capabilities of your CD recorder today!

The software that came with your computer or with your CD-Recorder is a "lite" version. Visit www.roxio.com to upgrade your CD-burning software today, and take advantage of the power that Easy CD Creator 5 Platinum or Toast 5 Titanium gives you.

Chris Gorog
CEO/President, Roxio

About the Author

Martin C. Brown
http://www.mcwords.com

Martin C. Brown has been a Mac manager for eleven years for a variety of organizations, including a university, an ISP, and an advertising agency. He specializes in making computers easier to use and more accessible to people who are not computer literate and in integrating different machines into the same environment. A full-time author, he spends most of his time writing programming books, despite spending the bulk of his life trying to avoid getting sucked too far into the programming world. Martin is the author of eleven other books, including *iMac FYI, Perl: The Complete Reference and Debugging Perl*. You can contact him by email at mc@mcwords.com, or through the MCwords Web site.

Dedication

To my wife, who always lets me buy the latest toys.

Acknowledgments

At Muska & Lipman Publishing, I need to thank Allen Wyatt, my development editor; Andy Shafran, the publisher, and Molly Flynn, all of whom helped me develop the book and turn it from a bunch of manuscripts into a printed work.

Secondly, thanks to Neil Salkind, my agent, for thinking of me when the opportunity came up, and to Kristen Pickens and Stacey Barone, for keeping me in check, and David and Sherry Rogelberg for providing guidance.

I also need to thank technical editor Rima S. Regas, who very kindly kept an eye on all of us when it came to covering the technical details and for spotting those points where I wasn't quite as clear to all and gentry as I could have been.

Finally, a huge thanks to all those people on Cix in the Mac conference who kindly gave me pointers, questions, material, and suggestions for content. Special thanks go to Mike Felton, who very kindly supplied me with a screenshot for one of the chapters when I couldn't get my machine to play ball.

Contents

10—Diagnostic, Installer, and Autolaunch CDs 149

Section III Writing CDs for Business

11—Troubleshooting. 163

12—Verification and Testing 175

13—Mass Duplication 187

Section IV CD Writing Software

14—Using Toast (Mac OS) 195

15—Using Easy CD Creator (Windows). 207

Introduction

We tend to take CDs for granted these days. Twenty years ago, owning a CD player and going to the local store to pick up a CD was something special—and expensive. Now, it's run of the mill and we're used to buying music CDs at the local supermarket and putting the latest software and games onto our computers using the same silvery discs. We've also started to watch movies from a similarly sized disc called DVD.

Getting hold of all this software (music, computer programs, and movies) for your equipment is easy, but what do you do if you want to write your own CDs with your own music selections, copies of your family photos, and the latest holiday movie?

You can do all of that with CD-R technology and this book. It doesn't matter whether you are a home user who wants to make music compilations and exchange files using CD or a business creating CDs ready for professional duplication, you should find everything you need to know. From choosing the right drive to recording audio for transfer to CD we take you through every step of the process.

How This Book is Organized

The book is split into four distinct sections:

▶ **Section 1—"CD-R Fundamentals"** looks at the basics of CD-R, including how the technology works, the different formats we can use to store information, and details on how to choose and make the best use of your CD-R hardware.

▶ **Section 2—"Writing CDs"** covers the specifics of the CD writing process. In addition to instructions for creating data CDs for storing standard files, I also look at music CDs, using CD-R for backups and archiving, and also the best methods for laying out and organizing the information you put on CD to make it accessible.

▶ **Section 3—"Writing CDs for Business"** details the issues surrounding the use of CDs in a business, looking at the basics of verification and testing and mass duplication.

▶ **Section 4—"CD Writing Software"** describes the different software packages you can use to write CDs, create videos, back up your machine—all using the CD-R medium. Once it's written, we even show you how to create suitable labels!

Throughout the book, special attention is given to providing and supporting cross-platform solutions, and the book covers the CD writing process under Windows, Mac OS, and Unix/Linux.

Conventions Used in This Book

The following conventions are used in this book:

All URLs mentioned in the book appear in **boldface**.

All Linux/Unix commands will appear in boldface, as in **cdrecord**.

The book also features the following special displays for different types of important text:

> **TIP**
> Text formatted like this will provide a helpful tip relevant to the topic being discussed in the main text.

> **NOTE**
> Notes highlight other information that is interesting or useful and that relates to the topic under discussion in the main text.

Keeping the Book's Content Current

For updates, corrections, and other information related to the content of the book, go to Muska & Lipman's Web site at **www.muskalipman.com/cdrecordable**.

Section I
CD-R Fundamentals

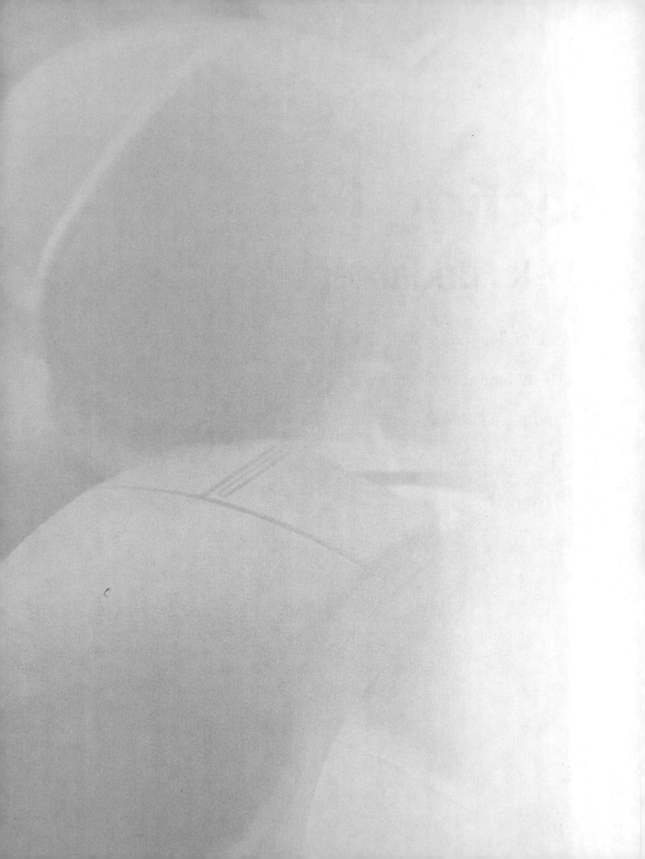

1

An Introduction to CD-R

We take them for granted now, but compact discs (CDs) are actually a relatively old technology. Developed in the 1980s by Philips, they were designed to solve a few of the problems inherent in the then-current range of recording technology. Vinyl—used for LPs (long playing records) and singles—was a destructive technology. Each time you placed that needle into the vinyl, you were wearing away the very information you were trying to read.

Magnetic tape and disk also had their problems. Place the medium near a magnetic source, such as a speaker or television, and the information was likely to be corrupted or even wiped out completely. Magnetic disks and tapes also, over time, wore out, for the same reason as vinyl—the tape or disk had to be dragged over a head that could read or write the information. Although it would probably take hundreds, if not thousands, of hours of usage for this to occur, it made tape impractical for long-term storage.

Then along came CD.

A CD is read using a laser—there's no physical contact, therefore no chance of the disc wearing out. Furthermore, you can place a CD almost anywhere without risk of the information being corrupted or lost. The protective plastic coating over the actual recording medium—an embedded metal foil—means that you can *just about* throw a CD around the room and use it as a coaster without risking too much damage. Because of the use of error correction, you can even scratch a CD without it affecting playback, but there are no guarantees. I don't condone trying any of these actions, but they all demonstrate the reliability of the CD format.

Perhaps the biggest advantage of the CD, especially from the point of view of prerecorded suppliers of information such as software companies and music publishers, is that it can't be recorded over. Gone are the days when you could accidentally overwrite your favorite tape or accidentally reformat the disk containing all of your accounts data. Another major benefit for software producers was that instead of having to supply twenty floppy disks to handle all their software, they could supply just one CD-ROM.

Then along came the recordable CD.

What is CD Recording?

CD-R, or CD recordable, is a relatively recent invention. It means that instead of being limited to buying only prerecorded CDs, you can now record your own CDs using CD-R and CD-RW media. Traditional CDs are produced by creating a "master"—a physical template that is used to "stamp" the information into the metal foil and plastic that make up the CD. With CD recordable, you use a special type of compact disc and a special CD writer to write information to the disc.

CD-RW is yet another advance. With CD-R, you can write the information to the disc only once, but with CD-RW you can rewrite (hence the acronym) information to the disc. When placed into a standard CD-ROM drive, the CD-RW acts just like a CD, so the data can't be corrupted. It's supported for only a limited number of write operations, usually 100 or 1,000, but it means that you have all of the flexibility of CD media with all of the practicality of other removable storage formats such as Jaz, Zip and Magneto-Optical.

CD recording is the act of writing information to a CD-R or CD-RW disc, and it's this process that we'll be covering in this book.

What Can You Create on a CD?

The compact disc is a bit like paper—it's just a method for storing information. What's important with CD, just as with paper, is what you put on it. A piece of paper can hold a simple drawing, a letter, or a prize-winning painting. A CD can hold lots of letters, books, computer software, and audio and video data. Just like a piece of paper, a CD can also hold a combination of these things, so you can have an interactive encyclopedia that includes the software, text, and audio and video clips designed to demonstrate and explain different entries.

The CD is a digital medium, but since most forms of data can be easily converted into a digital format, we can store just about anything on a CD. This includes, but is not exclusive to, audio (what most people think of as CDs), video (using the Video CD format, a precursor to DVD), and computer data (better known as CD-ROM, compact disc read only memory).

Regardless of the format of the information on the CD, the way in which it is recorded and how it can be recorded remains constant. A standard CD records approximately 650 MB of information, although the total storage is governed by what you store on the CD and how you write the CD. However, as a rough guide:

1. For computer data, it's a direct relationship to the amount of storage space on a CD. A typical hard disk is measured in GB, which is equivalent to 1,024 MB. To put the storage capability into perspective, though, 650 MB is enough for hundreds of thousands of pages of information, 100 high-quality scanned images or up to 3,000 low-quality images.

2. For audio CDs that you use in your stereo system, personal CD player, or car, you can record seventy-four minutes of stereo music. That's about the same length as an album, and the same effective length of prerecorded tapes and vinyl once you take both sides into account. You can also record audio information in different formats (MP3, for example) and then store hours of audio on a single CD.

3. For video, the limits are not quite so clearly defined, as it depends on the size, quality, and content of the video as to how much you can store on a Video CD.

Later, we'll go into more detail about how you can store different types of information on CDs.

What Can You Do with a CD-R?

You probably think that CDs are, as a rule, pretty boring—you put audio CDs into your stereo system and CD-ROMs into your computer to install new software. With CD-Rs, you might be equally confused that all you can do is store computer data. In fact, you couldn't be more wrong. Providing you have some imagination, you can place anything you like onto a CD, and in any format.

Here are some examples of what you can do with CD-Rs:

▶ **Create your own music compilations**—Imagine recording the favorite tracks from some of your albums all on one CD for your car or home.

▶ **Put hours of music onto a single CD for playing on your computer**—Imagine having one CD with a whole day's worth of music on it.

▶ **Offload data**—CDs are a great way of storing old data in an accessible format. You could put onto a CD copies of all of those letters you wrote ten years ago but never used, freeing up space on your machine.

▶ **Back up your machine**—Using tape can be a pain if you urgently need information that you just deleted. If it had been written to CD, you could have retrieved it in seconds.

▶ **Create "info" discs**—We live in an information world, so wouldn't it be great if you could place loads of information onto a CD that you could put into your machine each time you wanted to look something up? Your own personal encyclopedia!

▶ **Create a digital library**—You can now download books from the Internet, and there are plenty of titles to choose from. You could put the entire Bible, dictionaries and other reference works, even *Alice in Wonderland* and novels from modern authors like Stephen King, all on a CD that you could read and use any time. You'd never run out of material to read again!

▶ **Organize all your photo albums**—If you scanned all your photos into your computer with a scanner, you could write the images to a CD and then use a piece of software to catalog them. Then, next time somebody asks to see your wedding photos, you don't have to dig around in the cupboard looking for the box. Just take the CD from the shelf and start viewing!

▶ **Create safe video archives**—Imagine putting your wedding, christening, or office party video onto a CD. You'd never run the risk of accidentally taping *The Simpsons* over it!

▶ **Create software installation sets**—You've probably got hundreds of installers that you've collected from other CDs, the Internet, and even old floppies. Why not put them all onto CD, so the next time you need them, they are instantly at hand, and all in one place.

▶ **Create recovery discs**—There's nothing worse than having a problem on your machine, and no way of recovering because you can't fix the "active" disc. But you create a bootable CD that includes not only a core operating system, but also the diagnostic tools and virus checkers you'd want to have available. Then, when something goes wrong, boot from the CD and you've got everything you need to get your machine working again.

This is just the tip of the iceberg!

Why Use a CD?

Probably the biggest advantage of CD over other removable storage formats is the safety. CDs (and CD-R/RWs) are very difficult to damage. Minor scratches normally don't affect the surface or the ability to read the information again from the CD, which makes them less prone to minor aberrations than most types of disk media. CDs are also unaffected by magnetic fields, something that can corrupt information stored on magnetic media such as Jaz, Zip, floppy, and even tape.

However, that's not to say that CDs are indestructible. Handle a CD incorrectly and it's easy to get oil and finger smudges on the disc that affect the laser's ability to read information from the disc. Furthermore, oil and finger prints are difficult to remove from the disc. Throw a CD around like you would with a tape and it's likely to get scratched or shattered. CDs are also prone to certain types of handling—you can't sit on one for example, and carrying one around in a pocket without some sort of case or cover is just asking for trouble. The real benefits of CDs' impervious properties are more to do with the way the information is stored on the disc itself.

It is very difficult to corrupt the information that has been written to CD, CD-R, and CD-RW media. If you record information on a CD-R, it cannot be deleted or destroyed without physically destroying the CD. Even with CD-RW, you need special software to be able to make changes. With a Jaz or other rewritable media, it's as easy to overwrite and delete information as it is with the data on your hard disk. Because of this reliability factor, CD-R and CD-RW media are great when you want to write information that you don't want easily deleted. For example, archives, backups, and software installers are a few examples of information where you would want to be able to guarantee the reliability.

There's also one final point—at 650 MB, you can store a lot of information on a single CD. Putting hundreds of images and hours of audio onto a CD is not out of the question. Better still, CDs are supported nearly everywhere, on most computers, and for audio, on most stereo systems.

Copyright and Ownership

So far, we've talked about saving material you have created yourself or own because you purchased it somewhere. However, whatever your feelings about copyright and ownership may be, the law is a touch more specific and you'll end up in hot water unless you pay attention to what you are copying and distributing. There are laws in all countries governing what you can and can't copy, what you can distribute (whether you charge for it or otherwise), and restrictions on how you use different files, media, and data on the CD-ROMs that you create.

Here's a brief but important look at the issues surrounding copyright, both of material that you want to use on your CDs and your own material that you want to distribute. This material is offered for informational purposes only and is not intended as, nor is a substitute for, competent legal advice. I'm not a lawyer, so if you are unclear as to the exact rules surrounding the ownership and copyright of information, then talk to a lawyer *before* you put the information on the CD.

What Can You Copy?

The simple answer to this question is nothing, unless you create all of it yourself. Most works of authorship (including software programs) are copyrighted by somebody. Although certain works may be "in the public domain," it can be difficult to discern which works those are. All of that said, there are some rules which you can live by that should help you to avoid any problems:

- ▶ **Copyright rules *always* apply.** It doesn't matter how you obtained the file or work that you intend to put on your CD—whether it was downloaded or originally supplied on CD. Unless the copyright has expired or the use you plan to make falls within one of a couple of exceptions to the copyright owner's exclusive rights, you'll still need permission from the copyright owner before you use it.

- ▶ **Copyright rules apply even if the work does not carry a copyright notice.** Copyrights vest automatically in the author of a copyrightable work. Just because the work or file that you want to copy does not have a copyright notice doesn't mean that it is unprotected. Nor is it necessary for a work to be registered with the U.S. Copyright Office as a precondition to copyright protection. Copyright is automatically granted to the work's creator when the work is produced, and copies of the work do not have to be marked with an explicit copyright statement for the copyright to be in force.

- ▶ **Shareware does not mean "no copyright."** Files and information distributed as shareware are not devoid of a copyright—instead, they are usually distributed along with a license that gives you the right to redistribute the work providing you keep to a few conditions. For shareware software, it'll probably declare that you can distribute the files providing you don't charge for the distribution more than the operating costs (media, postage, etc.). For images and text, you will probably be given a right to use the item, but won't be allowed to charge for the item on an individual basis, although it can be included in another work, such as the clip art you use in a document.

- ▶ **Copyright applies on the original work in whatever form.** One of the rights that belongs exclusively to the copyright owner is the right to prepare adaptations or derivative works. Modifying, morphing, or translating a work or image does not convert your unauthorized copy into a new original and, therefore, will not insulate you from an infringement claim.

▶ **People who are the subjects of image/audio files have rights.** If you have taken a photo of someone, or recorded their voice in an audio file, you may need permission to use their image or voice. There are some exceptions to this rule—for example, people who are incidental to the shot of a public street scene probably do not have a reasonable expectation of privacy on the public streets and they would probably not be able to successfully object to an editorial use of that image. However, a "model" shot intended for advertising or commercial use, including that of a family member, will require permission.

▶ **Copyright applies to individual items.** If you want to include a selection of photos on your CD, you must get permission to include each item. Being granted permission for one file does not automatically give you the right to copy or distribute other works in the series or any other item copyrighted by the same author.

Keep to these basic rules and you should be okay. Because these are a little over-restrictive for some of the common uses of CDs and other removable media, there are a few exceptions.

Backups

The first exception relates to backups. Although computer software is copyrighted, most software licenses allow you to make a copy of the software onto CD (or other media), providing the copy is for personal backup use. The only rider to this particular exclusion is that you cannot then distribute the backup that you have made, as that would break the copyright law.

This exclusion means that you can back up your files to CD without violating copyright law. It also means that you can make a duplicate copy of a software CD for backup purposes. But both items should remain in your possession at all times. Keeping an OSB (off site backup) at your friend's house won't protect you, but keeping one copy with a storage company or safe-deposit box is allowed.

Audio CDs and "Personal" Use

Audio permissions are a bit of a gray area at the moment with the explosion of downloadable material and the proliferation of technology like personal CD-R recorders and MiniDiscs (MD). It is probably legal, as a "fair use," to make a copy onto tape, MD, or CD of any music for which you already own a legitimate copy. For example, if you want to make your own compilation albums based on the tracks from a number of other albums you own, it's allowed. But taking a copy of a friend's album for your own listening pleasure is against the rules.

In the case of tape and MD, prices are artificially kept high because a small portion of the funds goes to the record companies, and they therefore reclaim some of the money lost from an original item sale. With CD-R, you can use the special CD-DA (compact disc digital audio) media for recording audio compilations. Although this is identical physically to the CD-R media you would use for computer data, the price is also higher to give the record company some royalties. Legally you are under no obligation to use the special media—the introduction of the CD-DA media is more to protect the media companies than you—and normal CD-R media will work just as well, and for a lower cost. Be aware that some software will actually refuse to write audio files to anything other than CD-DA media.

Getting Permission

If you don't own the copyright on a piece of material because you are not the creator, or if the work is not in the public domain, is not shareware, or if your use does not qualify as "fair use," you must obtain permission from the creator before redistributing the files on your CD. If you need to get permission, keep the following in mind:

▶ **Always get permission in writing.** Don't rely on a face-to-face meeting, gentleman's agreement, or phone call to memorialize your agreement—if your use is later challenged, you would have nothing to prove that permission was ever granted.

▶ **Always get a signature or proof of the creator's authority.** If you are writing and expecting a letter, then make sure it's been signed. If you decide to get permission by e-mail (which is allowed), make sure that the e-mail address of the author can be verified and traced back to him or her in case of litigation.

▶ **Always *ask* nicely *before* you copy the files to the CD.** Don't do it afterwards, even if you are certain permission will be granted.

▶ **Always describe in detail what it is that you want permission for.** If it's an image, give the image reference number; if no number is available, describe the picture adequately enough for it to be identified. If it's software that you want to put on the CD, quote the version number that you want to include and get permission for each version; don't assume that permission for the first gives you rights to all subsequent versions.

Remember at all times that you are trying to protect *yourself* from litigation by the copyright owner, which could ultimately cost you a substantial sum of money, whether or not you have made money by including their material.

Asking nicely before the event will probably get you permission; asking afterwards or, worse, demanding permission will probably get you nowhere!

Certifying Your Ownership

If the work is your own, you may want to include a copyright notice on each copy you make available for distribution, and you may want to register your claim of copyright with the U.S. Copyright Office. The first costs you nothing other than the space the notice consumes, and the second is a relative bargain. Although copyright is automatically granted to you when the work is created, taking these steps will provide you with certain advantages in the event you are forced to enforce your copyrights. Oh, and remember that other people may want permission to include your work!

Copyrighting a Text-based Document

If you want to add copyright to a document, including a word processor file or spreadsheet, open the file in the correct application and then add...

> Copyright © [year] by [name], All Rights Reserved.

...at a conspicuous location in the document. The **[year]** should be the year in which the work was completed, and **[name]** should be your name, or the name under which you want the work copyrighted. Choosing the right **[name]** is important—in the U.S., most work created by an employee on company time belongs to the company as work-made-for-hire.

If it's an important piece of work on a word processing document, consider adding the copyright statement to the footer of each page. For most other documents, one notice in a conspicuous location will probably suffice.

When you are distributing source files as part of the source for an application, make sure that each file has its own copyright statement. Also, be certain that the software itself is able to generate the same copyright statement on request, so that both the source and compiled versions of the software retain the correct copyright information.

Copyrighting a Visual Document (Photo/Video)

If you are copyrighting a photo or video, you will need to embed the copyright notice into the image somewhere. There are a couple of ways of doing this, but the most obvious is to simply place the copyright text over the picture itself, as shown in Figure 1.1.

Figure 1.1
An image showing its
copyright statement.

Copyright © 1999 by Martin C Brown, All Rights Reserved

This solution obviously presents a problem if you want to distribute a file that others may want to use in its entirety, without your copyright notice. Here, the obvious solution is to add a border to the document on one side that contains the copyright statement—now, the image holds the copyright, without it actually affecting the image.

If you are distributing JPEGs or GIFs, you can also add a copyright statement to the comments section of the image—this won't show up in the image in any way, but because it's embedded in the image file, the file will always retain copyright.

2

CD–A Technical Overview

Before we look at how to produce, write, and use CD-R and CD-RW media, it's worth taking a little time to go over the basics of the format from a physical perspective. There are lots of different attributes that affect how you use and write CDs, from the physical characteristics of the media you are using to the drive type you use and how it connects to your machine. Getting the right combination will ensure that the CDs you do write are error-free and you don't end up making a lot of pretty "CD coasters" in the process!

In this chapter, we'll concentrate on the different CD formats that are available and how they work. By understanding this basic process, you can begin to make decisions about the sort of CD-R device you want and what you want to use it for.

What Is a CD?

The CD was jointly introduced by Sony and Philips around 1980, and was revolutionary at the time. It provided a significant increase in audio quality, plus some other neat tricks over vinyl and tape—such as direct track access and near-instant track access. It was also seen as an ideal format for the average consumer when distributing music and, later, software. Unlike vinyl, tape, and disks, a CD is virtually impossible to corrupt or ruin at a data level, because it is a read-only format and is read without physically touching the disc. With vinyl, playing the record once degrades the quality of the audio, and with magnetic media, placing it next to a strong magnetic source such as a TV or monitor can ruin the contents.

The CD itself is 12 centimeters (4.7 inches) in diameter and about 1 millimeter (one twenty-fourth of an inch) thick. The CD is made of a polycarbonate plastic which helps to protect the layer embedded in the plastic where the information is actually stored. The CDs on which you buy software (CD-ROMs) and music (audio CDs) use an embedded aluminum film layer—you can get a better idea of the physical layout from Figure 2.1. Some, but not all, CDs also have a labeled side. The label is either screen-printed onto the surface of the polycarbonate or onto a paper layer that is bonded to the plastic. CD-R, CD-RW, and DVD formats have a slightly different layout, which we'll look at shortly.

Figure 2.1
Structure of a CD.

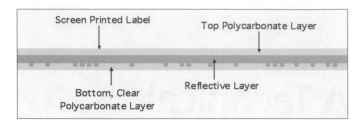

How Information is Stored

To understand how a CD stores information, it's best to think of it in terms of a type of media that you're already familiar with, so we'll choose the audio CD. With a vinyl record (ask your parents if you don't know what one is!) the sound is "read" from a physical groove in a piece of plastic by a metal or diamond needle. The vibrations caused by the groove on the needle are amplified in order to produce the audio that you hear when you play the record. On an audiotape, the sound is recorded by using a variable magnetic signal—the strength of the signal represents the audio and, like the vinyl record, is then amplified in order to produce the music that you hear when you play the tape.

Both of these formats are classified as "analog"—this means that the sounds are defined by a continuously variable signal level—this is represented by the physical groove on vinyl or the magnetic signature on a normal cassette tape. With analog there are no upper or lower limits and there is no fixed limit to the number of the levels within a given range. Think of analog in the same way as you think of an analog clock—the hands on an analog clock can be at any position on the dial. Between 2 p.m. and 3 p.m., for example, the hour hand could be anywhere between those two numbers, but it's impossible to measure it precisely. I could use a ruler, a micrometer, or even a scanning electron microscope and get slightly different measurements in each case, and a millionth of a second later the measurement will have changed!

Digital information, just like your digital watch, is more explicit and specific, but not necessarily as precise. All digital information is recorded using binary numbers. Binary numbers are made up from a series of 0s and 1s. A binary digit can be represented by two states, just like a switch that is either on or off. When the switch is off, you get a 0; when the switch is on, you get a 1. On their own, binary digits don't mean much, but a string of binary digits can be used to represent a number. If you look at Figure 2.2, you'll see what I mean.

Figure 2.2
Binary numbers.

128	64	32	16	8	4	2	1	
0	0	0	0	0	0	0	1	= 1
0	0	0	0	0	0	1	0	= 2
0	0	0	0	1	0	0	1	= 8+1=9
0	1	0	1	0	0	0	1	= 64+16+1=81

In the last example, the string 01010001 is equal to 81, because 64, 16, and 1 added together make 81.

All CDs store the information digitally, using the same strings of 0s and 1s to make up the information on the CD. When an audio CD is produced, the original music will have been "sampled," a process which measures the level (volume) and frequency of the sound. It's this combination of level and frequency values that is used to represent the sound on your CD. This is the main difference between vinyl, tape, and audio CD. Instead of converting the analog sounds into a physical representation (groove or magnetism), with an audio CD the level and frequency values of a sound source are converted into a stream of binary digits, and these then translate into physical pits in the aluminum layer in the disc, as shown in Figure 2.3.

Figure 2.3
Data storage on a CD.

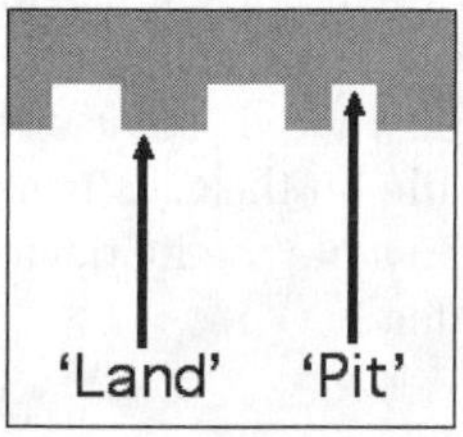

Because the binary system has only two values, 0 or 1, we can store them by recording the difference between two values. On a CD, it's the difference between the surface of a disc and the pits. So, now we have a binary stream, and a method for storing that string of 0s and 1s physically on a disc. To read the information, all we need to do is read the pits to get back our binary data.

A CD is actually made up of a big spiral track, similar to that on a vinyl record, although there is no physical groove. The information is read from the track using a laser—where there is a raised area, called "land," the laser light is reflected back and indicates a 1. Where there is a pit, the light is scattered and therefore not reflected back to the sensor, resulting in a 0. You can see this graphically in Figure 2.4.

Figure 2.4
Reading pits on a CD.

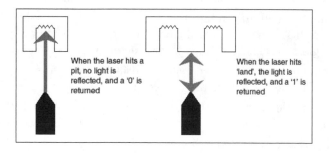

When the laser hits a pit, no light is reflected, and a '0' is returned

When the laser hits 'land', the light is reflected, and a '1' is returned

When you put a CD into a CD drive, the disc spins and a head reads the pits recorded onto the disc. The head can move in only plane—from the inside of the disc to the outside (and back). The head doesn't actually move along the CD or follow the tracks—it just reads the track information as it passes under the head. The track and pits on a CD are very small, so the head has to move only a very small distance to read each track, but it will move that distance many times each second. The track is separated by just 1.6 µm (1 µm = one millionth of a meter, or one thousandth of a millimeter) and the pits are separated by 0.83 µm. The entire track on a seventy-four minute CD is more than three miles long! In the case of our audio CD, the binary stream is converted back into the numbers representing frequencies and volumes. Built into your CD player is a digital-to-analog (DAC) converter, which translates these numbers back into the analog signals required to drive the speakers on your stereo system—that's how you hear the sound. There is other information stored on the disc along with the individual tracks. A catalog details the track number, its length, and its physical location on the CD, so that when a CD player first loads the disc, it knows where to start reading the track from, and how to move between the individual tracks.

When reading a CD-ROM in your computer, no digital-to-analog conversion needs to take place. This is because computers work entirely by using binary numbers—all we need to do is read the information from the file. Just like the audio CD, though, there is some additional information on the CD that tells the computer the location of each file on the CD, its name, size, and other attributes, just as on a floppy disk, hard drive, or a removable media device like Jaz or Zip. We'll be looking in more detail at recording formats in Chapter 3.

Mass Producing CDs

The production process for a CD-ROM or audio CD is relatively simple and completely different from the processes we'll see for CD-R and CD-RW media later in this chapter. Because the data is stored using a series of physical pits in the aluminum surface embedded in the disc, it can actually be "pressed" using a mold, in much the same way as the vinyl system it replaced.

What actually happens is:

1. A glass "master" is made by using a laser to etch the pits into a photo-resistive layer on a piece of glass.

2. The master disc is used to create a metal "stamp"—this is a negative impression of the final disc, just like the negative used in camera film. The stamp is used to physically stamp an impression of the CD into the plastic.

3. The stamp is fitted into an injection press, where molten polycarbonate is introduced to the mold. The resulting plastic disc has a physical layout of pits identical to the original glass master. This pitted layer is actually the "top" of the final disc.

4. A layer of aluminum is placed over the disc—this will form the reflective surface of the final CD and the film actually molds to the pitted surface of the polycarbonate.

5. A layer of polycarbonate is placed over the aluminum—this is the clear layer that is on the bottom of the disc, through which the pits will be read by the laser.

6. The label is screen printed or bonded to the top layer.

The process takes seconds, and a typical press will use multiple stamps to allow a number of CDs to be produced simultaneously. The cost of producing CDs in this way is relatively inexpensive from a raw material perspective, as the individual CDs cost less than ten cents. However, it may cost thousands of dollars to have a glass master etched, and a few hundred dollars for each stamp produced from that master. The whole process is designed to mass-produce thousands of copies of a single disc, a somewhat different approach to what's required when writing a CD at home or in the office, when we probably want only one or two copies of the same information written to a CD.

Note that throughout the actual CD-making process we are dealing with a physical representation of the information. It's the polycarbonate that is molded to form the pits of the disc. This is an important point to remember, because CD-R and CD-RW discs work slightly differently.

What is CD-R?

A CD-R is identical in size to a CD, and its basic construction, that of a 12-centimeter diameter plastic disc, is also the same. However, unlike a CD, which is read-only, a CD-R starts off "blank," but you can write information to it using a special CD-R drive. It can be written to only once, though—it's a type of WORM (write once, read many) storage—due to the properties of the CD-R media. It is this single fact that makes CD-R ideal for archiving information; you can write the data to the disc and not worry about accidentally overwriting the information at a later date.

The CD-R format uses the same basic principles as a mass-produced CD— a combination of reflective and nonreflective areas on the disc to store information. With a mass-produced CD, it's the physical pits that have been stamped into the plastic that make up the information stored on the disc. With a CD-R, we need to use a different system to actually write information to the disc. We can't, in the safety of our own homes, produce a glass master, create a metal stamp, or have an injection mold system to produce the CDs, so we need a different method of writing the pits onto the disc.

The solution is in the makeup of the CD-R medium itself. We already know that a commercial CD is made up of two plastic layers sandwiched with an aluminum reflective layer. With a CD-R, there are four layers, as you can see in Figure 2.5.

Figure 2.5
Makeup of a CD-R disc.

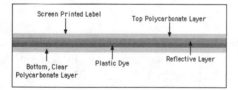

The top and bottom layers are made of plastic, just like a commercial CD, and sandwiched between them is a reflective gold, aluminum, or other metal layer used to reflect the laser light. In addition to these layers, between the reflective layer and the bottom plastic coating is a layer of plastic dye. In a CD-R, there are no pits in the plastic or reflective layers. In fact, there are no physical artifacts to the disc at all—it's actually the dye that helps us store information.

Writing Data to a CD-R

The dye is naturally opaque, which means that when a laser reads the disc, the light can't penetrate the dye, and therefore the light is not reflected back by the metal layer, so the disc returns a 0. To write a 1 to the disc, a different type of laser burns the dye, permanently altering its characteristics so that it is now transparent. Now, when a laser reads the disc, the light travels through the dye, hits the reflective layer, and is therefore identified as a 1. See Figure 2.6 and Figure 2.7 for some examples.

Figure 2.6
A "0" on a CD-R.

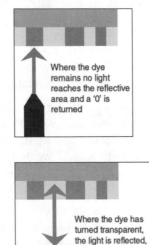

Where the dye remains no light reaches the reflective area and a '0' is returned

Figure 2.7
A "1" on a CD-R.

Where the dye has turned transparent, the light is reflected, and a '1' is returned

Although we're dealing with a different physical system, the CD-R works identically to a CD—instead of pits and land, it's the dye that makes the difference between the 0 and 1. The track and pit size is identical, too, which means that we can record information on a CD-R disc, and then read the information back from that disc in a standard CD-ROM drive.

Although it's not important to remember in this instance, a CD-R in essence works in reverse compared to a commercial CD. With a normal CD, the entire surface is effectively 1, as the physical pits represent a 0, because the light is scattered and not reflected right back. With a CD-R, the surface is naturally 0, as it's only when the laser in the CD-R drive burns the dye that a 1 is written, allowing the light to be reflected back.

What is CD-RW?

A CD-RW disc goes one stage further than CD-R. CD-RWs can be written to more than once; in fact, you can modify the information in a CD-RW disc a number of times. In a CD-R, the dye layer can be changed from its opaque to its transparent state only once. A CD-RW disc uses an amorphous crystalline layer that can be changed between its transparent and opaque states by using laser light at different intensities. Because we can change the crystalline layer between these two states, we can also change the reflective properties of the disc at different points, and therefore simulate the pits and land found in a CD.

In all other respects, the CD-RW disc is identical to CD-R and CD. It's made up of four layers: the same three basic layers we already know about—a top and bottom polycarbonate layer, and a layer of reflective metal sandwiched between the two. The crystalline layer, just like the dye in CD-R, is placed between the reflective layer and the bottom transparent layer of the CD. You can see the basic layout in Figure 2.8.

Figure 2.8
A CD-RW disc showing its crystalline layer.

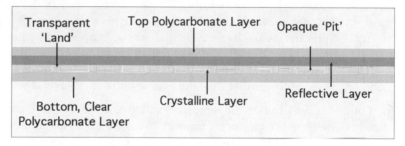

Writing Data to a CD-RW Disc

It's the crystalline layer in the CD-RW disc that is so critical. The crystalline layer is normally transparent, but when the laser hits it, the reaction changes the property of the layer to opaque. Using a different power level, the crystalline layer can also be turned back into its transparent state. Using a combination of the two power levels, the drive can "reset" and then rewrite the new data to the disc.

This "reset" stage is significant because it slows down the speed of writing to a CD-RW disc. With a CD-R, you write the information to the disc in one long controlled burst, and the actual speed at which you can write is constant. With a CD-RW drive, overwriting existing data is a two-stage process—you must first set the layer to its original state before writing the new data. Using CD-RW is always slower than using CD-R because of this process.

When it comes to reading the information, the same basic properties apply as with CD-R—where the crystalline layer is transparent, the light is reflected back and a 1 is registered; where it's opaque, a 0 is returned instead. Again, this means that a CD-RW can be read in any normal CD-ROM drive. This means that you can write data to the disc and then distribute it to others without fear of them modifying the information. But unlike CD-R, you can change the information once you get the disc back—a brilliant way of distributing large volumes of information that change regularly without wasting discs.

What is DVD?

Although I won't cover the use of DVD or its many rewritable forms in this book in much detail, it's worth taking a look at the next generation of technology. The DVD—digital versatile disc—is really just an extension of the original CD format. Like CDs, which were originally developed with audio storage in mind, the DVD format was developed with a specific purpose; this time, it was the storage of video.

A DVD disc is identical in physical size to a CD—12 centimeters—but the laser used to read information from the DVD is much narrower. The narrower laser allows the track and pit density to be increased significantly. You might remember that with a CD, the tracks are 1.6 µm apart, with a pit separation of 0.83 µm. With DVD, the tracks are 0.74 µm apart and the pits are 0.4 µm in size. This increases the basic storage capacity from 650 MB for a CD to 4.4 GB for a DVD. If you were to unwind a DVD track, then it would be about 21 miles long. That's enough for more than two hours of video. We'll look in more detail at DVD-Video standard in a moment.

In addition to increasing the basic density of the recordable layer in the disc, the developers also developed systems that allowed multiple reflective layers to be embedded in a single disc, without significantly increasing its thickness. This is accomplished by inserting an additional reflective layer that is offset slightly to the main layer, so that you can actually "read" the second layer through the gaps in the first. Because you can read only the information between the gaps, the second layer is slightly smaller than the primary, so a dual-layer disc is about 8 GB in size.

As a final improvement, the developers also decided to allow DVDs to be double-sided—which immediately doubles the basic storage capacity to 8.8 GB on a single-layer disc. Although for most purposes a single-sided, single-layered disc is more than adequate, a double-sided and double-layered disc allows you to squeeze almost 16 GB of information onto a disc. That's enough for eight hours of high-quality video. Although there aren't many films that are that long, it does allow some companies to supply two or more features on a single disc.

Discs that are both double-sided and dual-layered are not currently very popular. The first reason is that they are very difficult to produce commercially at a cost that would be acceptable to most consumers. The technology and precision involved in sandwiching four layers together at the correct offset, and without interference, is very complex.

At the moment, the most common formats are either a dual-layer disc or a double-sided, single-layer disc. The dual-layer disc is the format used to store most movies because it allows for the movie, multi-channel audio, and some extras (see the section entitled "DVD-Video" later in this chapter) without requiring to turn over the disc. The double-sided discs are used by companies that want to store multiple features on a single disc—for example, Warner Brothers put eight episodes of the television show *Friends* onto each DVD, four to each side. The reason for this is that currently a double-sided disc must be manually flipped over—with something like *Friends*, flipping the disc over between episodes is not a problem.

If they used a dual-layered, single-sided disc, they wouldn't be able to store both the episodes and the menus and other features required onto the disc. Other companies use the double-sided facility to provide both a 4:3 (normal TV ratio) and 16:9 (or other widescreen format), one to each side. As a general rule, they try to avoid spreading a movie over more than one side, although some early DVDs (*Starship Troopers* for example) used double-sided discs that had to be flipped half way through the film.

You can see a list of the different DVD and CD formats and their raw, audio, and video storage sizes in Table 2.1.

Table 2.1
Capacity of the different DVD, DVD-RAM and CD formats

Name	Physical Size (cm)	Sides	Layers	Raw Capacity (GB)	Audio (app. hours)	Video (app. hours)
DVD-5	12	Single	Single	4.38	8.51	2.20
DVD-9	12	Single	Dual	7.95	15.44	4.00
DVD-10	12	Double	Single	8.75	16.99	4.40
DVD-14	12	Double	Mixed	12.33	23.95	6.20
DVD-18	12	Double	Dual	15.9	30.88	8.00
DVD-1	8	Single	Single	1.36	2.64	0.68
DVD-2	8	Single	Dual	2.48	4.82	1.25
DVD-3	8	Double	Single	2.72	5.28	1.37
DVD-4	8	Double	Dual	4.95	9.61	2.49
DVD-R 1.0	12	Single	Single	3.68	7.15	1.85
DVD-R 2.0	12	Single	Single	4.38	8.51	2.20
DVD-RW 2.0	12	Single	Single	4.38	8.51	2.20
DVD-RAM 1.0	12	Single	Single	2.4	4.66	1.21
DVD-RAM 1.0	12	Double	Single	4.8	9.32	2.42
DVD-RAM 2.0	12	Single	Single	4.38	8.51	2.20
DVD-RAM 2.0	12	Double	Single	8.75	16.99	4.40
DVD-RAM 2.0	8	Double	Single	1.36	2.64	0.68
CD-ROM	12	Single	Single	0.635	1.23 (74 min)	0.32
CD-ROM	12	Single	Single	0.686	1.33 (80 min)	0.34
CD-ROM	8	Single	Single	0.18	0.35 (20 min)	0.09
DDCD-ROM	12	Single	Single	1.27	2.46	0.65
DDCD-ROM	8	Single	Single	0.36	0.7	0.18

The 80-minute CD-ROM is not compatible with all CD drives, whether in a computer or as part of a stereo system. However, it does offer some additional flexibility if you are transferring music from tape (which regularly ran to 90 minutes). The DDCD-ROM format is a new double density format being pioneered by Sony—it offers exactly double the capacity of normal CDs but will require special equipment to use. There are also a number of future formats, many of which are still in the laboratory at the time of going to press. These include a system that uses up to six shades of gray, rather than the simple on/off technology of current CDs, and a multiple layer format called FMD (fluorescent multi-layer disc) which can currently hold up to 50 times the data of a single layer DVD. When these products come to market is anybody's guess.

Writable DVD

There are lots of competing standards for writable DVD, with different manufacturers supporting and marketing the competing formats. The DVD-R standard, the DVD equivalent of CD-R, exists and is actually split into two basic standards, DVD-R(G), for general use, and DVD-R(A), for use as an authoring mechanism before production of the final DVD-ROM.

The main focus of development, however, has been on the standard DVD (in DVD-Video, DVD-Audio and DVD-ROM) and a rewritable DVD (DVD-RW, DVD+RW, and DVD-RAM) format. The rewritable DVD formats work in the same fashion as any other removable media and should therefore be considered as similar in principle to the CD-RW standard.

There is currently no standard DVD rewritable format, and there is heavy competition to standardize a format that can be used both for computer-based storage and for use as a replacement for the aging VCR. You can see a compatibility summary between the different formats and standard DVD-ROM drives in Table 2.2.

Table 2.2
DVD compatibility

	DVD-ROM	DVD-R (General)	DVD-R (Authoring)	DVD-RW drive	DVD-RAM drive	DVD+RW drive
DVD-ROM disc	Reads	Reads	Reads	Reads	Reads	Reads
DVD-R (General) disc	Usually Reads	Reads, Writes	Reads, Doesn't Write	Reads, Often Writes	Reads	Reads
DVD-R (Authoring) disc	Usually Reads	Reads, Doesn't Write	Reads, Writes	Reads, Doesn't Write	Reads	Reads
DVD-RW disc	Usually Reads	Reads	Reads	Reads, Writes	Usually Reads	Usually Reads
DVD-RAM disc	Rarely Reads	Doesn't Read	Doesn't Read	Doesn't Read	Reads, Writes	Doesn't Read
DVD+RW disc	Usually Reads	Usually Reads	Usually Reads	Usually Reads	Usually Reads	Reads, Writes

DVD-Video

Most people have probably come across DVD in its DVD-Video format. This is rapidly replacing VHS tape as the best format for releasing movies and other features. DVD-Video has a number of advantages over the old magnetic tape, not least of which is the improvement in visual and audio quality. The resolution of the video on a DVD is much higher than that possible with standard VHS tape, and it even outperforms Super VHS and most professional video formats, giving you better than broadcast-quality pictures.

Also, because a DVD disc is read using a laser, it doesn't degrade over time. VHS tape starts to lose quality the first time you use it, and for videos that are watched more than fifty times, the difference is noticeable—as anybody with children and Disney videos will probably testify!

The way video information is stored on DVD is also technically advanced. Like an audio CD, a movie is converted into a digital format. In its raw form, this digital stream would be too large to fit onto even the high-capacity DVDs. For example, a 25 fps (frames per second) video uses about 35 MBps (megabytes per second). That would mean that a standard 4.4 GB DVD would hold just 128 seconds of video, and a double-sided, dual-layer would hold only 468 seconds (just about enough for a *Tom & Jerry* cartoon).

To get round this limitation, DVD-Video uses a standard called MPEG (Motion Picture Experts Group). MPEG looks at the source video and records only the differences between each frame. The amount of information that changes between each frame is actually fairly small, so this reduces quite significantly the amount of information that has to be stored. In addition, MPEG also compresses the information in each frame so that blocks of identical color are referenced only once. By the time your MPEG compression has finished, you have a data stream of between 150 KBps and 1.5 MBps. Even at the top rate, a 4.4 GB DVD would hold fifty minutes of video. For most movies, you'll easily get eighty minutes onto a single-sided, single-layer disc.

One of the most significant features of DVD is that the sheer capacity of the medium allows us to include so much more information on each disc. A standard single-layer DVD has enough room for a ninety-minute movie and cinema-quality surround sound. Using a dual-layer disc, it's possible to have the movie, the sound in multiple language versions, another separate director's commentary audio track, and other "mini" features like "making of" and outtakes.

The format also lends itself well to video. Watching a film on videotape, I'd have to fast forward to a particular scene, which takes seconds, even minutes, if what I want to watch is at the end of the tape. Like CDs, the tracks on a DVD can be selected instantaneously, so I can skip forward to a particular part of a movie immediately. On a standard film, this isn't much of an improvement, but for videos that store multiple episodes it means you can skip straight to a particular episode.

DVD systems also support a menu facility so that you can select which track you want from an onscreen menu, and that menu can be static or video-based—because you can skip instantly to another track, you can have multi-layer menus and access to all sorts of information. On a typical DVD, this might include the original movie, a "making of" feature, interviews with the crew and stars, information on the special effects, and even an archive of pictures taken on the set during filming.

At the end of 2000, writable DVD equipment to be used as a replacement for VHS VCRs had only just started appearing in Japan, and at a price of about $4,000. There have been a number of reasons for this delay—the primary reason is directly related to the need for compressing video information in real-time and having a writable DVD that can keep up with the process. There is equipment that is able to do this, but not at consumer prices, so other alternatives—such as writing the compressed video to an internal hard disk before writing it out to DVD-RAM—have to be used instead. It'll be some years before DVD-RAM completely replaces the humble VCR.

DVD-Audio and SuperAudio-CD

DVD-Audio is an extension of the audio CD format. It increases the sampling rate and the frequency range of the source audio to improve the quality. By increasing these two elements, the audio quality is increased to the levels used by the studio when it's recorded, and this information is then recorded onto standard DVD media. This resolves one of the issues with CDs for professionals and audiophiles who have always maintained that CD has been an approximation of the source, rather than a faithful reproduction of it. Because of the increase in the size of the audio stream, you don't quite get the hours of music quoted in Table 2.1, but there is still enough space for hours of multi-channel audio on a single-sided, single-layer disc.

The SuperAudio-CD (SACD) format pushed by Sony uses the same basic techniques as DVD-Audio to increase the quality of the music stored on the disc. SACD, though, works differently from DVD-Audio and the focus has been placed more on the quality of the audio and the facility to have multiple active channels, both for surround sound and for better reproduction of concerts and other live events.

SACDs are not compatible with DVDs in any way, and you currently have to buy two different players to listen to each type of media. It's likely that either both formats will survive and dual-support drives will appear or one will come out on top in the same way as VHS won out over Betamax. Note that, at the moment, no computer can read DVD-Audio or SuperAudio-CD discs at all; it's currently designed only with hi-fi usage in mind.

DVD or CD?

Although DVD has a larger storage capacity and is practically available to most end users only in a rewritable DVD format, the same basic principles of layouts and file formats apply to DVD as they do to CD-R/CD-RW. There are some limits, however. DVD-Video discs cannot be written with easily accessible equipment on a home or typical work PC or Mac. However, at the beginning of 2001, that was all about to change. Apple, in partnership with Pioneer, has developed a drive that will write DVD-R discs that can be played in an ordinary DVD video player without the need for any extra equipment. Aside from the technological advance of a consumer-oriented machine being able to write DVD video compatible discs, the other major achievement is that this can be done using the AltiVec extensions in the G4/733MHz CPU. This negates the need for the expensive MPEG encoding hardware, which normally increases the price, while also allowing the writing to take place at two times normal speed (i.e. two minutes of data is written during one minute of real time)—previous systems have taken hours to write just a few minutes of video.

As the product becomes more mainstream, the prices go down, and the speed of computers goes up, we're likely to see much more of this kind of equipment. Even so, DVD is still fairly limited and expensive as a home-based audio and video alternative to CD-R. If you need inexpensive video capability, then CD-R still has its place, and most professional authoring systems will actually allow you to write DVD-player compatible video CDs.

If you want the larger storage capacity of DVD, then the DVD-RAM drives currently fitted as an option to Apple's G4 and some PCs is a good idea. However, these devices lack the software support offered to CD-R and CD-RW users, and it's still expensive to use your desktop PC to create DVDs that you can play in your DVD player. Since there is no reliable and universally agreed standard for rewritable DVD, my advice is to steer clear of rewritable DVD.

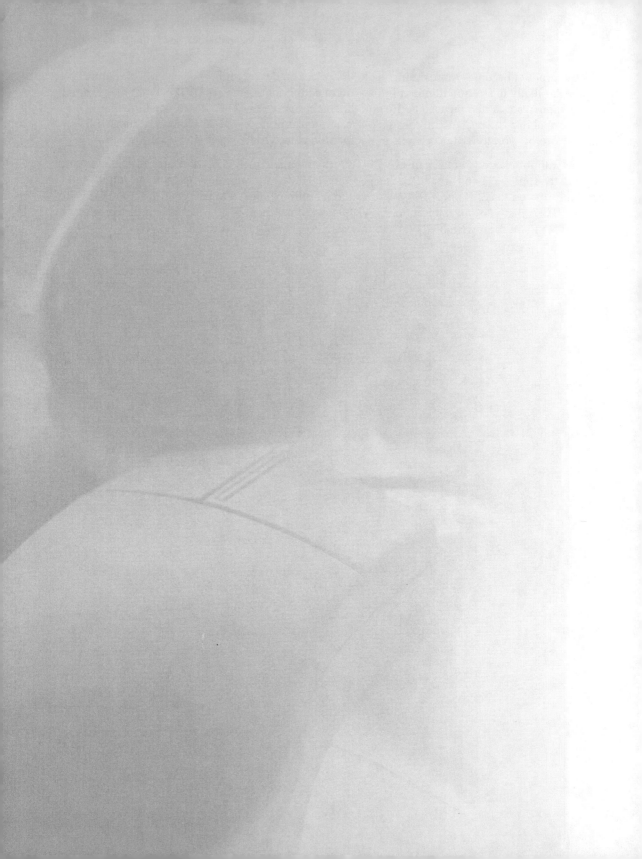

3

Choosing a Drive

Now that you know the basic mechanics of how CD, CD-R, and CD-RW work, you need to decide on the drive you want to use to create your CDs. Choosing a suitable drive is a complex process, and picking the right one depends on what machine you have, how expandable that machine is, and what you want the drive to do once you've got it.

There are four basic questions that you need to ask yourself:

▶ **What sort of media do I want to use?** There are CD-R, CD-R/RW, and combined DVD and CD-R/RW drives available. The type that you choose will determine what sort of media you can use, and the types of CDs that you create. See "Drive Types."

▶ **Do I want an internal or external drive?** This is partly related to the interface type you choose—some interfaces are internal only—but the answer will also be determined by what sort of machine you have and whether you have any spare space to fit the drive internally. See "Internal or External."

▶ **How will I connect it to my machine?** Different machines have different interfaces and methods of communicating with a CD drive. The type of machine you have, and the speed at which you want to record CDs will help to determine the type of interface. See "Interfaces."

▶ **How fast do I want it?** Different types of CD drives write information at different speeds. Again, the speed is partially governed by the interface type you are using, but if speed of writing is an issue, then you need to know how that speed is measured. See "Writing Speeds."

We'll cover the issues raised by each of these questions in the following sections.

Drive Types

There are three types of drives on the market that can write to CD-R, and two types that can use CD-RW. Which one you choose is determined by what you want to do with it. The three types are CD-R, CD-R/RW, and DVD/CD-R/RW:

▶ CD-R drives only allow you to write to CD-R. CD-R only drives are becoming rare, as most types move toward a combined CD-R/RW format.

▶ CD-R/RW drives allow you to write to CD-R, just as a CD-R drive does, and to read and re-write CD-RW, just like any other removable drive. These are the most popular drives at the moment because they provide the best flexibility—you can use the CD-R ability for archiving and the CD-RW facility to fill the space normally occupied by a Zip, Jaz, or other removable device.

▶ DVD/CD-R/RW drives are identical to CD-R/RW drives, allowing you to use both CD-R and CD-RW media. However, they also allow you to read DVD-ROM discs and to play DVD videos. They are not DVD-RAM drives—they allow you only to read DVD media, not write to it.

It's worth remembering that all the different drive types can read ordinary CD-ROMs at varying speeds. The DVD standard was developed with backwards compatibility for reading CD-ROMs, so if you get a DVD/CD-R/RW drive, you should be able to do just about everything with the drive. See "Writing Speeds" later in this chapter for more information on the relationship between writing, rewriting, and reading CDs.

Internal or External?

OK, we've chosen a drive type. Now, you need to decide whether you want to install the drive into a spare slot in your machine or whether you want to have an external drive that sits in its own case, with its own power supply, on top of, or beside your machine or monitor. Choosing an internal or external drive will also affect how you expect to connect the drive to your machine. An internal drive fits inside your computer and connects either to a spare IDE port or onto the SCSI chain inside your machine. To fit the drive, you'll need to open up the case of your computer and probably remove some blanking plates and other equipment and cables to actually fit your drive. If you're not sure of how to do this, or whether you even have the space, take your machine to a local computer dealer for advice on the best option.

Using an internal drive has a number of advantages, which I've summarized below:

▶ **Saves space**—Because it's inside your machine, it doesn't take up any more room on your desk, and you don't need to find any space to locate it.

▶ **Saves clutter**—An external drive has additional power cables and the connection cable that connects to your machine. If it's all inside, there aren't extra cables to worry about.

▶ **Reduces power sockets**—Because the power is supplied by the power supply in your machine, you don't need an extra socket.

The downside to an internal drive is that you must have both the physical space—in the form of a 5 1/4-inch drive bay—and a spare interface connection in order to fit one. The physical space depends on the type of machine you have—PC or Mac—and what equipment you already have fitted in your machine. Most common desktop PCs come with one hard drive and a CD-ROM drive and usually have space for an additional hard drive and CD-ROM or other 5 1/4-inch device. Some may have many more, and others offer no expansion capabilities at all. Most Macs, including the iMac, iBook, and even the G3, G4, and Powerbook G3 machines, do not support additional internal CD-ROM drives. In these cases, you'll have to use an external drive.

If you determine that you have the physical space, then you need to find out if you have the spare interface connections inside your machine to support it. Most modern PCs have four IDE ports—two devices can be fitted to each of two channels. In a standard PC with one hard drive and CD-ROM drive, you should have two spare connections available. If your PC supports SCSI devices, then you can connect up to seven SCSI devices on one chain, or up to fifteen if you have Wide SCSI. See the sections in this chapter on IDE and SCSI devices for information and advice on how to configure these types of devices.

If you don't have room to fit an internal device, or don't think you have the technical know-how to open up the case of your machine and fit an internal drive, then you should consider getting an external device that connects through an SCSI, parallel, USB, or FireWire port on your machine—see "Interfaces" in this chapter for more information. External devices also have a number of other advantages over their internal counterparts:

▶ **Easy to install**—If you're not comfortable with the insides of your PC, an external drive is the right choice. Because it plugs into one of the external ports on your PC, it's very easy to add to your system. You also don't have to worry so much about configuring the drive to work with your system.

▶ **Portable**—With an external CD-R/RW, you can disconnect it and use it on other machines. If you have a parallel, USB, or FireWire unit, you can even disconnect and reconnect with the machine switched on. If you have more than one computer, this is a great way to share the drive between the machines.

Remember, though, that any external device will also require its own power cable—the computer won't supply power to the drive for you. You also need to ensure that you have a spare port to which to connect the device.

Interfaces

Once you've decided on the type of drive that you want to use and whether you want an internal or external device, you need to think about how it will communicate with your computer. The exact type of connection is dependent on the type of machine and whether you are fitting the drive internally or externally. Use Tables 3.1, 3.2, and 3.3 to help you decide what interface you can use with your machine and operating system.

Table 3.1
Interfaces and
internal/external
drive compatibility

Interface	Internal	External
Parallel	No	Yes
IDE	Yes	No
SCSI	Yes	Yes
USB	No	Yes
FireWire	No	Yes

Table 3.2

Interfaces supported on PCs running Windows and Linux

Interface	Win95	Win98/SE	WinNT	Win2K	WinMe	Linux
Parallel	Yes	Yes	No	Yes	Yes	No
IDE	Yes	Yes	Yes	Yes	Yes	Yes
SCSI	Yes, with SCSI card	Yes, with SCSI card	Limited support with SCSI card	Yes, with SCSI card	Yes	Yes
USB (built-in)	No	Yes	Limited support with some USB cards	Yes	Yes	Limited Support
FireWire	Yes, with suitable card	Yes, with suitable card	Limited support with some FireWire cards	Yes, with suitable card	Yes, with suitable card	Not Yet Supported

Table 3.3

Interfaces supported on Macs, according to type

Interface	68k/Non-PCI PowerPC (61/71/8100)	PCI PowerPC (72/73/75/85/9600)	iMac/iBook	PowerBook G3	G3/G4
Parallel	No	No	No	No	No
IDE	No	No	No	No	Yes, but only if it replaces existing CD/DVD drive
SCSI	Yes	Yes, but only if it replaces existing CD-ROM drive	Yes, with USB or FireWire to SCSI adaptor	Yes	Yes, with suitable card
USB	No	Yes, with suitable card	Yes	Yes	Yes
FireWire	No	Yes, with suitable card	Yes, on iMac SE/iBook SE	Yes, on Power-Book G3 (2000) or older units with FireWire PC Card	Yes

Parallel

A parallel drive connects to the parallel port that you normally use for communicating with your printer. The speed of a parallel device is much slower than all the other solutions because of the limitations of the interface itself. Using a parallel device shouldn't affect your connectivity to your printer, since most devices provide a "pass-through" port to allow your computer to continue talking to the printer. This is not compatible with all printers (notably those from Hewlett-Packard), so your results may vary. If in doubt, unplug the printer or CD-R/RW drive when using the other piece of equipment. However, printing and writing a CD at the same time are not supported, and you can support only one storage device per parallel port on your machine—and most PCs have only one port.

The main advantage of a parallel-port CD-R drive is that it can be connected to almost any PC, even if it's several years old. If you have a PC that is less than two years old, it probably comes with a USB port, and providing you are running one of the supported operating systems (Win95, Win2K, WinMe), you shouldn't have any problems using USB instead of parallel.

IDE/EIDE

IDE (integrated drive electronics) and its newer, enhanced brother, EIDE (enhanced IDE), is the interface standard used to support hard drives and CD-ROM drives inside modern PCs and Macs. The IDE system supports two channels, primary and secondary, and two devices on each channel, the master and slave. Don't worry too much about the terminology, as there is no difference between a master and slave device, it's just the way each device is identified.

TIP

If you've purchased a PC that comes with a CD-R/RW drive already fitted, then it probably uses the IDE interface. You shouldn't need to perform a configuration of the drive; it should be ready to use when you opened the box. If in doubt, check with your dealer.

In all PCs, you can use all connectors to fit up to four devices in your machine. If you are connecting a CD-R/RW device, then place it on a different channel from your hard drive. This will ensure the maximum transfer speed between the two devices and should help to avoid any problems when writing CDs. If you are adding the CD-R device to a computer that already has a CD-ROM drive, then put the CD-R as the master device and the CD as the slave. Although, in theory, it shouldn't make any difference, on some machines the slave device is given a lower priority and, therefore, lower transfer speed. Newer machines do not exhibit this problem.

In a Mac, things get more complicated. The IDE interface is relatively new to all Macs, and all Macs made up until the end of 1998 support only a single device on each IDE channel, making a maximum of two devices. Since one device will be the hard drive, and the other will be the CD-ROM or DVD-ROM drive, you will need to find an external CD-R drive. The only Macs that support four IDE devices are the second generation G3 and all G4 desktop machines. Unfortunately, neither of these machines supports more than one 5 1/4-inch drive internally. Unless you want to replace your existing drive—which I don't recommend—consider using a USB or FireWire device instead.

SCSI

The SCSI (small computer systems interface) has been around for many years and allows you to connect up to seven devices to your machine on the older, "narrow" SCSI standard or fifteen devices on the "wide" standard. Unlike IDE, SCSI interfaces typically provide both internal and external connectors, so if you have a SCSI interface but not the physical space inside your machine, you can still connect a SCSI device to your machine.

SCSI is not fitted to many PCs as standard, and it's only recently that standard SCSI support has been dropped from Macs. If you are going to connect a SCSI device, remember to set the correct SCSI number (use the System control panel under Windows or SCSIProbe under Mac OS) so that it does not conflict with another device. Also, if you are connecting the drive externally, try to make the CD-R the first device connected to the chain. At all times, also remember that you must have a termination block on the last SCSI device in the chain.

USB

The USB (universal serial bus) standard is relatively new and, thanks to the iMac, which was the first machine to use USB as standard for its keyboard and mouse, there is a flood of devices that support the USB interface. Unlike SCSI, you can connect and remove USB devices without turning either the device or the machine off. You can also connect a number of USB devices (up to 127) to one USB port. Although it's unlikely that you'll want to connect 127 CD-R drives to your machine, it does mean that you can have scanners, printers, keyboards, mice, Zip, Jaz, and CD-R drives all connected to your machine at the same time without worrying about conflicts or other problems.

USB is standard on all new PCs and has been fitted to new PCs for the last few years. It's also fitted as standard to all new Macs, including, of course, the iMac, iBook, and the G3/G4 desktop machines. Most computers come with only two USB ports, which means you'll need to use a USB hub to connect more than two devices to your machine. If you have an iMac or G4, then the keyboard and mouse use only one port, and there's a spare port on the keyboard and another spare on your machine.

The only problem with USB is that it is relatively slow. USB transfers at only 12 Mbps (megabits per second), equal only to 1.5 MBps (megabytes per second)—this means that the highest speed CD-R drive that you can safely use on your machine is a 4x. Although, in theory, it should support an 8x device, the transfer speed cannot be assured during the period of writing CD. There is a new standard, USB 2.0, due out some time in 2002 that will increase the speed by thirty to forty times, to between 360 and 480 Mbps.

FireWire

The FireWire standard is similar in principle to the USB standard. Like USB, it allows a number of drives, up to sixty-three per port, to be connected. However, the transfer speed is much higher at 400 Mbps (50 MBps), with a future FireWire 2 standard starting at 800 Mbps (100 MBps). The FireWire name is actually used by Apple, which is one of the main supporters and users of the technology. Other companies call the same technology by different names—Sony, for example, calls it i.Link. The technical name is IEEE1394.

When writing CDs, the increased speed of FireWire allows it to support CD-R/RW drives up to 16x, the maximum available at the time of this writing. Incidentally, because of the high speed of FireWire, it can be used for all sorts of data transfers, and DV (digital video) camcorders can export their recorded video over a FireWire link into your PC.

FireWire is now fitted as standard to all but the low-end Macs—even the new DVD iBook has a FireWire port. On older PCI Macs, PCs, and PowerBooks/Notebooks, you can get cards that will allow you to connect external FireWire devices.

Writing Speeds

The speeds quoted for all CD drives based on the speed of the original CD-ROM drives in computers and are expressed as a multiplier; for example, you buy a 52x CD-ROM drive. The original CD-ROM drives transferred information at 150 KBps—that means that it would take seventy-four minutes (the length of a standard CD) to transfer all of the information from the CD to your computer's hard disk. The 52x CD-ROM drive can transfer 7.8 MBps—that means it would take just 1.5 minutes to transfer all of the information from the CD to your hard disk. Note that even with a 52x CD-ROM drive, you are still using a low-performance device when compared to the hard disk in your machine. Your hard disk will probably be running at 33 MBps, with newer machines operating at 66 MBps or higher.

The same basic rule applies to CD-R drives. The first CD-R drives took seventy-four minutes to fill an entire CD-R; then came 2x drives, which took about thirty-eight minutes; and now a 4x takes just over eighteen minutes. Modern CD-R drives generally work at 8x (nine minutes) or 12x (six minutes), and there are 16x drives trickling onto the market in early 2001. The speed obviously affects how long it will take to write your CD, and how long your machine will be tied up writing the information. But, if you are not filling an entire CD with information, then the times will be shorter. I've summarized the speeds, transfer rates, and the times taken to write an entire CD, and each MB and minute of a CD, in Table 3.4.

Table 3.4
CD speeds and
transfer times

CD Speed	Data Rate (KBps)	Entire CD (min)	Time to write 1MB (s)	Time to write 1 minute (s)
1x	150	74.00	6.83	60.00
2x	300	37.00	3.42	30.00
4x	600	18.50	1.71	15.00
6x	900	12.33	1.14	10.00
8x	1200	9.25	0.85	7.50
10x	1500	7.40	0.68	6.00
12x	1800	6.17	0.57	5.00
16x	2400	4.63	0.43	3.75
20x	3000	3.70	0.34	3.00
24x	3600	3.08	0.28	2.50
30x	4500	2.47	0.23	2.00
36x	5400	2.06	0.19	1.67
40x	6000	1.85	0.17	1.50
50x	7500	1.48	0.14	1.20
52x	7800	1.42	0.13	1.15

For example, from this table we can see that if you have 200 MB of data to write to a CD, using an 8x CD-R drive, you would write the data in about 170 seconds (200×0.85), just shy of three minutes. Similarly, if I were writing thirty-seven minutes of audio on the same 8x drive, it would take just over four and a half minutes of actual writing time.

For a CD-R/RW drive, the information is generally quoted using three figures, as in 8x/4x/16x. The individual figures relate to the CD-R, CD-RW, and CD-ROM speeds, respectively. In this case, the drive would write CD-R at 8x (nine minutes), CD-RW at 4x (eighteen minutes), and read CD-ROMs at 16x.

Speeds of DVD-ROM drives are very different. A 1x DVD-ROM drive transfers information at about 1300 KBps, roughly equivalent to a 9x CD-ROM drive. A DVD also spins three times faster than a normal CD player. When reading CD-ROMs, however, a DVD-ROM drive will usually increase the spin speed further so that most achieve at least 12x when reading a normal CD. Information is read from a DVD at a higher rate because of the increased density of the media. This also means, confusingly, that the equivalent CD rate and the actual rate at which CD-ROMs are read is different. In effect, a DVD-ROM drive works at DVD speeds when reading a DVD disc and CD-ROM speeds when reading a CD.

DVD times are quoted separately to CD reading and CD-R/RW speeds. For example, you might have a 16x/40x DVD-ROM drive, which works at 16x DVD speed and 40x CD-ROM speed. If it's a CD-R/RW/DVD drive, then all four speeds will probably be quoted—for example, 12x10x32x8x, which refers to CD-R, CD-RW, CD, and DVD times, respectively. See Table 3.5 for a DVD speeds, transfer rates and comparable CD speeds.

Table 3.5
DVD speeds and comparable CD rates

DVD Speed	Data rate (MBps)	Equivalent CD Rate	Actual CD Rate
1x	1.32	9x	8x-18x
2x	2.64	18x	20x-24x
4x	5.28	36x	24x-32x
5x	6.6	45x	24x-32x
6x	7.93	54x	24x-32x
8x	10.57	72x	32x-40x
10x	13.21	90x	32x-40x
16x	21.13	144x	32x-40x

Note that the equivalent CD rate applies only when reading information from a DVD—when reading from a CD, the actual CD rate applies.

Because DVD and the higher speed CD-R and CD-RW drives use a higher transfer rate, you find that you need to use either IDE (for internal) or SCSI/FireWire (for external) interfaces. The USB interface is not fast enough to supply the drive with information for writing, and you may end up wasting a lot of CD-R media. The highest USB-based CD-R I would recommend is 4x—anything above that speed and you may experience problems.

We'll have a closer look at the mechanics behind this problem and ways in which you can resolve it in Chapter 11.

4

CD, CD-R, or CD-RW?

Having digested all of the information in Chapters 2 and 3, you're probably wondering which media you should be using. All the formats (with the obvious exception of DVD and its variations) store the same amount of information—650 MB, or seventy-four minutes of audio, and once written, the discs all share the same basic properties. CDs in any form are great ways of storing information—they are nearly indestructible, last a lifetime (within reason…), are exceedingly practical, and if designed and written properly, they provide an excellent way of storing information.

The first thing to consider with all three formats is which is the most practical for *your* needs. CD has its place and it's difficult to imagine what the world would be like without aisles of audio CDs in the record stores—or, indeed, buying and swapping tens, or even hundreds, of floppies when installing the latest piece of software or playing computer games.

Death to CD!

If CD-R and CD-RW is so great, why aren't companies releasing their software on these formats? Wouldn't it be great, for example, if we could add tracks to an audio CD we already own? Or, how about updating the drives that came with your printer with the latest version you've just downloaded over the Web?

There are really three reasons why CD will always be a viable format in the current climate. The first is actually a technological limit—until about six years ago, writing to a CD using either the CD-R or CD-RW format was either impossible or so expensive that it just wasn't practical. CD technology, on the other hand, is more than twenty years old and it's already the dominant force in the audio and computer industries for the distribution of information.

The second reason concerns the practicality of creating the media in the first place. As we saw in Chapter 2, writing a CD-R or CD-RW requires a special type of drive, while creating a CD is a physical and, therefore, easily automated, process. It takes a couple of seconds to "press" a CD, but even with the fastest CD-R/RW drives it takes a few minutes.

The third reason is directly related to the final product. A CD is difficult to destroy or even mildly corrupt, and the information stored on it cannot be modified in any way. For the consumer—and by that I mean YAJ (Your Average Joe)—the industry needed something that was more reliable than the write protect tab on a tape or floppy disk to protect the information stored on it.

CD as a technology and an industry is not likely going to die anytime soon—in fact, as the number of computers in homes and businesses around the world increases, the requirement for CDs is likely to increase as well. Even with the introduction of DVD, CD will probably remain the major technology for audio and software distribution. DVD is more expensive to produce, and the storage capacity is far beyond the requirements of most applications.

With all this in mind, the basic CD format is beyond the realm of most individuals since it's designed to create hundreds of thousands of copies of the same disc, which is why it's so ideal for audio and software distribution. The information can't be deleted, users can't ruin the data, and the format of the disc is such that it's also physically difficult to damage the disc. However, it's completely impractical for the home user to think about using CDs as a storage method.

That doesn't mean that we won't be covering the basics of the process for creating CDs in this guide. Writing a CD-R or CD-RW and the techniques and tricks you employ to do that apply just as much to CD production as to CD-R production. In fact, aside from the method of duplication, the final format and contents of both formats is identical.

Death to CD-R!

So, if we're sticking to CD technology, the next question is why use CD-R when we have a better and far more practical solution in the form of CD-RW. Ten years ago, nobody would have wanted to use a floppy disk that they could only write to once, so why do we still need CD-R technology?

The simple answer to that is related to how and why we use the different removable storage technologies that are available and the sort of information that we now work with. Ten years ago, floppy disks were really the only form of removable storage—there were some technologies, like those used by the SyQuest drives, which were really just a single hard disk platter placed into a plastic shell, but they were rare and expensive. At the time, most computer data was made up of simple text and graphics. I still have the disks I used in college, and all of my coursework for more than two years would fit onto a couple of floppy disks.

Nowadays, we are a far more digitally minded nation. We don't just store simple text and graphics—we have photo-quality images and video on our machines. Even simple documents can take up 100 Kb. These files just don't fit onto a floppy disk, and in the case of images and video, most of the time we don't make modifications to them, either. We could store them on Jaz or Zip disks, but these are expensive, and designed for fast read/write access. That makes them an expensive proposition for storing large volumes of data that won't ever change. We could also store them on CD-RW disks, but these, too, are expensive compared to CD-R media, and we still don't need rewrite ability.

This is where CD-R fits right in—we can write large volumes of information to a CD and never again worry about losing it, accidentally overwriting it, or otherwise damaging the contents. It's the perfect format for archiving—it's cheap, reliable and, because it works like any other CD, it's easy to get the information back when we need it.

Of course, CD-R can be used for much more than just archiving computer information. We can also create our own audio and video CDs, but the same reason remains: CD-R is easy to use and difficult to corrupt.

Death to CD-RW!

OK, so CD and CD-R have their place, but if there are faster and higher-capacity removable formats like Jaz out there, why do we need CD-RW?

There is one primary reason for using CD-RW over the other formats: compatibility. All PCs and Macs sold today include a CD-ROM drive, or at least a drive capable of using CD media. But not everybody has a Jaz, Zip, ORB, MO, SuperDisk, or any of the other disk formats. If I've got the latest game demo, my holiday pictures, or that video of my brother spraying milkshake from his nose on Jaz, I'd probably need to take the Jaz drive with me so that my friends could use it.

If I were to write the same information to a CD-RW disc, I wouldn't have to worry about taking the drive, and I wouldn't "waste" a CD-R disc when I wanted to change the information. In the business world, you could distribute that large multimedia presentation on CD-RW, and when it needs updating, you just change the information on the disc.

For me, personally, there's one other reason for using CD-RW: space. I very rarely use removable media of any kind; I prefer to have all of my information instantly accessible from a hard disk on a server. My situation is not unique, as most companies work in that way as well. What is different is that I do need to write CD-Rs, and occasionally, I also need to swap large amounts of information with another machine that's not connected to my network.

I could use a Jaz or Zip disk, but as I've already described, CD media is more practical because I know that the other machine has a CD drive. However, if I decided to go for a Jaz system, I'd need another box, power socket, and more cables coming out of the back of my machine just so I could swap data. Since my CD-R drive also handles CD-RW, and it's internal, it makes much more sense—and much less clutter—to do that instead!

Compatibility

Although you might think that all the different CD formats are essentially the same when it comes to reading the information, you'd be wrong. Because of the different methods used to write and store the information on the CD, some CD players and readers have trouble reading the information back.

Mass-produced CDs are the most compatible of all the different formats. Because the information is stamped into the disc, and there is nothing but clear plastic between the laser and the reflective layer, any CD drive should be able to read the information.

With CD-R, problems can occur because of the dye layer. Older CD drives and players used a laser that could sometimes be affected by the dye in the CD-R, causing the information to either be hidden or corrupted when it was read from the disc. The CD mechanisms produced since about 1998 use a slightly different laser and are therefore able to read the information easily.

The CD-RW medium is the most prone to problems. The crystalline layer can also be misread or even physically corrupted by the lasers used in some older mechanisms. Again, since 1998 most drives made have resolved the problem, but don't be surprised if your five-year old stereo system has problems reading CD-R and especially CD-RW media.

Comparing CD to Other Removable Formats

We were looking earlier at why you would want to use any of the different CD types for storing and exchanging information. One of the reasons I gave was cost, so to quantify my statements, I've produced Table 4.1. This compares all of the major removable disk technologies, from the point of view of the cost of the drive, the media you use, and how much it would cost using that combination to store 10 GB (a typical size for a home computer's hard disk) and 100 GB (a typical size of a file server's hard disk).

Table 4.1
Removable drive and media cost comparison

Drive	Media Size (MB)	Drive Cost	Media Cost	Based on 10 GB Storage				Based on 100 GB Storage			
				No. Media	Total Cost	Cost/ MB	MB/ $	No. Media	Total Cost	Cost/ MB	MB/ $
Floppy Disk	1.44	$50	$0.50	7112	$3,606	0.356	3	71112	$35,606	0.348	3
SuperDisk	120	$150	$9.80	86	$993	0.096	10	854	$8,519	0.083	12
Zip	100	$100	$9.00	103	$1,027	0.108	9	1024	$9,316	0.092	11
Zip	250	$180	$16.00	41	$836	0.082	12	410	$6,740	0.066	15
Jaz	2048	$349	$90.00	5	$799	0.078	13	50	$4,849	0.047	21
Magneto Optical	640	$470	$30.00	16	$950	0.093	11	160	$5,270	0.051	19
Magneto Optical	1300	$750	$34.00	8	$1,022	0.099	10	79	$3,436	0.033	30
ORB	2200	$280	$27.00	5	$415	0.04	25	47	$1,549	0.015	67
CD-R	640	$290	$1.80	16	$319	0.031	32	160	$578	0.006	177
CD-RW	640	$290	$7.00	16	$402	0.039	25	160	$1,410	0.014	73
DVD-RAM	5200	$690	$50.00	2	$790	0.077	13	20	$1,690	0.016	61

You can see very quickly from the table that CD-R is the most cost-effective media for storing information, costing just three cents per MB for 10 GB and less than one cent per MB when storing 100 GB. In comparison, although Jaz stores more and is generally quicker than CD to use, it costs more than twice that price at 10 GB and about eight times more than CD at 100 GB.

Of course, prices will fall all the time and CD-R and CD-RW media are getting cheaper almost daily. Jaz, on the other hand, has already reached its plateau, and prices have been steady for some time now. DVD-RAM is also coming down in cost but is currently less popular, as it requires special drives to read the information when compared to CDs.

A Word About Reliability

If you've followed the progress of CD-R technology at all, you will have seen a lot of conflicting stories about how long the media lasts. CDs—those pressed at a factory—have a quoted lifetime of about fifty years. Those people who bought CDs when they first came out are probably still listening to them today!

There were some worries in the early '80s that can be directly attributed to some teething problems in the production process. One particularly bad batch of CDs started to fail, either because the top layer was not thick enough or the wrong type of ink had been used during screen-printing, and it had actually etched into the plastic surface of the disc. In both cases, over a relatively small period of time the plastic would wear down and the reflective aluminum surface would start separating from the bottom layer of the disc. These problems have long been solved, and although it can still happen, the probabilities are very low.

For CD-R, the same basic rules apply—in some cases the discs are badly made and the reflective layer can literally be rubbed off the bottom plastic layer. There have also been problems with the dyes used in the layer that is written to the CD. Different types and different colors of dyes have been tried and they don't all work to the same quality or ability. This can result either in discs that can't be read just months after they were first produced or in discs that fail completely during the writing process.

With CD-RW, the main problems were related to the age of the technology. Early discs used an almost experimental crystalline layer that would result in a limited number of changes on the disc. Unfortunately, they would sometimes also result in changes when exposed to strong sunlight, not what you want at all. Modern crystalline layers are much more reliable and you're unlikely to have too many problems.

Choosing a Brand

Whatever type of media you decide to buy, think about what you are buying—saving ten cents a disc on a pack of twenty-five made by somebody you haven't heard of, compared to the cost of twenty-five from a reliable brand like Sony, TDK, or Verbatim, is unlikely to save you money in the long run. If you end up throwing a couple of the cheap discs away because they didn't write properly, you haven't saved any money at all. Worse, if you find that, six months to a year later, your disc isn't readable, you may have lost more than just the cost of the disc.

As a rule, buy a brand name you know and trust. If you are buying CD media for the first time and are worried about the long-term effects and reliability, buy only a couple from each manufacturer and try them with your drive. If you find that one works better than another—and believe me, it can happen—then stick to it.

We'll actually be looking at using CD-R/RW discs for backups and archiving in Chapter 7. We'll go over some of the ways in which you can protect yourself from losing vital information, either from bad media or from a drive/media incompatibility.

Handling and Cleaning

One of the best ways to keep your media in working order is to treat it properly. Although CDs are *almost* indestructible, they are not quite there, so it's possible, completely by accident, to damage a disc beyond use.

What NOT to Do

The following is a list of what you *shouldn't* do when handling CDs:

- ▶ **Don't place them face down**—if you want to put a disk down temporarily, put it down label side first. Better still, put it back into its case.

- ▶ **Don't leave your CDs in a hot place, in bright sunshine, or in damp conditions.**

- ▶ **Don't put your fingers onto the bottom of the disc surface**—this is the surface through which the information is read, and, although CD drives have mechanisms to recover from some errors, greasy fingerprints is not one of them.

- ▶ **Don't leave your CDs in your machine for long periods of time**—the heat inside your machine can sometimes warp the disc. When you've finished using a CD, or you're about to switch your machine off, take the CD out and put it back into its case.

- ▶ **Don't mail your CD in a normal envelope without any form of rigid packing**—Bubblewrap is not even enough to stop the disc from getting damaged. Instead, either insert a piece of hard cardboard, use a hardback envelope, or use one of the special CD mailers that are available.

- ▶ **Don't carry CDs around in your pockets**—they are likely to get scratched and if you sit down with one in your pants pocket, it will probably get broken.

- ▶ **Don't put CDs into your microwave oven**, whether you want to keep them or not. They might start a fire or damage your oven beyond repair. (The aluminum in a CD causes microwaves to go bonkers.)

- ▶ **Don't scratch or draw on either surface of the disc.**

- ▶ **Don't use a ballpoint or other hardtipped pen to label a CD-R/RW.** Instead, either use one of the special felt tip pens available or use one of the CD labeling technologies that we'll look at in Chapter 20.

Long-term Storage

When storing CDs for long periods of time, try to find a suitable location that is cool, has a low humidity, and is not in direct sunlight. Storing CDs on the shelf above your radiator across from a window is not a good idea!

If you have a lot of CDs, then think about purchasing one of the various high-volume solutions such as drawers or flip folders. Drawers allow you to store the CDs and their jewel cases safely, and most can be stacked and joined together to make large libraries. The flip folders use special CD pockets in standard ring binders that allow you to store up to eight disks on a single, double-sided page. If you archive and use a lot of different CDs during the day, this might be the best solution, but remember to keep the folder in a sensible place.

Picking Up and Handling CDs

When you pick up a CD, you should do so using one of two methods:

▶ Grab the disc by the edges using one or two hands, avoiding surface contact with either the top or bottom of the disc.

▶ Put your finger through the hole in the middle of the disc.

And, when retrieving or placing discs in their cases:

▶ When putting a CD into its jewel case, rest the case on a flat surface and then place the disc on top of the central ring. Then, still holding the edges, push down the middle of the disc until it latches.

▶ To remove the disc, grab it by the edges, and then push on the latch holding the hole in the middle. This will release the disc so that you can lift it away from the case.

▶ Don't try to "lever" the disc away from its case. If you can't remove it from the case using the method above, you're not doing it right!

Cleaning

If your disc surface does get dirty, you can clean it by using a lint-free cloth such as that used by photographers on their lenses. Don't try to wipe it on your jeans or t-shirt, as you'll probably end up scratching the surface and making the situation worse.

When you do wipe, use a straight motion from the center of the disc to the outside, as shown in Figure 4.1. Don't use circular motions or "rub" the disk, as this will affect the plastic surface and either wear it down or scratch it. If you need to, use some alcohol-based cleaner to get stubborn stains off, but avoid using normal solvents such as acetone (nail polish remover) or lighter fluid—both will eat the plastic off the disc!

Alternatively, you can get some special cleaning kits. These consist of some fluid and a manually operated powered spinner. You put the fluid and the CD into the spinner—the rotating action cleans the CD and, with suitable cleaner, will actually repair the surface of scratched CDs. Cleaning kits like this cost between $10 and $40 and can be a wise investment if you use a lot of CDs.

Figure 4.1
Use a straight motion from the center of the disc to the outside to clean it.

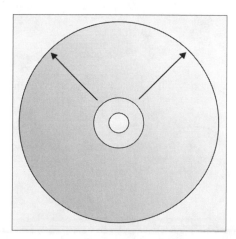

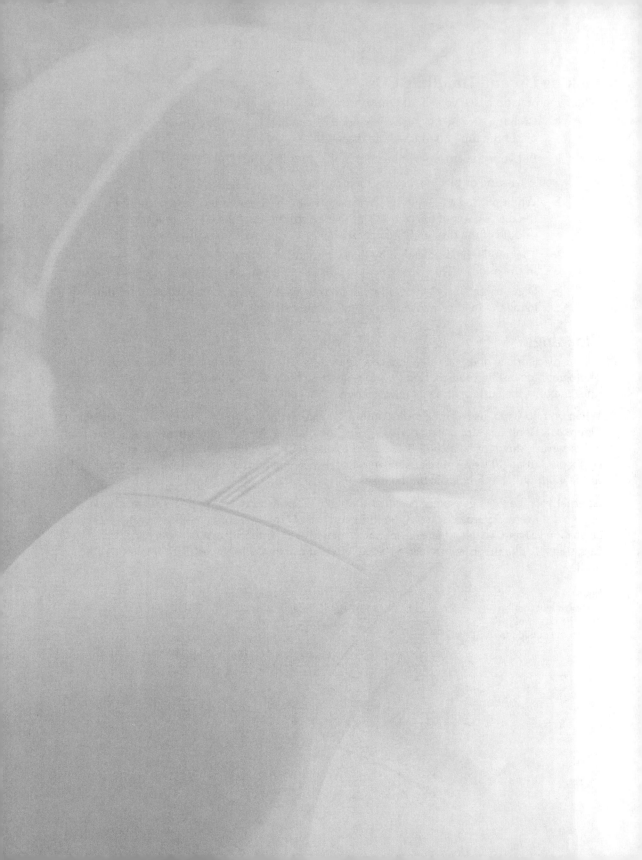

5

Software Overview

Now that you know about the hardware and the reasons why you should think about using CD-R media, it's time to take a closer look at how you store different pieces of information on the CD itself. There are two aspects of this process—the first is choosing the right recording format for the data that you want to store. For example, if you are creating your own CD compilation albums that you want to be able to play on your home stereo system and in your car, then you need to record audio discs. If you are archiving information, then you probably want to use standard files and folders.

We'll be looking at the organization of what you want to write in the next chapter and at the specifics of writing audio CDs, backups and archiving, and bootable and installer CDs in subsequent chapters. Before we get there, however, we'll have a look at the basic recording formats, writing methods, and a quick overview of some of the software that we can use when writing CDs on Macs, Windows, and Unix.

Recording Formats

Before you think about what you are going to write and how you are going to write that information to the CD, you need to consider the different recording formats available and the format of the sources that you will need to supply in order to correctly write that information to the CD.

For example, if you want to create a CD from that pile of MP3s you downloaded from the Web, what format should you use? The answer is not immediately obvious—if you want to play it on your home stereo system or in the car, then what you need is an audio CD, but if you want to play it on your PC, then it could be either an audio or data CD. The difference is entirely in how the information is written onto the disk.

There are, in fact, a myriad of different formats that you'll probably find listed in your CD-R software that can be used for writing CDs. In fact, most of them can be reduced to only a few formats. For the moment, we'll look at the three main formats you'll probably use: data, audio, and mixed-mode. There are other formats, such as the Video-CD and CD-I formats, and we'll cover those when we look at the specifics of writing different data to CD in Section 4, "CD Writing Software."

Data CDs

A data CD is recorded using what is referred to as the "Orange Book" standard. This defines the method for writing the data onto the disc so that the tracks can be read and recognized as raw data. The Orange Book standard defines how the information is stored on the disc, but it doesn't describe how the individual file layout is recorded—that's handled by a series of file-system standards. All the different file-system standards allow you to organize the information using the same layout as you would use on your hard disk or removable storage format, so you can have a hierarchy of files and folders (directories) at different levels in order to structure the files you store.

NOTE

The recording format used for commercial or mass produced CD-ROMs is called the Yellow Book format.

The basic data-recording format is the HSFS (High Sierra File System) or ISO9660. This is the format supported by every operating system for reading CDs. HSFS is *very* basic; it supports only 8.3 character filenames—that is eight characters, a period and an optional three-letter extension. HSFS is also very limited in the number of levels of directories it supports, but it does provide for file versions. (Multiple versions of the same file have **;x** appended to their name, where the **x** is the version number.)

Because of the limitations of the HSFS system, a number of extensions have been introduced that allow you to overlay a more practical file system on top of the basic HSFS system. These extensions are designed to allow support for such items as long filenames or the multi-stream files used on the Mac. The primary extensions supported are the Joliet, Mac (HFS/HFS+), and Rock Ridge extensions.

The Joliet format was developed by Microsoft as a method for supporting the long filenames used on the FAT16/FAT32 file systems used by Windows. The Joliet file system allows long filenames of up to 64 characters with no limitations on either spaces or periods, or on the number of folders or potential directory levels that you can create.

The Mac extensions support the HFS/HFS+ file systems, allowing you to write Mac files, including the data and resource fork entries to store Mac files and applications. If you want to store Mac-specific files, then you will need to use the Mac extensions—the Joliet format does not handle the forked data streams properly.

You can also get hybrids that allow you to use both the Joliet and Mac extensions so that you can create mixed-format discs. What happens is that both sets of extension information are recorded onto the disc and when the disc is inserted, the host chooses the most suitable set of extensions according to its operating system. Unfortunately, there isn't a completely cross-platform compatible format. Although the UDF format that we'll look at later in this chapter does support all of the artifacts of a file system, it's still far too limited to be of any practical use.

Rock Ridge extensions were specifically developed for the Unix platform. Unix has supported long filenames (up to 255 characters) and very deep folder structures for many years. When CD-ROMs were introduced, Rock Ridge extensions improved on the standard ISO9660 format by supporting the 255 character name limit and directory trees up to 64 levels deep.

CD-Audio

Audio discs are written in what is called Red Book audio format, and some CD programs still actually refer to the format in these terms. The Red Book format defines the way in which the individual tracks that make up an audio CD are laid down on the disc and also the format of the index used to describe the disc contents. If you put an audio CD into a stereo system, generally the first thing that is reported is the size (in minutes and seconds) of the disc and the number of audio tracks that it contains.

The track information is stored in an index that also describes the physical location on the disc of the start of each track—it's this information that allows you to instantly jump to any track on the CD. Without the index, the CD player would not know where to start playing even the first track, let alone any of the others.

Audio CDs are created by writing the raw audio stream to the disc from another audio source. The CD writing software translates the source format into the raw format during the writing process. Source formats can include the WAV format used on PCs and the AIFF format used on Macs, as well as the MP3 format currently popular for storing and downloading music on the Internet. We'll look at the different formats in more detail in Chapter 9, when we look at writing audio CDs.

Mixed-Mode Discs

A mixed-mode disc is exactly what the name suggests—it's a disc that is made up of one data track and one or more audio tracks, all stored on the same disc. This enables you to store software and some audio on the same disc and is a common format often used for multimedia and game discs. The layout of a mixed disc is slightly different from a typical data or audio CD, and there are two different methods for writing the tracks to CD.

The first method is the standard mixed-mode disc; here, the data track is recorded first and then subsequent audio tracks are recorded afterward, as shown in Figure 5.1. This is often the format used for computer games, as it allows the software to be recorded on one portion and then CD quality audio to be recorded on the same disc. This gets around the problem of having to decode an MP3 or other audio stream straight from the CD. Instead, we just use the audio CD playing capabilities of the CD drive to hear music while we destroy aliens!

The second method is CD-Extra (or Plus or Enhanced). This works in the same fashion as an ordinary mixed-mode disc, except that the audio tracks are written first, and the data track is written last on the CD, as shown in Figure 5.2. This allows the audio portion to be played in an ordinary CD player, while still allowing the data to be read on a computer.

Figure 5.1 (left)
The layout of a mixed-mode disc.

Figure 5.2 (right)
The layout of a mixed-mode CD-Extra disc.

Mixed-mode discs have their place, but they also have their problems. Mixed-mode discs are not compatible with all CD mechanisms, whether they are in audio players or CD-ROM drives. Generally a CD-Extra disc should be used only when there isn't a solution that uses audio files on a standard file system partition.

NOTE

The CD-Extra format is how some bands and promotional discs can be released, allowing you to listen to tracks and view videos and band information, all without changing the disc. I've also seen them used as a way for multimedia companies to promote their services—they can put the audio presentation on the disc along with the multimedia demo so that the boss can listen to their promo in the car!

Writing Modes

Beyond the actual format that you want to use for recording, you also need to decide on the mode in which you write the disc. The mode will affect both how the information is written and what you can do with the CD once the recording has been completed. Different writing modes are also more suitable for certain formats than others. There are four basic modes—disc-at-once, track-at-once, session, and packet writing.

By the way, just in case you've been wondering, all CDs are physically written to from the inside out, not the outside in, regardless of either the format or mode you are using. This means that when recording, information is written beginning near the hub of the CD and continuing toward the edge. The reason for this is very simple when you think about what happens when a CD is put into a drive and how the drive determines where to start reading. Let's say, for example, that we put a 7-centimeter disc (or so-called "CD-single") into a player. If the drive searched from the outside in to find the information, then the amount of time required to "load" the CD would be directly proportional to the time taken to search for a valid track all the way from the outside of an ordinary 12-centimeter disc to the outside of the 7-centimeter disc. This obviously isn't practical; otherwise, loading a CD-single would take seconds, perhaps even a minute, instead of being nearly instantaneous.

However, all CDs, whether they are 12 centimeters, 7 centimeters, or oddly shaped (see sidebar) have tracks near the central spindle hole. If we look for a track there, then it doesn't matter what size the CD is, because we can always read that first track. The significance of this has an effect on how we write the disc. All formats are written from the inside out, but because part of that process *must* include the information that tells the CD player what type of information is on the disc, and also additional information about sizes, track lengths and so on, the process is a little more complex than simply writing a stream of bits to the disc.

Non-circular CD-Rs

Although most people will want to use the normal circular 8-centimeter and 12-centimeter discs, it is possible to get CD-R discs that are not of a normal size. A popular format is the business card CD—this is the same size as an ordinary business card, but instead of being made of paper, it's made of the same polycarbonate/aluminum combination used in normal CD-Rs. You can also get CDs mass produced using the same unusual shapes and sizes.

Using business card CDs, when you give out your card, you're not just giving out your contact details. You could include your company's presentation, your resume, or even some examples of your past work. People are less likely to lose your card, or forget to call you back, if they get to use that card in their computer!

The requirement of inside-to-outside writing also affects how mixed-mode discs are written—if you want a disc that is mixed-mode and compatible with both computers and audio CD players, then the audio tracks *must* be written first. This is because an audio CD player will look only at the inside track; it won't search the rest of the disc for a track it can play. Most CD-R software will account for this requirement, but check back to the "Mixed-Mode Discs" section earlier in this chapter for more information on how mixed-mode discs work.

Track-at-Once Mode

In track-at-once mode (otherwise known as CD-ROM Mode 1), the CD-R drive records onto the disc one track at a time. This is the basic mode supported by all CD-R drives and is the default mode used by most applications. What happens is that each section of data that you have selected to be written to the disc—including individual tracks on an audio CD or individual files or directories on a data CD—is written, but before writing the next track, the laser is turned off. An example of this process is shown in Figure 5.3.

Figure 5.3
Writing discs in
track-at-once mode.

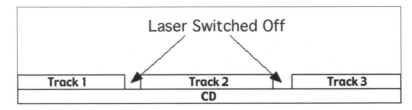

The result is that between tracks there is a blank portion of CD-R that cannot be used and obviously cannot be read. Although for data discs this gap has no effect, on audio discs it can create an audible click because the CD player reads the blank track as a series of 1s. Not all CD players do this, but it can be a significant problem.

NOTE
In fact, if you look very carefully, you can actually see the effects on a final CD-R disc of using track-at-once mode—the blank track is visible to the naked eye if you look very carefully!

Disc-at-Once Mode

In CD-disc-at-once mode, the entire data stream is written to the CD in one long process. It doesn't matter whether you are writing a number of files, directories, or audio tracks, the laser is never turned off from the first bit written to the last bit written in the stream. This doesn't mean that the tracks are unidentified—you don't end up with seventy-four minutes of nonstop music that you can only search, not skip through—as the track positions are written to the disc as normal. You can see a sample of the completed disc in Figure 5.4.

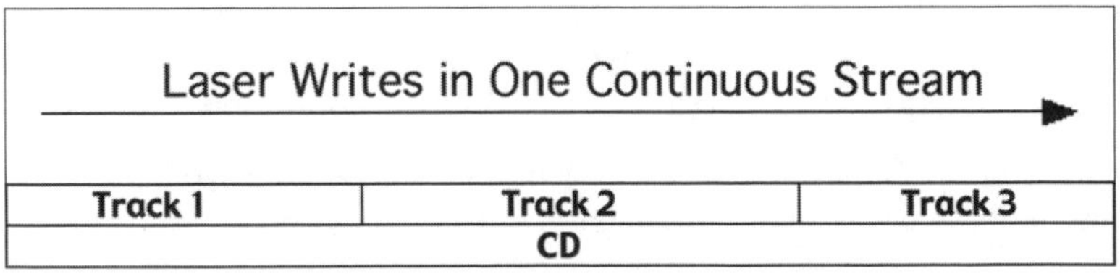

Figure 5.4
Writing discs in
disc-at-once mode.

> Laser Writes in One Continuous Stream
>
> | Track 1 | Track 2 | Track 3 |
> |---|---|---|
> | CD | | |

Disc-at-once mode requires a change in the way the CD-R laser operates, and although it's standard on most modern drives, older drives or those at the lower end of the market may not support the disc-at-once mode. If your CD-R drive doesn't support disc-at-once mode, it's not the end of the world. Just be aware that you may have trouble playing audio CDs written with your drive.

Sessions

Sessions are a bit like the individual tracks on an audio CD, except that each individual track will appear to the host computer as a separate volume. That is, if you wrote a CD with two sessions, you would appear to have two separate discs, even though both are contained on the same single CD. Using sessions, it's possible to write 120 MB of information to a CD-R, and then later write another 120 MB of data without "losing" the unused space on the disc. You can see a sample of the layout of a multi-session disc in Figure 5.5.

Figure 5.5
The layout of a multi-session disc.

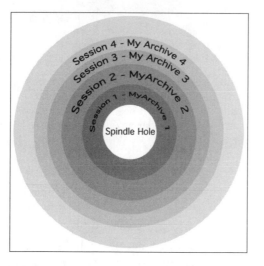

The multi-session mode (otherwise known as CD-ROM/XS Mode 2), as it is properly called, can be very useful in situations where you want more than a simple logical separation of information like that provided by a directory. For example, Sun supplies its operating system on multi-session discs because it allows the company to separate the bootable partition used to start up a machine from the software archives that contain the operating system that will be written to the disc.

The use of multi-session discs has been on a serious decline for a long time as the amount of information that people have needed to store has increased, thereby reducing the possibility of writing a small amount of data to the CD-R. It's also been affected by the introduction of CD-RW and other rewritable removable storage technologies such as Zip and Jaz.

Multi-session discs are also difficult to handle in some situations. Some drives won't read any but the first session, regardless of the operating system you use. Even if your drive supports it, selecting the session that you actually want to read can be difficult. Under Windows, you need to use the Roxio Session Selector, or a similar tool, as shown in Figure 5.6. Under Mac OS, all the sessions are generally mounted at the same time and then appear on the desktop just the same as any other volume.

Figure 5.6

Using Roxio's Session Selector to select an alternative session.

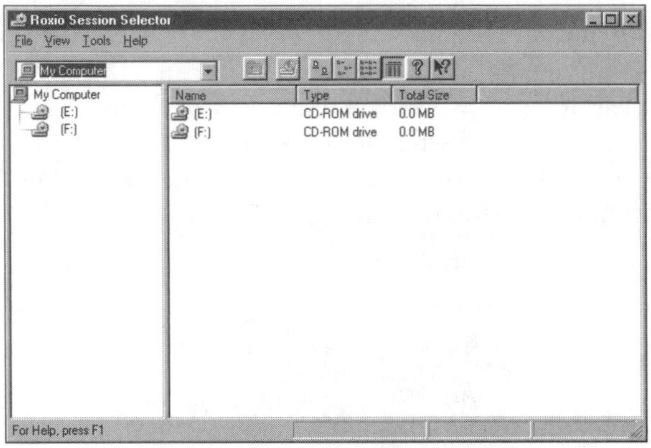

Multi-session discs are also workable only with data—audio CDs, as we've already seen, rely on a steady stream of information, and sessions appear as completely separate blocks of data on the CD when read by your CD-ROM drive. An audio CD player only knows how to read one data block, even when it contains multiple tracks. Sessions also use up more space than a single-session disc written in track- or disc-at-once modes. This is because some additional space is required for the file system and layout information of the session in question. It can be small (about 5 MB), but the size requirement increases as the size of the individual session increases.

With all that in mind, it's worth remembering that multi-session CDs exist and they can in many circumstances be very useful. They can provide a useful level of separation when the other modes and formats aren't enough. Sessions are also a common way for multimedia and games developers to provide cross-platform solutions where the files for one platform are hidden from another. For example, you might write a main session that contains the game installer for both platforms, and then supply one session containing the Mac game files and another session containing those for the PC. Although this method has been dropped in recent years due to the use of cross-platform compatible game systems, it shows that sessions still have their place.

Packet Writing

Packet writing is a relatively new invention used for writing to CDs. Unlike all the methods discussed up to this point, packet writing allows you to use the CD-R or CD-RW just as if it were any other type of removable media. With the other modes, the information has to be written to the disc in a rigid format and the final layout of the disc must be calculated before it can be written to. With packet writing, information is simply added sequentially to an existing disc.

One of the benefits of the packet-writing process is that you can write information to a CD-R and then later delete it. You don't actually delete or "blank" the portion of the disc in question; instead, the directory table is just updated so that the file in question is no longer accessible. This means that a CD-R that has been packet written may ultimately store less than one written in track- or disk-at-once modes.

The major benefit is really the accessibility and ease of use—you can just drag and drop files onto the CD as if it were a floppy, Jaz, or hard disk. This is great for those situations when you want to have an active backup of a set of files without the hassle of specifically using the CD-R software to write the files each time. I've installed a number of packet-writing solutions where client files come into a production environment, and as part of that process, the files are immediately copied to a "daybook" CD-R. Now, it doesn't matter if the machine crashes or if the hard disc fails before the normal nightly backup has taken place—the files are safe and sound on the CD-R that's being used as a daybook. Each CD is then locked away in a safe each night, and it's possible to go back to the files received on a specific day just by accessing the corresponding CD-R.

Unfortunately, packet writing has its disadvantages, too. Discs written using packet writing are written in UDF (universal disc format) format, which is not compatible with all systems. In fact, only Windows supports the drag-and-drop operation of packet writing through the directCD application. At the beginning of 2001, Apple released a packet-writing system (called CD Burner), but it supports only a small selection of drives, although it's likely that the number will increase. Obviously, the support includes the new iMacs and G4 desktop models announced at the beginning of the same year that include a CD-RW drive. The Retrospect backup and archiving application does support (actually, it requires) the packet-writing capabilities to allow for easier backup. Mac OS 8.6 and higher support UDF discs (UDF is part of the DVD specification), but older versions do not. UDF support is coming for Linux and there are some drivers available, but UDF is not yet universally supported—expect this to change significantly in the future. The other disadvantage is that packet writing and the UDF format are suitable only for writing data discs. This is because audio CDs rely on a block of information at the start of a disc that specifies the track locations and lengths. Because this information is unknown, and because it has to be at the start of the disc, audio CDs that are compatible with a standard audio CD player can't be produced in this way. This shouldn't be a problem, since you're unlikely to want to drag and drop the audio onto the CD.

NOTE

Knowing that the UDF format is used on DVD might make you wonder how audio and video are stored on the disc, since we obviously can't use the same method used on audio CDs. In fact, DVD audio and video tracks are stored as large files on the disc—when your DVD player is showing your latest film, it works in the same way as a computer, opening the file and then reading the contents. Because the information is stored in individual files, it's easy to see how DVDs support multiple features. See Chapter 2 for more information on DVD.

An Overview of Creating CDs

Writing information on CDs has become very popular in recent years. This has led to a wide range of software programs that, in terms of usability, run the gamut from extremely simple to very complex. Fortunately, for most people's needs, there are very simple solutions available to get your data onto CD.

As an introduction to the process behind writing a CD, we'll look at the three main tools used under Mac OS (Toast), Windows (Easy CD Creator) and Linux (CDR Toaster and cdrecord).

NOTE

Late in 2000, Adaptec handed the Toast and Easy CD Creator packages over to a new company called Roxio. Roxio Easy CD Creator 5.0 Platinum contains a number of enhancements over the previous Adaptec Easy CD Creator Deluxe package. First and foremost, it has gained a whole new interface to most of the applications, although the core operation of the applications remains the same. The instructions included here cover Roxio Easy CD Creator 5.0 and Toast 5.0 Titanium, but should also work with the previous version.

Writing a CD with Toast

Toast is one of the oldest CD recording programs. The Mac was actually the first platform that made CD writing a reality, largely due to its built-in support for the SCSI standard, which allowed an easy migration of the professional market in CD technology to the mainstream business world. As such, Toast is one of the most capable of the CD writing packages on the market and has for a long time supported both the mainstream data and audio formats as well as the hybrid, CD-Extra, CD-I and other specialist formats.

The main window for Toast is shown in Figure 5.7. The top section contains buttons to select the type of CD that you are going to write, while a smaller panel at the bottom tells you the current status of the CD recorder attached to your machine. You can see from the screenshot that I'm about to write a selection of files and folders that are just under 211 MB in size. All I had to do was drag and drop the folders onto the main window and Toast automatically added them to the top of the current CD project.

Figure 5.7
Creating a CD
using Toast.

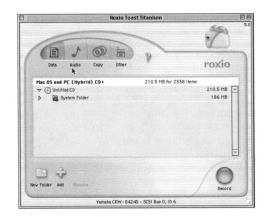

You can, of course, also write data CDs, audio CDs, CD-I, Video CD, and a multitude of other formats. A screenshot of the popup in Figure 5.8 shows the main list. Hidden beneath those major formats are the abilities to record Joliet-compatible discs and to write from pre-built CD-ROM images.

Figure 5.8 (left)
Disc formats
supported by Toast.

Figure 5.9 (right)
Getting ready to write
a disc with Toast.

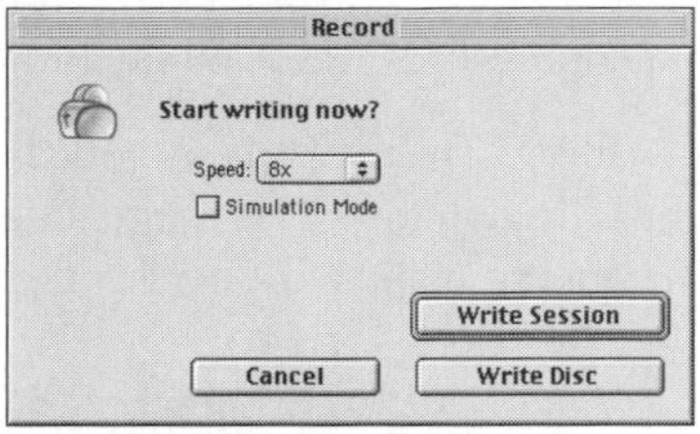

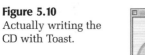

Once you're ready, click on the Record button and then choose how you want to write the CD using the buttons shown in Figure 5.9. If you want to write a single session, click on the Write Session button, but if you want to write and "close-off" the CD, then click on the Write Disc button instead. Note that you can write an individual session only if the amount of data you want to write leaves enough room to add further sessions later.

That's it—Toast will fill the memory cache, then the disk cache, and finally start writing the CD. Toast will give a progress report showing the amount of information written and how much more time is required to complete the writing of the CD. You can see a sample of this in Figure 5.10.

Figure 5.10
Actually writing the
CD with Toast.

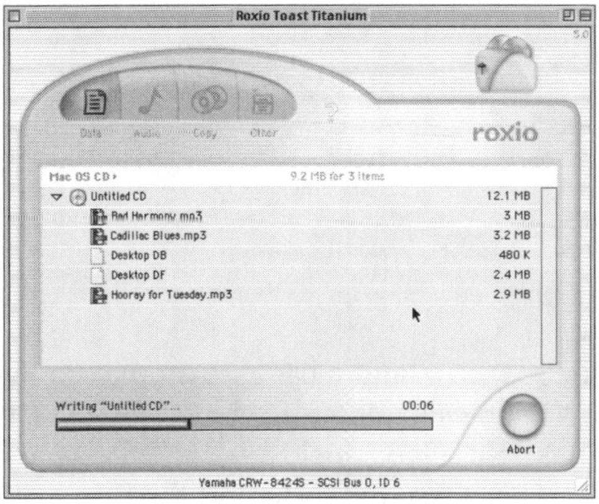

Once the process is complete, Toast will automatically verify that the CD has been written correctly by comparing the contents on the CD with that of the source material. This is a simple, but efficient, way of checking that the writing process has been completed successfully. You can skip this stage, but I don't recommend it. Once everything has been completed successfully, Toast will eject the new CD from the drive ready for you to use.

Writing a CD with Easy CD Creator

Easy CD Creator comes as standard with many of the CD-R drives available for the PC and is the premier CD writing software. The Easy CD Creator package is actually made up of a number of tools, from the main Easy CD Creator application that writes CDs through to sound recorders/editors, SoundStream (for recording audio from CDs and analog sources, including the removal of hiss from analog sources) and PhotoRelay (for creating catalogs of your photo collections).

The operation of Easy CD Creator is largely similar to Toast—you select the files that you want to place onto the CD, give the CD a name, choose a writing speed, and let Easy CD Creator get on with it. You can see the main window for the Easy CD Creator application in Figure 5.11.

Figure 5.11
The main Easy CD Creator window.

The window is split into four panels, with a button bar at the top of the window. The top two panels operate just like any other Windows Explorer-like browser—the left-hand panel lists the disk and directory structure and the right-hand panel shows the files and directories within the currently selected directory. You use these panels to find the files that you want to add to the CD.

In this case, I've selected and then dragged and dropped the list of directories on the right-hand panel into the CD Project panel, which is on the bottom left of the main window. I could have just selected the folders that I wanted to copy and pressed the big Add button in between the top and bottom panels to the selected files and/or folders to the CD Project. These bottom two panels operate in the same fashion as the top panels, except that they show the final CD Project as it will be written, rather than the layout of an existing disk.

At the bottom of the window is a scaled bar that shows how much space the files and directories that you have already selected will take up on the final CD—it actually shows figures for both 74-minute and 80-minute discs. You can control the format of the CD by right-clicking on the main CD icon in the bottom left panel and choosing the Properties option from the resulting menu. From the CD Project Properties dialog box, you can adjust the CD's name, file system, and the mode used to write the track to the CD. You can see the General panel in Figure 5.12. We'll examine the other panels in more detail in Chapter 16.

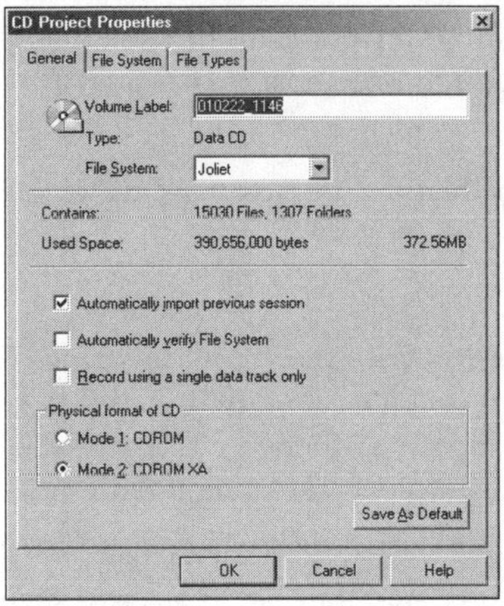

Figure 5.12
Controlling the methods used to write the CD.

Once you're ready to write the CD, click on the red record button in the center button panel—you'll be presented with the dialog shown in Figure 5.13. From here you can control the writing speed and the number of copies that you want. If you click on the Options button, you can also control the writing method (i.e. disc- or track-at-once mode) and whether to test, write, or test and then write the CD when you click the Start Recording button.

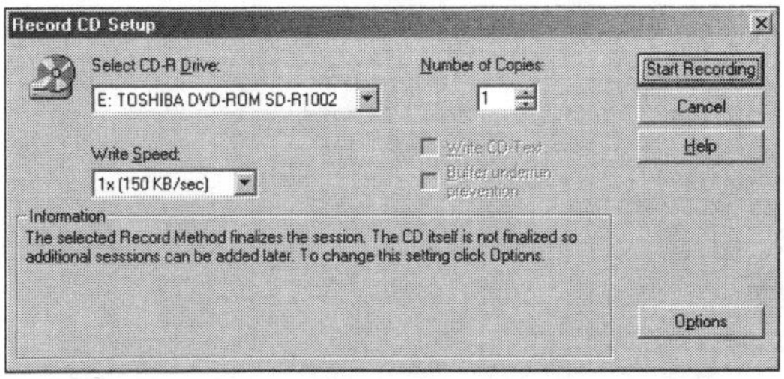

Figure 5.13
Getting ready to write the CD using Easy CD Creator.

The last window shows the progress of the writing process. Easy CD Creator first attempts to locate a suitable drive to use as a source for the files that will be written to the CD. This allows you to write information to a CD from a slower source such as Zip, Jaz, or even a network drive. If necessary, Easy CD then copies the files to a suitable drive before actually writing the track to the CD. You can see from Figure 5.14 that I'm at the start of the copying process.

Figure 5.14
Writing the CD with
Easy CD Creator.

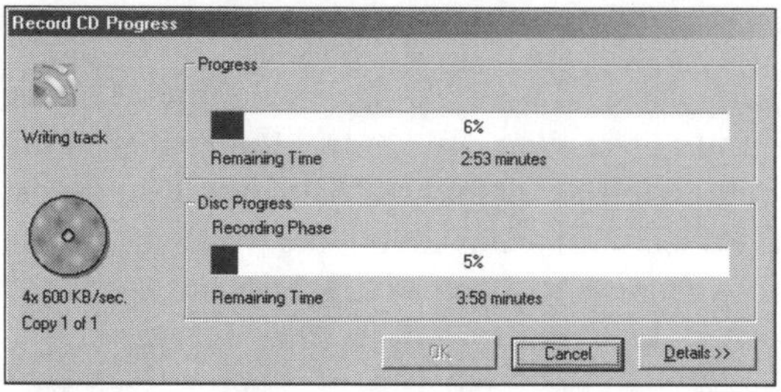

Although this multi-stage process can be quite time-consuming (especially if it has to copy the files from another drive or over the network), it does ensure that the CD will be written correctly.

We'll be looking in more detail at all of the features of Easy CD Creator in Chapter 16.

Writing a CD with Unix/Linux

There is really only one tool that provides you with the ability to write a CD under Unix, and that's **cdrecord**. This is a very raw program and it's generally used with some kind of interface (or front-end). My favorite is CDR Toaster, although there are many others available. With CDR Toaster, when recording a data disc, it's as simple as selecting the directory that you want to record and then clicking go!

You can see the main (and, in fact, the only) panel for CDR Toaster in Figure 5.15.

Figure 5.15
The CDR Toaster
interface to cdrecord.

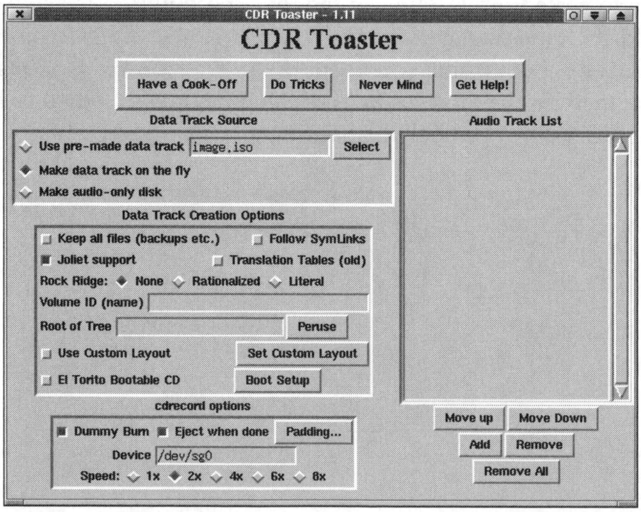

Although this window looks quite complex—and contains a number of inside jokes—the application is actually very easy to use. The window is split into five sections. The top panel (Figure 5.16) contains the buttons and popups that control the operation of the **cdrecord** tool. For example, the Have a Cook-Off actually writes the CD, while the Do Tricks button is actually a popup button set that allows you to read existing CDs and CD-ROMs for copying and audio production, as well as blanking a CD-RW disc.

The Data Track Source panel (Figure 5.16) controls the source and destination format, allowing you to use an image, a data disc, or an audio disc. The Data Track Creation Options panel (Figure 5.17) controls the specifics of the writing process, including picking the location of the directories and files and whether to follow symbolic links. It even supports the ability to create a bootable CD.

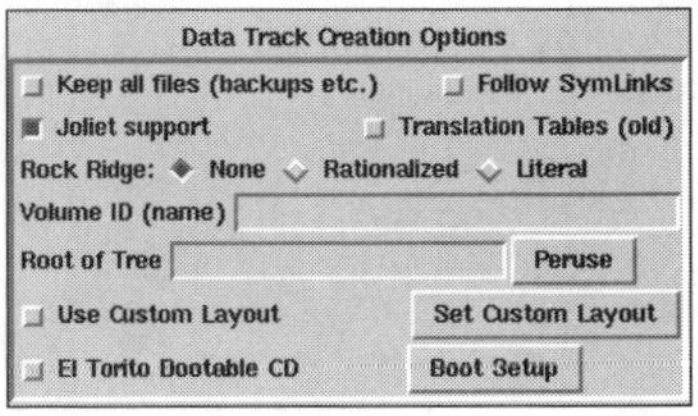

Figure 5.16 (left)
The Data Track Source panel in CDR Toaster.

Figure 5.17 (right)
The Data Track Creation Options panel in CDR Toaster.

The cdrecord options panel (Figure 5.18) controls the process of actually writing the CD—for example, selecting the correct device, specifying the writing speed, and whether padding should be used. The last panel (shown in Figure 5.19), Audio Track List, allows you to add and control the order of the audio tracks that you want to write to the CD.

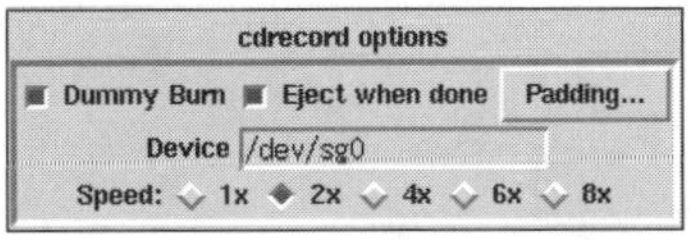

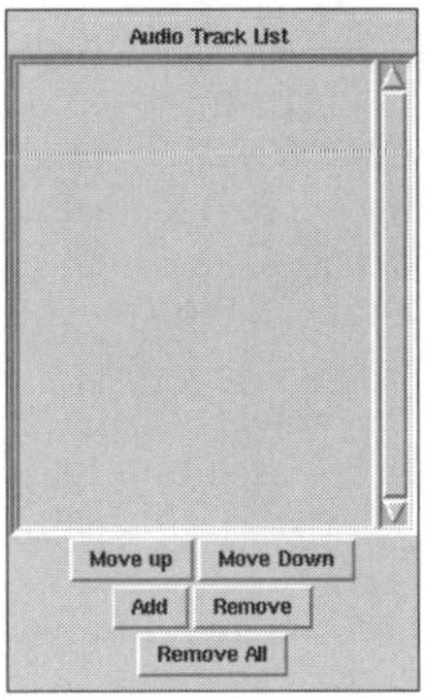

Figure 5.18 (left)
The cdrecord options panel in CDR Toaster.

Figure 5.19 (right)
The Audio Track List panel in CDR Toaster.

To write a data CD, copy all of the files and directories that you want to write into a new directory. If you are limited by space, create symbolic links using **ln** to the files and directories you want to include and then click the Follow Symlinks option in CDR Toaster—this will force the files/directories that have been linked to be written to the disc, instead of merely adding the link itself.

Once you're happy with the file layout, fire up CDR Toaster and put the path to the directory that you want to write into the Root of Tree box—you can use the Peruse button to select the directory interactively (see Figure 5.20). Set the speed at which you want to write the CD, and then check that the device name is correct (see Chapter 17 for more information). If the "Dummy Burn" is selected, then no CD will be written; it'll just go through the motions. You can use this to check that the speed you have selected will not fail.

Figure 5.20
Selecting the directory to use as the root source for data CDs in CDR Toaster.

All you have to do now is click on the Have a Cook-Off button and the process will start. CDR Toaster will spawn a new terminal window (using **xterm**) which will show the output from **cdrecord**, a truncated version of that output is given below:

```
Disk type:  Long strategy type (Cyanine, AZO or similar)
Manuf. index: 25
Manufacturer: Taiyo Yuden Company Limited
cdrecord: WARNING: Track size unknown. Data may not fit on disk.
Starting to write CD/DVD at speed 8 in write mode for single session.
Last chance to quit, starting real write in 1 seconds.
Waiting for reader process to fill input buffer ... input buffer ready.
Performing OPC...
Starting new track at sector: 0
Track 01:  5 MB written (fifo 100%). 1.58% done, estimate finish Mon Nov 20 19:18:02 2000
Track 01: 15 MB written (fifo 100%). 3.15% done, estimate finish Mon Nov 20 19:11:41 2000
Track 01: 25 MB written (fifo 98%). 4.72% done, estimate finish Mon Nov 20 19:09:13 2000
...
Track 01: 591 MB written (fifo 100%). 95.97% done, estimate finish Mon Nov 20 19
:04:52 2000
Track 01: 601 MB written (fifo 100%). 97.54% done, estimate finish Mon Nov 20 19
:04:52 2000
Track 01: 611 MB written (fifo 100%). 99.11% done, estimate finish Mon Nov 20 19
:04:51 2000
Track 01: 616 MB written (fifo 98%).Total translation table size: 0
Total rockridge attributes bytes: 0
Total directory bytes: 0
Path table size(bytes): 10
Max brk space used 67e4
317824 extents written (620 Mb)
```

Track 01: 620 MB written (fifo 100%).
Track 01: Total bytes read/written: 650903552/650903552 (317824 sectors).
Writing time: 541.742s
Fixating...
Fixating time: 34.256s
cdrecord: fifo had 10254 puts and 10254 gets.
cdrecord: fifo was 0 times empty and 6548 times full, min fill was 87%.
Done. Press Enter

A lot of this information is really for statisticians, but it can be helpful to know how much room is left on the disk and how long it takes to write the given CD. We'll be looking at **cdrecord** and CDR Toaster in Chapter 17.

Advanced Software Tools

Writing the CD is really only part of the process. There are a huge number of other programs that you will probably want to use as part of your CD-R tool kit. The tools we've quickly looked at here only solve the problem of actually writing the CD itself. But what if we want to record some audio, rip some tracks from a CD, or even collate a load of scans into a folder?

For that, we need additional software. Some of the tools you need will probably come with the CD-R drive or software that you've purchased. There's also a huge range of packages available on the Internet for recording music, encoding audio CDs to MP3s, and organizing your files and images.

As a rough guide to what you can expect, here's a list and brief descriptions of some of the packages that we'll be looking at throughout the rest of the book:

> ▶ **Retrospect**—A backup/archiving and recovery tool that allows you to back up your machine to CD.

> ▶ **CD Spin Doctor**—Records audio from your tape, record, or other analog source and then removes the hisses and crackles ready for writing the files to CD.

> ▶ **SoundStream**—Records and organizes files for creating audio CDs.

> ▶ **PhotoRelay**—Organizes and catalogs your images for easy browsing.

> ▶ **Take Two**—A backup system for Windows that uses your CD drive instead of a tape.

> ▶ **CD Label Creator**—Creates jewel case and CD labels for your CD-Rs on a PC.

> ▶ **Toast Audio Extractor**—Rips (copies) the tracks from an audio CD.

> ▶ **VideoStudio**—Create video CDs with titles and menus.

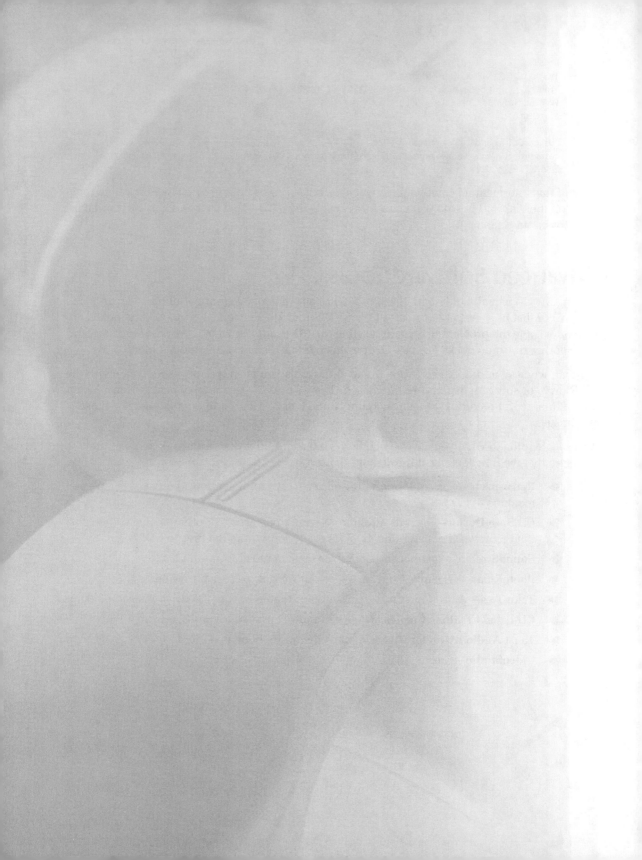

Section II
Writing CDs

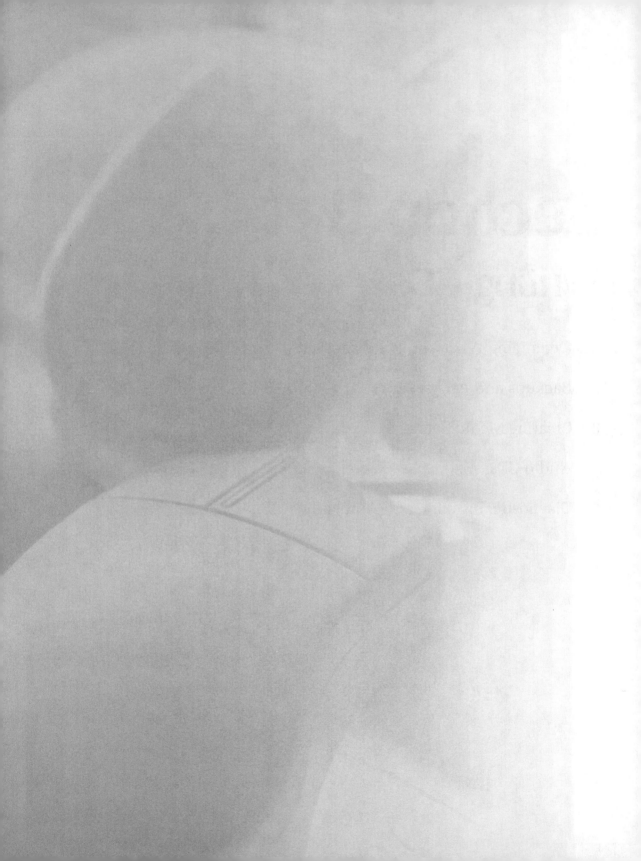

6

Organizing What You Read and Write

Before you decide to start writing CDs, you need to think about how the information and data that you expect to write is organized. This affects every CD that you will ever write. From the basic data CD to audio and even multimedia CDs, you need to be thinking about the layout (both locally and on the final CD).

Finding the Space

Before you start thinking about how you are going to organize the files that you want to write to CD, you need to create some space for the files. Although you might be writing an existing folder to a CD, it's still a good idea to copy the files you expect to write on the CD to a separate folder. This will allow you to delete some files that you perhaps don't need without actually affecting your original (for example, backup files).

Using a different location will also allow you to change the layout and organization of the files that you are writing. This can be especially important when you are archiving files, as you'll probably want to create a layout that allows you to find the files quickly, rather than one that is project or client oriented.

Before looking at ways in which you can free up some space, you need to know how to check the current space situation. Under Windows, double-click on the My Computer icon on the desktop, and then select your hard drive (drive C) or another hard drive or removable disk that you want to use for storing CDs before writing them. Now, press Alt-Return or right-click on the drive icon and choose Properties from the popup menu. The resulting window—an example of which is shown in Figure 6.1—shows the amount of free space you have. You'll need 650 MB for a full CD.

Section II Writing CDs

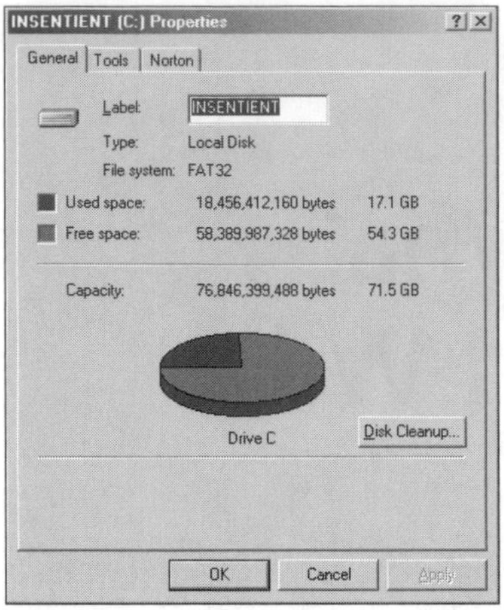

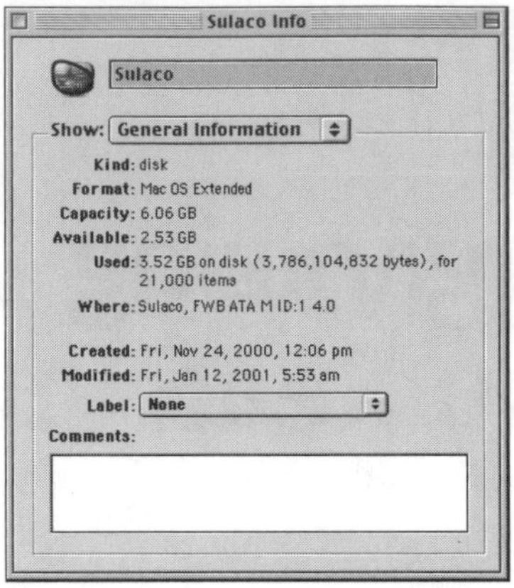

Figure 6.1 (left)
Checking the disk
space on your
Windows machine.

Figure 6.2 (right)
Checking for disk
space on your Mac OS
machine.

On the Mac, choose a volume—probably your hard drive—and then choose File > Get Info or press Command-I. This will show the amount of free space (and used space) on the disk. See Figure 6.2 for an example.

Under Unix, use the **df** command (with the **-k** command line option to show values in kilobytes) to show the amount of space on each of the mount points on your system:

```
$ df -k
Filesystem      kbytes  used  avail capacity Mounted on
/dev/dsk/c1t0d0s0   492977  71011 372669  17%  /
/dev/dsk/c1t0d0s3  2052764 1207478 783704  61%  /usr
/dev/dsk/c1t0d0p0:boot
        10533   1668   8865  16%  /boot
/proc        0    0    0   0%  /proc
fd           0    0    0   0%  /dev/fd
mnttab       0    0    0   0%  /etc/mnttab
/dev/dsk/c1t0d0s6   246493  26301 195543  12%  /var
swap       791308    0 791308   0%  /var/run
swap       791412   104 791308   1%  /tmp
/dev/dsk/c1t0d0s5  2863911 1845645 960988  66%  /export/contrib
/dev/dsk/c1t0d0s7  2052764 1072098 919084  54%  /export/home
/dev/dsk/c1t0d0s4   492977 430213  13467  97%  /export/proxy
/dev/dsk/c1t2d0s0  5159582 1532953 3575034  31%  /usr/local
/dev/dsk/c1t3d0s0  4406142 613487 3748594  15%  /export/mail
/dev/dsk/c1t2d0s1  3651902   130 3615253   1%  /export/cvs
/dev/dsk/c1t3d0s1  4405342 1149237 3212052  27%  /export/http
/dev/dsk/c1t4d0s2  8813061 456046 8268885   6%  /export/data
/dev/dsk/c1t5d0s2  8813061 8284692 440239  95%  /export/share
```

If you have access only to your home directory, you can supply the name of your home directory to find out how much space there is on the drive holding the directory:

```
$ df -k .
Filesystem      kbytes  used  avail capacity Mounted on
/dev/dsk/c1t0d0s7  2052764 1072097 919085  54%  /export/home
```

I've got about 900 MB on this machine to play with—more than enough for a new CD. If you don't have the space, you need to start looking at ways of trimming down the amount of files on your machine, so let's look at some of the more common areas where you can save some space.

Clearing Files You Don't Need

If you want to create a copy of the files and folders that you want to copy onto CD—something I recommend in all situations except when creating a backup of an existing folder—you may find yourself running short of space and needing to create some before you can start setting up your new CD. Here are a few tips on where to look for files to delete.

Internet cache: When you view Web pages, some of the information from those pages is kept on your machine so that it doesn't have to be downloaded again when you next view that page. This speeds up your Web browsing, but it also requires space on your machine in order for the files to be cached ready for use next time. To empty the cache, go into your Web browser and find the Cache panel—you should find a button that will allow you to clear the current cache. You can see examples from Internet Explorer and Netscape under Windows, Mac OS, and Unix in Figures 6.3 through 6.6.

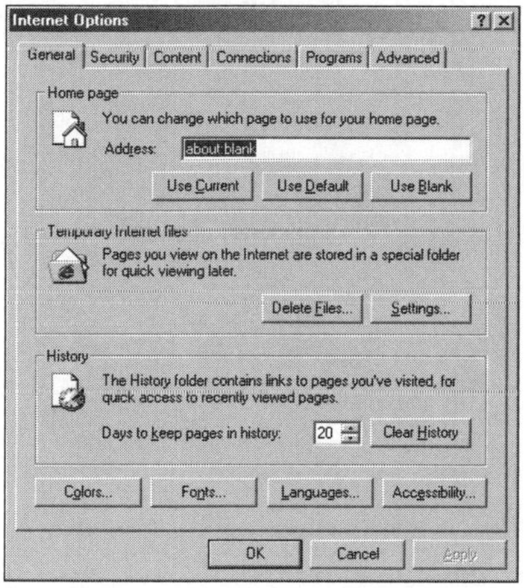

Figure 6.3
Clearing the Cache with Internet Explorer under Windows.

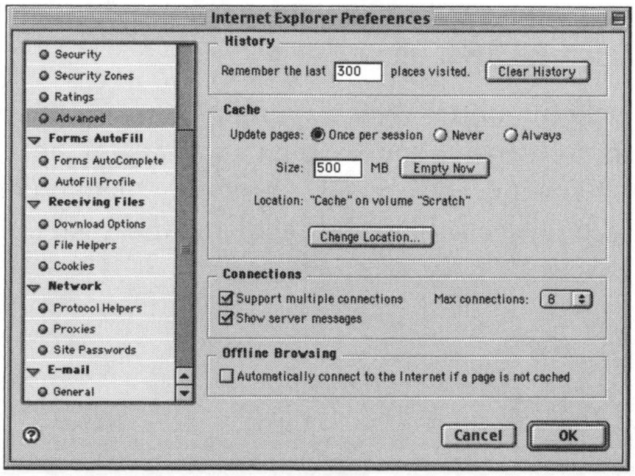

Figure 6.4
Clearing the Cache with Internet Explorer under Mac OS.

Figure 6.5
Clearing the Cache
with Netscape under
Mac OS.

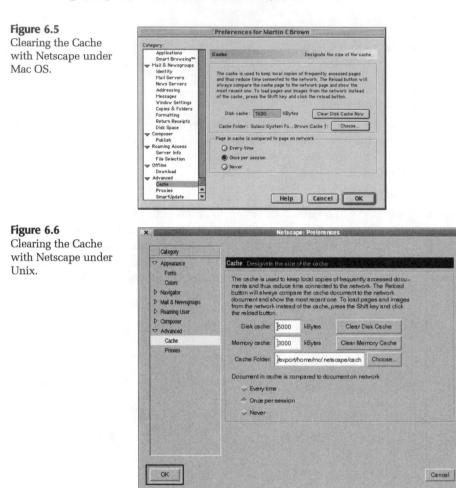

Figure 6.6
Clearing the Cache
with Netscape under
Unix.

Wastebasket/Recycle Bin: We're all guilty of doing this, but it's amazing how many people drag items to their wastebasket, Trash, or Recycle Bin and leave it there without ever emptying the trash—imagine what would happen if we did this in the real world! Emptying your trash can often frees up a lot of space without actually eliminating any necessary information from your machine—after all, you marked it for deletion.

To delete items from the Recycle Bin under Windows, right-click on the Recycle Bin and choose Empty Recycle Bin from the popup menu. You are then asked if you are sure you want to delete the items in the Recycle Bin. If you are, click on OK. Assuming that you have quite a number of files in the Recycle Bin, you should see a dialog box showing the trash flying out and dissolving.

Under Mac OS, choose Special > Empty Trash to empty the wastebasket. You may get a dialog asking you to confirm the process—just click OK and let it run. You might also get warnings about locked or hidden files that couldn't be deleted. You can bypass these messages by holding down the option key as you select Empty Trash.

Under Unix, there is no such thing as a central trash can, but one may be emulated by the windowing system you are using. You usually have to right-click and select the Empty Trash option to delete the files permanently from your machine.

Temporary Files: Lots of software creates temporary and backup files as it is working. It's easy to lose track of exactly how many of these files are created during a typical day and how much space they use up. To delete those files, you need to know what they are called. Under Windows, most temporary files have a TMP extension, while backup files often have the extension .BAK—you should delete these files only when you are sure that you don't need the backup copies anymore.

Under Mac OS, things are slightly more complicated. Temporary files generally are created by applications, but they are also usually deleted as soon as the application quits—or during the next startup. The only time these files are left around are when the application crashes. For example, Microsoft Word creates files with TMP extension, as it does under Windows. Other applications, including Photoshop and QuarkXpress, can create large temporary files—check the application folder to see if any files were created. Especially with Photoshop, check the disk you have selected to use as a Scratch Disk.

Under Unix, there are no standards for the naming of temporary files (although **emacs** gives temporary files a leading and trailing hash sign, and backup files end in a ~ character). However, there are temporary directories in /tmp, /usr/tmp and /var/tmp and even ~/tmp that hold temporary files. Although you won't always have access to these directories, they can use up space. Also, be aware that some temporary directories reside in swap space and therefore don't take up any normal disk space. You might also want to check for any "core" files created when programs crash. These can be quite large and take up a lot of room.

Virtual Memory: You should consider disabling the virtual memory system on your machine only if all your other attempts to clear enough space have failed. Disabling virtual memory may mean your machine is unable to work and you may be limited in the applications that you can open. These methods only work on Windows and Mac OS—you *cannot* disable virtual memory on a Unix machine.

Under Windows 95/98/Me, go into Control Panels and open the System control panel. Once the System control panel is open, click on the Performance tab. Now, click the Virtual Memory button. Within the new window, click on the "Let me specify my own virtual memory settings" radio button and then the Disable Virtual Memory checkbox—see Figure 6.7 for an example. You'll be warned about the dangers and limitations of switching off virtual memory—read them, they mean it! Now, restart your machine and you should be able to claim back the memory previously being used for virtual memory.

Section II Writing CDs

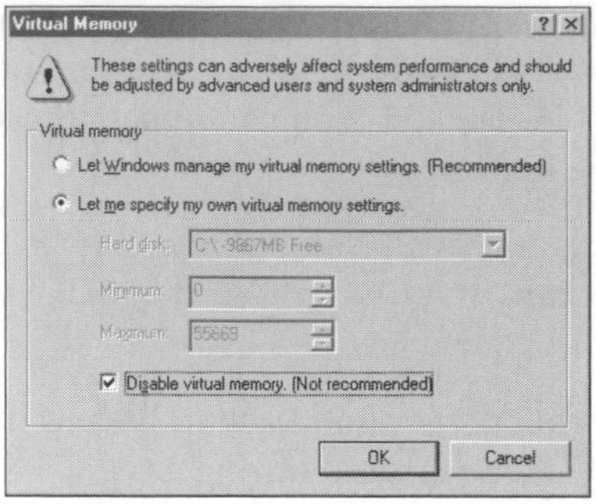

Figure 6.7
Switching off Virtual
Memory under
Windows Me.

Under Windows NT and Windows 2000, you need to go to the Performance panel in the System Control panel and then set the paging file size range to zero for each drive attached to the machine.

Using Mac OS, you need to go to the Memory control panel, click the Off radio button under Virtual Memory, and then restart your Mac. You can see a sample of the Memory control panel—here with Virtual Memory switched on—in Figure 6.8.

Figure 6.8
Switching on Virtual
Memory on the Mac.

If you have Windows 98 or Me, then you have a handy tool called Disk Cleanup, which will sort out the first three items—Internet Cache, Recycle Bin, and Temporary Files—for you. Windows Me will also clear up installer files and application logs. To use it, select Start > System Tools > Disk Cleanup. You'll get a dialog like the one in Figure 6.9. Select the checkboxes next to the types of files that you want to clean up and then click OK.

Figure 6.9
Using the Disk
Cleanup tool.

Creating CD Partitions

Under Windows, creating special partitions in order to store the temporary files before you use them is not really a practical solution—Windows machines don't operate in a way that makes this suitable. Although it can be done, it's not easy. It requires that you either purchase special software (such as Partition Magic), so that you can adjust your existing setup, or install a new hard drive and partition it when setting the drive up. Otherwise, you'll need to re-install your system and re-partition your only drive. This is a complex procedure and shouldn't be attempted unless you know what you are doing. If you need additional space, find out from your dealer about USB or FireWire disk drives or about a Jaz or removable storage device.

On the Mac, historically, the easiest way to create a CD is to create some additional partitions on your main disk if you have room or on a secondary drive connected to your machine. Each of these partitions should be 650.4 MB in size. You'll need a recent version of Drive Setup or a hard disk tool such as FWB's Hard Disk Toolkit to format the drive into individual partitions. If you have an iMac, iBook, or a B&W G3, G4, or PowerBook G3 (2000) machine, you can connect a FireWire or USB drive to your machine and partition it accordingly.

On a Unix box, there is no point in partitioning a disk especially for use when writing CDs. You don't ever write a volume from a Unix machine to a CD; you just write a directory straight to the CD instead. If you are concerned about space, though, it's easy enough to add to your machine a new disk for storage—check your documentation for information on how to do this.

Although partitioning isn't really necessary anymore (even on a Mac), it can be a useful way of ensuring that you get the maximum use out of your CDs. I used CD partitions on a Mac for years for archiving at an advertising agency. When we archived a project, it often made three or five, and, in one case, eight CDs.

Because the hard disk partitions matched the size of the final CD so perfectly—even including the file system—we could cram the information onto the CD more easily. It also meant that I could copy and organize a series of CDs before writing them, while still leaving the original structure on the server. The final benefit was that the CDs were also backed up, twice, to DAT tape—because the CDs were there as partitions on a hard disk, I could simply select all the partitions to back up and let it run. Not only was it quicker, but I could also leave it running without having to manually insert each CD.

Of course, today we could do this with folders, just by keeping an eye on the size of each folder to make sure we don't go over the limit. Partitions are still useful—we'll use them when we create installer and boot CDs—but it's more convenient to use disk images or some form of removable storage like a Zip, Jaz, or SuperDisk drive.

Using Removable Storage

If you have some form of removable storage (excluding a CD-R/CD-RW drive), then you can use the removable storage as a staging area. Of course, you need a staging area that is as large as the CD you expect to create. Using a floppy disk is probably a bad idea, and unless you are creating a small CD, even a SuperDisk (120 MB) or Zip (100/250 MB) is probably too small. However, an Orb or Jaz is perfect—I used a 1.3 GB (650 MB per side) Magneto Optical system for years, which was ideal because the size of the MO almost perfectly matched the size of the final CD!

The advantage of removable media of any kind is that because it's on a separate disk, you have to copy information to it, rather than move it. It also means that you can have a number of CDs "on the go" being populated—when you have something to add or change, just pop in the removable disk and copy it over.

Using Network Drives

There are occasions when using a network drive is the best solution for your organizational problems. For starters, you'll probably have more space on a network drive than on your local machine in order to keep and organize the files. Because of the available space, you can use a network drive as a staging post for a number of CDs simultaneously. Alternatively, a network drive can be used as a way of providing a central area on your network for storing files before they are written to CD.

Everybody can copy files to the network drives ready for archiving—it relieves the pressure from you to find archive material. The downside is that it also relies on you to check the network volumes to determine when a CD needs to be written. That can make it a bit of an administration nightmare, but it also provides a useful service to your users without so much hands-on interaction.

Using Disk Images

Under Mac OS, you can use the Disk Copy utility to create a disk image. This is mountable and accessible just like any other Mac volume. You can use images as a way of creating a temporary, CD-sized volume onto which you can copy files before they are written. You still need disk space—Mac OS doesn't magically create a CD-sized volume for you out of nowhere—but it does enable you to create volumes that can be prepared with an operating system and diagnostic tools, which can then be written to a bootable CD.

To create a CD-sized disk volume, open Disk Copy, which should have been installed within your Utilities folder. Choose Image > Create New Image. You'll get a slightly modified standard file dialog box like the one shown in Figure 6.10. Under the Size popup, select the size of the image that you want to create—you can create any sized image up to 2 GB. The list includes three CD-ROM specific options—an 8-centimeter disc (173 MB), an almost full 12-centimeter CD (595 MB), and a full 12-centimeter CD (651 MB).

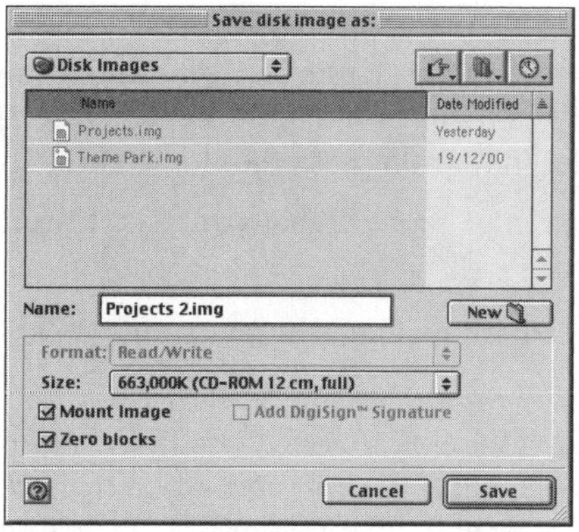

Figure 6.10
Creating a new
disk image.

You need to give the image a name—this will be given to the volume when it is mounted and written to CD. Select a disk where the image can be saved—you'll need about 5 MB more than the image size you've requested. Unless you've changed any of the checkboxes, the image will be created and then mounted onto the desktop. You can now start copying files, and even installing an operating system, straight onto that volume. It'll be written to the disc image—once you've copied everything across, you just ask Toast to write a volume to a CD.

I use disk images frequently for the same reason that I used to use partitions. I know that the 651 MB disc image created by Disk Copy is the maximum amount of space available on the final CD. I also know that I can set up everything about the CD—including a custom icon—by using the disk image, safe in the knowledge that once I'm happy with the disk image, that's exactly what will be written to the CD. Furthermore, I can have a number of disk images "on the go," and I can fill them up as I get new information—when they are full, I write them to CD.

Unfortunately, because of the way in which both Unix and Windows work, neither of these operating systems supports the ability to create special disk images like the Mac. Don't get confused into thinking that a "Create ISO Image" or similar option within your CD-writing software does the same thing. What it does is create a prepared image that can be used to write the same CD a number of times on different machines. You cannot copy files to an existing image like you can with a Mac OS disk image.

Files and Directory Structure

As I've said before—unless you have a specific requirement, the way you organize your source material is entirely up to you. However, there are some tips and techniques that I've found useful over the years that make collecting, writing, and using CDs much easier.

Your primary consideration should be how you expect to use the information once it's been written. With an audio CD, there's not a lot to the process. You can't subdivide tracks on the CD into different folders, so it doesn't matter what your layout is like. With an MP3 CD, on the other hand, things get more complicated—you'll probably want to organize the individual tracks on the CD into their albums or artists and then again, perhaps, in different music styles.

If it's an archive CD, you need to ensure that your structure makes it easy to find the information again afterward. Putting all of the letters that you wrote last year into a single directory probably isn't a good idea. What would be better is if you could split them into recipient directories so that when you go looking for that letter to Grandma, you could go straight to it.

These are all basic examples of the layout of your CD that you need to consider before it's been written—you can't change it afterward!

There are some general tips that you can follow that will make the process easier regardless of the type of CD you are using:

▶ **Use directories**—It's amazing to think that many people fail to use one of the simplest mechanisms for organizing information: the directory. Just by creating a few directories on your disk, and eventually on your CD, you can improve the chances and speed with which you can find information from a few minutes to just seconds.

▶ **Use sensible names**—Don't give your files or folders either silly names or arbitrary numbers of code names unless you have a good way of working out what they mean.

NOTE

I once came across a site that used a sequential number to store its letters. This meant that when looking for a particular letter to a client, they had to look up the client records, find the file number, and then open the file. There were 4,500 files in one directory that contained letters sent to about forty different clients and it took a few minutes each time for the secretaries to find an item. If that wasn't bad enough, they dutifully archived their letters to CD, but foolishly restarted the file numbers each time, so when they had to open file 4567 it meant checking through five or six CDs until they found the right 4567 document!

▶ **Use long filenames**—Gone are the days when we are limited to eight characters in a filename and the three optional extension letters. All platforms now support names of at least thirty-one characters in length—use them! Trying to determine what POAMIACM.GIF means three years after you wrote the CD is probably not possible (it's "Picture of a mouse in a cat's mouth," just in case you wondered!).

▶ **Arrange files by content, not type**—Creating a set of directories called "Letters," "Faxes" and "E-mails" will make it difficult to find a file at some later stage. Instead, create directories according to clients or projects.

▶ **Use a CD insert**—We'll look at creating custom printed labels in Chapter 20, but just writing a simple list of contents on a CD insert will help. Simply giving a CD a name—for example, Archive 001—without any form of description of the contents is asking for trouble. If you need to refer to the contents often, use a disk cataloging program that will match files on a disk with a disk's name.

▶ **Use directories**—It really will make a difference!

There are some other, more content specific issues to consider, which I've covered next.

Audio CD Layouts

When it comes to creating audio CDs, the important thing is not so much the layout, but where you store the source files and how they are organized. Once they are written to the audio CD, any structure you intended to have on the CD will disappear since you can't support directories on a standard audio CD. When it comes to the source material, order it by album and/or artist. This will make it easy to find the information you want when you write the CD. For example, you can see from the screenshot in Figure 6.11 that I've organized my MP3 files according to the artist and then the album title. Now, when I come to select the tracks for one of my custom CDs, I have to find only the artist and album, not hunt through hundreds of tracks in a single folder.

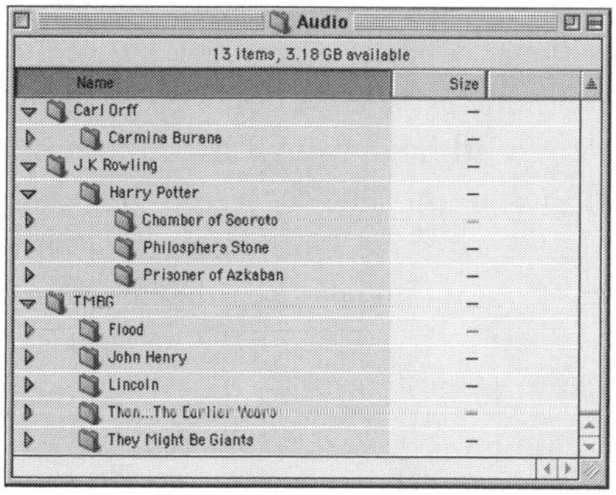

Figure 6.11
Arranging audio files
by artist and album.

Archive CD Layouts

Going back to an archive CD months (or even years) after you first wrote it is a brilliant way of appreciating just how bad your organization can be. Unfortunately, there is no right or wrong way to archive information on a CD. It's entirely dependent on your source material, but it's important to remember that it must be easy to retrieve the information. I have in the past archived accounts, ad agency projects, book projects, Web sites, and correspondence. In all these cases, the following issues have become apparent:

▶ **Organizing only by client/project name is not enough**—However unlikely it may seem at the time, you may well do work for a different client or, indeed, work on a similarly named project. It's also possible to work on the same project a number of times. Rather than just labeling folders and directories with the client or project name, also supply a date. This should be the date at which no further information is added. For example, a folder named "iMac FYI, June 2000" will have information only up until June 2000—information from July 2000 and beyond would be stored on a different CD.

▶ **Organizing with arbitrary folders is time consuming**—Try to avoid creating a CD that has only a few top-level directories. Many people archive information onto CD and then make the CDs available, either through a CD multi-changer or by copying them onto a big disk drive on a network server. Adding extra levels through which a user has to click to get to the information can prevent people from using the archived information.

▶ **Use subdirectories for different file groups**—Although I'm repeating myself here, it's an important item that can't be stressed enough. If you have a project folder for your latest brochure, don't just dump all of the files into a single directory. Create a project directory, and within that create "artwork," "image," "illustrations," "scans," and whatever other directories you need to divide the information up. Then, when you're looking for the image used on a specific project, you can go straight to it.

▶ **For big clients, use archive CD sets**—At the ad agency I worked for, we did work for Hewlett-Packard, Digital, Raytheon, and many others, and most of the time we could fill up two or more CDs just with the contents of a single project for a single client. Although it could be tempting to simply label all the CDs Archive XXX, it made it difficult when looking for an image used on an HP project. Instead, we had sequential numbering on a client-by-client basis, so we had a set of CDs for HP, another for Digital, and so on.

▶ **Don't shortchange your numbering system**—In the space of five years, I wrote about 350 archive CDs from all my client projects. If I had decided to label them HP Archive 1, HP Archive 2, and so on, it would have been a nightmare in our cataloging software when browsing for a CD and then a file. The reason is that computers will sort HP Archive 1, HP Archive 10 and HP Archive 2 one after another, even though we know that the order should be 1, 2, 10. You can see the effects better in Figure 6.12.

Figure 6.12
How computers sort
text/number based
directories.

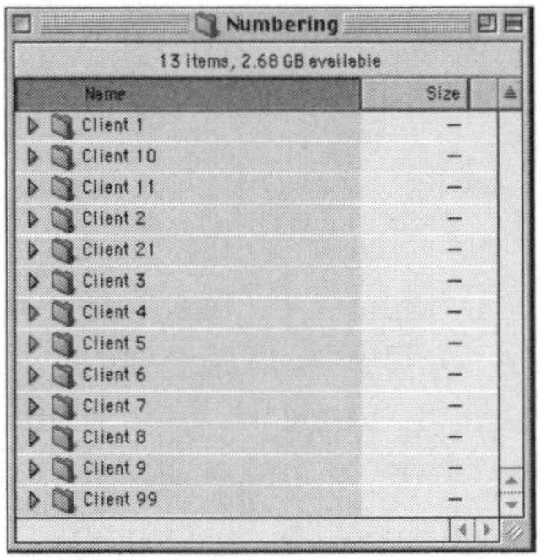

Instead, use a fixed digit numbering system. For example, use 001, 002, etc.—this will allow the titles to be sorted properly. The same applies to directories within those CDs.

▶ **Use international-style dates**—Continuing from our previous example, it's also important to use international dates, which are formatted 20001213 (year month day, no separators)—these, too, are ordered properly by the sorting algorithms used on files and folders. If you use traditional 13/12/2000 (day, month, year) or 12/13/2000 (month, day, year), then the sorting systems go haywire!

Installer CD Layouts

For an installer or other bootable disc, all you need to think about is how you organize the information on the CD so that it is easily accessible—I tend to use the same format on all my CDs, shown here in Figure 6.13 from a Mac OS bootable CD. Unfortunately, we don't have the same flexibility on other systems, so it's not really an option. See Chapter 10 for more information.

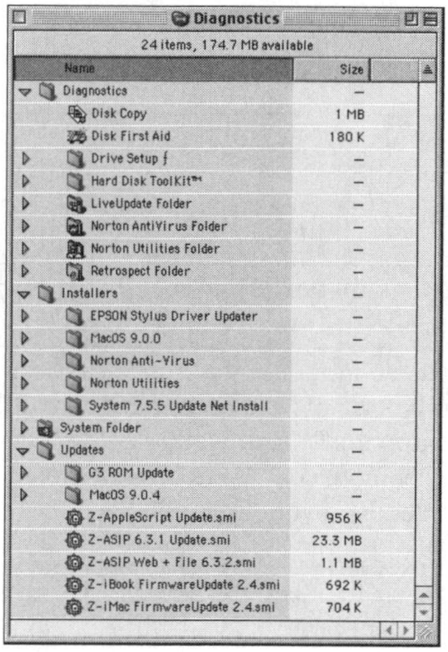

Figure 6.13
A simple install/boot/
diagnostic CD.

Name	Size
▽ 🗂 Diagnostics	–
🖥 Disk Copy	1 MB
📀 Disk First Aid	180 K
▷ 📁 Drive Setup ƒ	–
▷ 🗂 Hard Disk ToolKit™	–
▷ 🗂 LiveUpdate Folder	–
▷ 🗂 Norton AntiVirus Folder	–
▷ 🗂 Norton Utilities Folder	–
▷ 🗂 Retrospect Folder	–
▽ 🗂 Installers	–
▷ 🗂 EPSON Stylus Driver Updater	–
▷ 🗂 MacOS 9.0.0	–
▷ 🗂 Norton Anti-Virus	–
▷ 🗂 Norton Utilities	–
▷ 🗂 System 7.5.5 Update Net Install	–
▷ 🗂 System Folder	–
▽ 🗂 Updates	–
▷ 🗂 G3 ROM Update	–
▷ 🗂 MacOS 9.0.4	–
🔷 Z-AppleScript Update.smi	956 K
🔷 Z-ASIP 6.3.1 Update.smi	23.3 MB
🔷 Z-ASIP Web + File 6.3.2.smi	1.1 MB
🔷 Z-iBook FirmwareUpdate 2.4.smi	692 K
🔷 Z-iMac FirmwareUpdate 2.4.smi	704 K

Diagnostics — 24 items, 174.7 MB available

Image/Video Archive Layouts

When creating an image or video archive on CD, think about how the information will be accessed and where it comes from. On image CDs, you should label each CD with a unique identifier and then label each folder within each CD uniquely as well. This will improve the chances of you recovering the information through cataloging software, because it will require a unique location to find the image again.

For example, you might consider giving each directory on an image CD a name that is made up of the source type (35 millimeter, APS, large format, digital, etc.), a serial number (APS films actually have one built-in, so use it!), and a date, either when the film was scanned (*not* taken) or when it was transferred from the digital camera or video. Try to avoid giving the folders and directories labels according to a project (unless you can guarantee individuality). Instead, use the image cataloging software to record image-specific information such as the location it was taken, the date, conditions, subject, and so on.

Using this method means that when you come to access the film at some later stage, the catalog software has a unique identifier for each shot that will save you time when you need to access the original.

Section II Writing CDs

File Formats

You should take great care when putting files onto a disc that may be used by people other than yourself. Writing a CD that contains Office 2000 files, when the eventual user has Office 95, is guaranteed to cause problems. Although you can argue that converters are available, the simple fact is that most users don't want to have to find these items in order to use your CD—and it's unlikely that supplying them on the CD will be practical, either.

Table 6.1
Specific and common file formats

Current Format	Suggested CD Format
Unformatted Text	Use the plain text format (with line breaks) supported by most word processors and applications.
Formatted Text	Use Word 95 format, or better still, the RTF format that is supported by a larger number of word processors.
Formatted Documents (Text/Pictures)	Unless it needs to be in editable form, use the Adobe Acrobat portable document format (PDF). If it needs to be editable, export to a number of formats. For example, Microsoft Word supports RTF, as well as earlier versions of Word and WordPerfect. You can get more converters from Microsoft's Web site (**www.microsoft.com/downloads**) if you think you need to support additional formats.
Application Specific Formats	Unless you can afford to export to one of the alternative formats (raw text, JPEG, or other application-independent formats), you will have to use an application-specific format. For example, if you want to exchange a multi-layer Photoshop document, it must be saved as a Photoshop file. Equally, PageMaker, QuarkXpress and other page layout software also use their own formats, even though they do basically the same job. There is no alternative that is compatible with all three applications—just remember to give the files their correct extension (see "File Extensions" later in this chapter) and make it clear to the user what software is required to read the files on the CD.
Images	For simple photos, use JPEG with a 95 percent (high) quality setting. This will give a good combination of picture quality and size. If you want to use the image in a printed brochure, use TIFF. Although the TIFF format has both Windows and MacOS subformats, all applications are able to read either format without problems.
Sounds	Use the AIFF format for exchanging raw audio streams or the MP3 format if you want to exchange compressed audio. Remember, though, that MP3 is a lossy format and the quality will not be as good as AIFF
Movies	Use MPEG or AVI formats, but try to use one of the standard system codecs instead of a custom one. If you can, use a format like QuickTime, which is cross compatible on Windows and MacOS.

If you know your target audience, try to use file formats that you know they will be able to read. For example, if you are distributing a simple text document, use a plain text format—don't put it into a Word, Ami Pro, or AppleWorks document, as it would be unreadable by many of your users.

Try to pick a common denominator that will be readable by the majority, if not all, of your expected user base. I've listed some of the common file formats and a suitable common file format you could use in its place for compatibility in Table 6.1.

Naming Conventions

How you name your files, directories, and CDs is entirely up to you (although consider using the guidelines I've given). However, whatever you choose as a filename, remember it will ultimately affect your ability to access the information or open the file that you stored on the CD.

You need to consider three things when dishing out filenames: the file's name, the file extension, and how to handle cross-platform CDs.

The File's Name

The ISO9660 disc format supports a basic filename of 8.3 characters. The three characters are used to give the file an extension, which is used under Windows (and occasionally Unix) as a way of identifying the content type of a file. The first eight characters you could use for whatever you wanted.

Although we aren't restricted to the eight-character limit anymore on the main filename, it doesn't mean that you can knock yourself out on the name front. For example, naming a file "That picture I took while Laura was laughing about the duck" may be very descriptive, but it doesn't help you (or anybody else) understand what it is about. Equally, naming a folder "Digital Transmissions" is a bit too arbitrary—do you mean e-mails, faxes, or both?

File Extensions

I have to admit to being somewhat of a fan of file extensions, even allowing for their limitations, because I know the instant I see a file what type it is, because I recognize the three-letter extension. Under Windows, and probably in most situations under Unix, you can't avoid the three-letter extension—it'll be required and probably automatically added by the application that created the document. The extension is not compulsory—the extension of a file doesn't govern the file's content or format, only how it is recognized by the operating system and applications. To ensure that your files are identifiable, you should use the correct file extensions. Under Mac OS, though, a file extension is optional. Macs use a completely different way of identifying which application is required when opening a file. Although this information will be written and identified correctly on a Mac OS CD, if you create a cross-platform CD, or PC-only CD from your Mac, then neglecting to add extensions to your documents can cause all sorts of problems.

With no way of identifying the file's type, your Windows and Unix users may be unable to decide which application is required to open each file. It's therefore a good idea to remember to add the extension when you create the file, so that when you write it to CD, the information is already there.

Although it would be impractical to list all of the extensions and their corresponding descriptions in this guide (there are a few million possible combinations), there are some that you will probably need shown in Table 6.2.

Table 6.2
Common extensions for different file formats

Description	Extension
Word Document	.DOC
Word Template	.DOT
Excel Worksheet	.XLW
Excel Spreadsheet	.XLS
HTML Document	.HTM
JPEG Image	.JPG
Photoshop Document	.PSD
MPEG Video	.MPG
TIFF Image	.TIF
QuarkXpress Document	.QXP
Wave Audio File	.WAV
AIFF Audio File	.AIF
Acrobat PDF	.PDF
QuickTime Movie	.QT/.MOV
GIF (Graphics Interchange Format) File	.GIF
Zip (compressed/archived) File	.ZIP
StuffIt Archive	.SIT
Binhexed (text compatible) Mac OS File	.HQX

Cross-Platform CDs

If you are writing a CD that you expect to use or be used on more than one platform, you also need to consider the following when naming your files and folders:

▶ **On a Mac, avoid using forward or back-slash characters in your files.** The slash characters are used under PCs and Unix as path separators. You'll generally find slashes in filenames when used in dates or when used as separators between components. Try using hyphens to separate details or, if you are dealing with dates, use the format 11 Jun 2000 or 20000611—the latter option has the advantage that will produce a list ordered by date when sorted.

▶ **On a PC (or Unix), avoid using the colon in a name.** The Mac uses a colon as a path separator, and you can confuse a Mac very easily if it sees a colon in a filename.

▶ **Under Unix, avoid using files that use more than one period.** Although it won't make any difference under Mac OS, on a PC it can confuse some applications and some versions of Windows, because it expects only one period—the one that separates the file name from its extension. The most popular use for a filename with multiple periods is when used to separate multiple extensions, for example, on a compressed tar or cpio archive. See Table 6.3 for some of the commonly accepted abbreviations of many Unix archive formats.

Table 6.3
Unix Compound
File Extensions

Full Name	Long Name	Abbreviations
.tar.Z	Tarred, compressed	.tZ, .trZ
.tar.gz	Tarred, Gzipped	.tgz
.tar.bz2	Tarred, Bzipped	.tbz, .tb2
.pkg.Z	Solaris Package, Compressed	.pkZ
.pkg.gz	Solaris Package, Gzipped	.pgz
.pkg.bz2	Solaris Package, Bzipped	.pbz, .pb2
.cpio.Z	CPIO Archive, Compressed	.cpZ
.rpm.gz	RedHat Package, Gzipped	.rgz
.rpm.bz2	RedHat Package, Bzipped	.rbz

▶ **Limit names to thirty-one characters**—Mac OS supports only thirty-one characters in a file or directory name, but you can have unlimited full path lengths. Creating a file on either Unix or Windows with more than thirty-one characters will cause problems, especially if you expect those files to be referenced from another document (for example, within a page layout or HTML document).

▶ **Limit directory nesting to eight levels.** If you are using any of the extensions to the ISO9660 format (Joliet, Rock Ridge, etc.), you are not limited to eight directory levels, but that doesn't mean you can go crazy. In fifteen years of computing, I've never had to go more than eight levels, and for ultimate compatibility, you should avoid going beyond this limit.

Final Preparations

You've copied the files across, you have a reasonable structure to your files, and you are ready to start recording files and information onto your CD disc. Wait!

Before you start, it's worth taking a few minutes to ensure that your machine is in a suitable state to start copying the files over to CD. Any sort of delay or problem will lead to what are called buffer underruns (see Chapter 11). A buffer underrun while writing your CD means that your CD becomes a coaster and you need to start again. Although all of the steps below aren't necessary for every writing process, they can prevent you from starting a new line of high-tech coasters.

Check for Disk Problems

Although your operating system and software should be written in such a way that such problems don't occur, minor disk problems are a part of everyday life. If you want to check your disk for problems, you need to use some special software.

Under Windows, use Scandisk to check your drive. You may want to boot up in Safe Mode first (hold down the control key during booting and select Safe Mode from the menu) and then run Scandisk, but you'll have to reboot before you write the CD. Let Scandisk run its course—it'll take anywhere from five minutes to more than an hour, depending on the size of your disk and how full it is. To get a full checkup, make sure you check the Thorough radio button. You can see a sample of Scandisk in progress in Figure 6.14.

Figure 6.14
Checking a Windows disk with Scandisk.

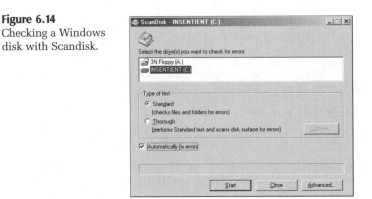

For Macs, you need to use the Disk First Aid (DFA) utility, which comes with your machine, under Mac OS. This will check all the volumes on your machine for problems. If DFA fails because it can't unmount the disk, you will need to boot up from your system CD that came with your machine. Insert the CD, choose Special > Reboot and then hold down the C key to force your machine to boot from the CD. Once again, you'll need to reboot using your hard disk in order to actually write the CD. You can see DFA in action in Figure 6.15.

Figure 6.15
Checking a Mac disk with Disk First Aid.

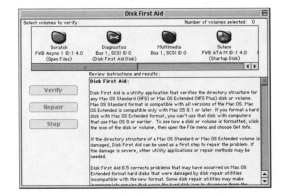

Unix is ultimately more reliable than either Mac OS and Windows, and disk problems of any kind are very rare unless you've had a system crash. You shouldn't need to manually check the disk, but if you are concerned, reboot the machine (using **shutdown -r now**) to force the disks to be checked upon startup.

Defragmenting your Drive

As you use the disk in your machine, it will gradually get fragmented. This happens because information is normally written sequentially to your disk. However, if you create file A, then file B, and then add more information to file A, file A will be fragmented—it's no longer in a sequential block because it has file B in the middle of it. This fragmentation causes problems when writing a CD because it makes the operating system and hard disk look around for the next block of information for each file. The interruption while it searches causes our buffer underrun problem.

Although defragmenting your drive can be an important part of the process, it won't be needed for every CD that you write. In fact, due to the buffers built into modern drives and the software that writes CDs, the effects of a badly fragmented drive are very rarely experienced. If you do find you are having problems, however, check out Chapter 11, where we look in more detail at how to defragment your drive.

Quit Unnecessary Applications

It really isn't a good idea to try to write your letter to Grandma or edit that photo while you are writing a CD. In fact, most CD-creation software will actually stop you from trying to use another application while you are writing a CD (Unix excepted). That doesn't mean, however, that your machine is quiet and unencumbered at the time you write your CD.

All machines have a certain amount of "background chatter" from applications. These can be official background applications—virus and disk checkers, for example—or just standard applications that you happened to have open when you decided to write the CD. Your word processor, image editor, and database program all perform functions while they are in the background, from checking network connections to auto saving and spell-checking a document.

You should quit the latter applications (just switch to them and choose quit). The former, "proper" background applications can probably be left alone. They are specifically designed to run in the background without causing too much trouble—but see Chapter 11 for more information on what to do if you have CD writing problems.

Viruses

Whether you are creating a CD for personal use or a CD that will eventually be used to create the master for CD distribution, you must ensure that the information you are going to write is virus-free. There have been sporadic reports of viruses being distributed on CD-ROMs from game and software manufacturers that are not discovered until after the CDs have reached customers' hands. Obviously, this isn't the best way to find out about (or resolve) the problem.

Section II Writing CDs

Instead, you should be checking your machine and the files that you are about to write to CD *before* starting the writing process. The easiest way to do this is to install virus-checking software on your machine. I recommend either Norton's AntiVirus product, or McAfee's VirusScan software. Regular updates and a development/discovery team that are constantly watching the world for new viruses and strains back up both packages. Both packages are also supported under Mac and Windows platforms and they'll check everything from system viruses to macro viruses.

If you get either package, then make sure that you:

▶ **Keep up to date with the latest virus definition files.** Most software comes with its own update system that will automatically update your system with new virus patches at periodic intervals. At the very least, you should be updating your system with new definitions weekly. If you are regularly burning CDs on a system that is connected to the Internet and is regularly used for downloading information from the Internet, you might want to consider checking each day. Although updates aren't always available this regularly, it will do no harm to check, even if nothing is downloaded. You can see a sample of the Mac Norton AntiVirus LiveUpdate package in Figure 6.16.

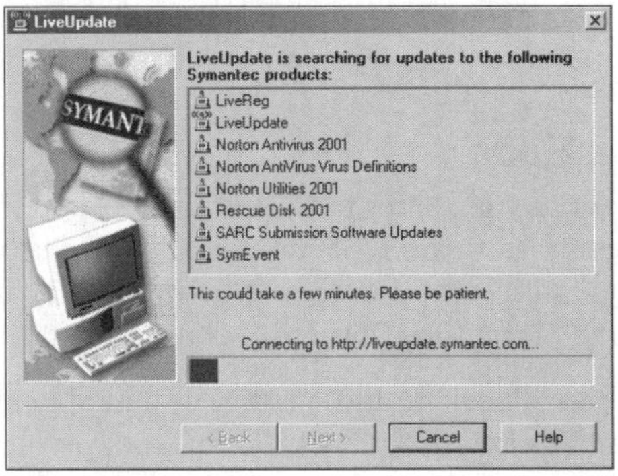

Figure 6.16
Updating your virus definitions with Norton AntiVirus LiveUpdate.

▶ **Check your machine for viruses on a weekly basis**. Having the latest definitions will not stop the viruses from infecting your machine. You still need to actually check your machine to verify that it has not already been infected.

▶ **Before you write a CD, even if it's only for your own personal use, check the contents of the directory that contains the files you are going to write.** Both of the packages mentioned above allow you to arbitrarily scan any directory—assuming you've followed the guidelines above regarding layout and file location, you should be able to scan the contents of the CD you are about to write. Figure 6.17 shows you the window searching a specific directory structure under Norton Anti-Virus for Windows.

Figure 6.17
Checking for viruses in
a specific directory with
Norton AntiVirus.

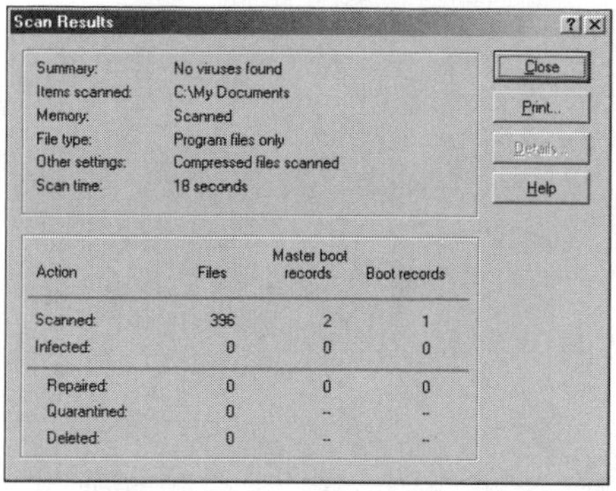

▶ **Try to avoid downloading and extracting/running software downloaded from the Internet on your CD writer.** Although it isn't the location or source of all viruses, a high proportion are distributed accidentally with files and e-mail attachments, often without people knowing.

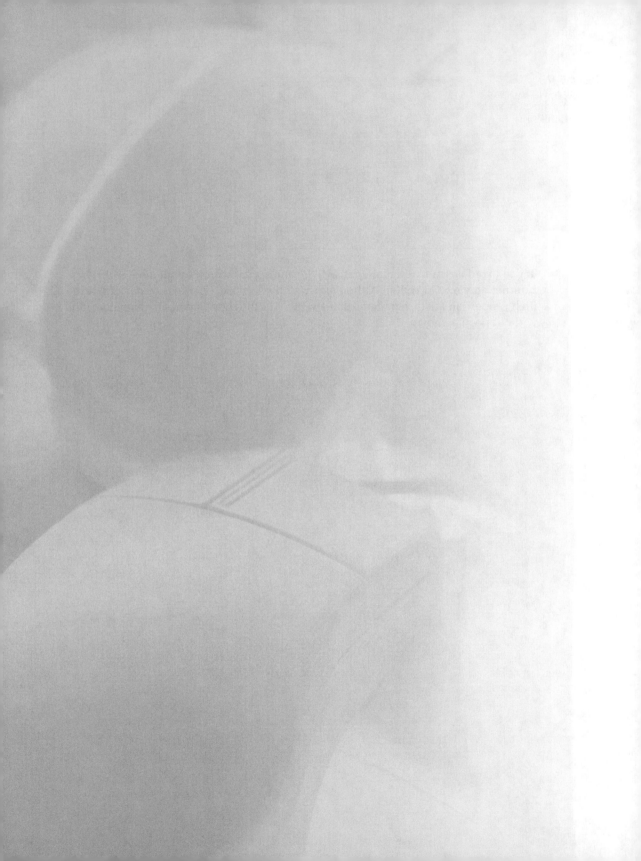

7

Backups
and Archiving

Although it's not everybody's favorite solution, CD-R/RW can be used as a method for backing up and archiving your machines. Part of the perceived problem with CD-R, at least for backups, is that it is not very easy to add information on an ad-hoc basis. As a general rule, CDs are written to and forgotten, not written to and then updated as you get more information. Although it's possible to use CDs in this manner, it's not the ideal use for the medium.

Despite its shortcomings, using CD-R for backups is better than having no form of backup at all, and it's convenient to be able to use the same device for backups, archiving, and creating CD compilations. When archiving, however, CD is an ideal technology. Most companies archive old but still useful information as well as the orders, invoices, and other documents that are required to be kept legally all onto CD. CD generally has a long life, and it's easy to copy information back off a CD compared to restoring the information from tape. Most computers now have CD-ROM drives, so it's easy to give a CD to just about anybody and let them access the information.

There are many factors to consider when backing up any machine using any type of media, such as choosing what you will back up and how often you will back up your machine. If you are only a home user, then doing a backup once a week of all your documents is a good idea. However, if you run a small company, you ought to consider backing up the information daily to ensure you don't lose important documents.

When archiving, you also need to think about the layout and organization of the information that you want to archive, and how and when you will archive the information. Do you generally archive once a month or wait until a project is finished? When you do actually archive, do you create only a disc or two? Have you thought about archiving that information to tape as well, just in case?

In this chapter, we'll try to cover all of these issues and look at the best ways in which you can use CD as your backup and archiving media. We'll take detours into some of the connected areas of the process, including the different levels of storage that you may need on your machine and discuss the different files and types that you should be including in your backup and archiving processes.

Backups

If you decide to use CD-R (or better still, CD-RW) for backups, there are a few things that you need to consider. The two most important elements are when and what you want to back up. Choosing what to back up can be difficult—do you record everything or only the files and documents that you have created? The choice actually comes down to how quickly you need to get running and under what circumstances you expect to have to do a restore.

When it comes to choosing a time for your backup, it all comes down to how frequently you expect your files to change and how much work you are willing to lose in the event of a system failure or other problem. These two factors—when and what—are also intertwined. The more you back up, the more time it takes during the backup process, but the less time it will take when doing a restore. If you are short on backup time, you can be highly selective about the files that you back up, but you also run the risk of forgetting to back up a file that you may need at some later date.

Irrespective of what and when you back up information, you also need to think about where you store the CDs once the backup has been completed. Putting them on the shelf with your books is not generally a good idea—in the event of a fire, you may lose everything. Finally, although it's not everybody's primary concern, you might want to think about what happens when you want to restore the information. If you have both Macs and PCs, what will happen if you back up files on a PC and then need to restore the information back onto a Mac?

We'll take a look both at the basic problems and effects of these two elements, as well as some backup methodologies that can be used to provide a secure backup for your machines.

Choosing What to Backup

Deciding what you should back up is possibly the most important decision you will ever make at work. What you back up not only affects how long it takes, and how much media you will need, but it also defines how effectively you will be able to get back on your feet when you need to recover information. We'll look at some general information on what you should back up on any machine, as well as some of the machine specific files that you should back up.

You should keep in mind the reasons that you want to do backups. There are probably three main reasons:

1. To provide a record of information for business or legal reasons.
2. To provide a backup copy in case I delete something accidentally and need to get it back.
3. To provide a quick method of getting my machine back into working order in case of failure.

The level of information you back up will depend largely on which of these statements most matches your needs. If it's reason 1 or 2, you can probably get away with backing up only your documents. If it's reason 3, however, you probably need to back up everything.

With CD-R/RW, we also have a different problem—the limited storage space of the CD itself. This makes the selection of files for backup far more important. With modern PCs having multi-gigabyte hard disks, a mere 650 MB on a CD does not seem very much. In fact, since most people deal with relatively small files from word processing and spreadsheets—even most databases won't use up all that space. Unless you are working with large images or video, it's unlikely that you will ever need the storage space of a CD for each night; instead, you should be able to use one CD for a number of backups over a period of time.

For an example of just how much information you can store on a single CD, you need only look at my own requirements. After four years of writing eleven books, numerous articles, and countless letters, all of the information from image scans and screenshots to illustrations, manuscripts, and Acrobat page proofs still fits onto a single CD!

Whatever the level of the information that you decide you want to store, you should at a minimum include the following files in your backups:

- ▶ **Data files, documents, letters, faxes, databases, and accounting information that you have created.** On a Mac, this might include the contents of your Documents folder, and on a PC, it will probably be your My Documents folder. On a Unix machine, consider backing up the entire home directory for all your users.

- ▶ **Any saved games from your favorite gaming software.** You'll need to find the saved games, which are almost exclusively stored within folders and directories of the games themselves. They can be difficult to find, but, speaking from personal experience, there is nothing more frustrating than losing that all-important game!

- ▶ **Any e-mail and Internet-related files that you have created.** For example, Outlook Express, Outlook, and Entourage (on Macs and PCs) all store the e-mail that you've sent and received in a single directory or folder. Under Unix, most of these files should have been under your home directory.

- ▶ **Any system-specific configuration and information files.** Under Mac OS, this means the Preferences folder in your System Folder, which contains all of the preferences for your machine, from simple viewing and desktop colors right up to the preferences for individual applications. Under Windows, most of this configuration information is stored in the registry, a special database of configuration settings. Under Unix, most of the configuration information will be under the /etc directory, but you might also want to keep a record of the /boot directory, which contains the running kernel.

- ▶ **System and application fixes and updates.** To get your machine working as quickly as possible, you will probably need to keep a record of the system updates, fixes, and new drivers and kernels that you install onto your machine during its lifetime. I prefer to archive these items onto CD (see "Archiving" later in this chapter), or even to create special boot and installation CDs (see Chapter 10)—but if you aren't archiving, then at the very least you should back up these files.

Section II   Writing CDs

There are, of course, exceptions to all of the examples given above. However, you should be able to make up a pretty good list of the files that you need to install, once you start thinking about the different files and documents on your machine that would be difficult to reproduce. Always keep in mind that it's not just the letters, homework, and business documents that you might create—those computer settings would take a long time to duplicate.

In most circumstances, the files that you should avoid backing up include:

- ▶ **System Folder on the Mac, or your Windows or WINNT directories on a PC.** Under Unix, it gets more difficult to decide where to draw the line. You probably should ignore /bin, /lib, /sbin and /usr. In all cases, these files and folders are easily re-creatable from the CD-ROMs on which your software is delivered—there is no point in backing up information that you already have on a safe format such as CD-ROM.

- ▶ **Internet cache files**—Your machine keeps a copy of some of the pages and graphics that you view on the Web in order to speed up your Web viewing. There's no need to keep these, as these are stored (and have since probably changed) on a Web site somewhere.

- ▶ **Temporary files**—All machines store some temporary files, from simple text files to Photoshop scratch files. You don't need to keep any of these, because they are only used when editing an existing document.

- ▶ **Swap files**—All three platforms support the ability to create swap files. Under Mac OS and Windows, the files reside on the disks of your machine. They are normally hidden from view, but your backup software will back them up just like any other file. Under Unix, swap files that exist as part of the standard file system are not normal, but they can still exist. Since these files will generally be at least equal to your machine's memory, it's not uncommon to find a swap file that is 96 MB or even 256 MB in size. These files don't contain any useful information, so backing them up just wastes space.

Although the above list is pretty explicit, there are exceptions to the rules. If restoration time in the event of a complete systems failure is important to you, you will want to back up your system files and applications to get your machine up and running as quickly as possible. Merely recording preferences and documents in this instance is not enough; it can easily take a day just to restore all of your system files, applications, and settings before you even start to recopy your documents and files.

In this instance, the first item in the list above should be included, rather than excluded, from your backup. However, the last three items can always be ignored—there really is no need to back up files that contain only temporary information that you likely will never need to refer to.

Remember this simple rule: The quicker you need to get your system up and running in the event of a failure, the more you need to backup. For complete recovery, back up everything!

Servers

Although CD-R might seem an unlikely choice for backing up a server, it does have some advantages over tape. In most instances, CD-R will just not be able to cope with the sheer amount of information. Even a relatively small server will have a 20 GB or 30 GB disk—that will require forty-eight CDs if the disk is almost full. If used by twenty people during the course of a day, you could easily use a CD or two during the course of a week in order to back up all the changes.

However, the advantage of CD-R over more traditional tape backup systems is the speed with which you can recover a server's OS and application files after a system failure. You can use CD-R to create a quick copy of the core files required to get you up and running again—it's likely that the whole backup will fit onto a single CD. In the event of an emergency, you could have your machine up and running again within hours, or even minutes. Compared to the time taken to reinstall the OS and then restore the settings and applications from tape, this is a significant improvement.

In order for this to work properly, you'll need to avoid backing up the user files, which you should have located in a strict directory location so that you can easily exclude it from the backup.

Clients

Whether individual client machines are backed up is entirely dependent on how machines are used. If clients are *dumb* (i.e., they are used purely for applications and don't physically store any information), then there is no point in backing them up. You could probably reinstall the OS and applications yourself faster than fiddling with backup discs. This, however, can be dangerous if your users are not disciplined about storing information on the server. Unless you somehow restrict access to the local storage, I can almost guarantee that at least one user each month will request a restoration of the files stored on his machine.

Furthermore, be aware that certain applications record information on local storage that may be considered vital by the user. E-mail is a case in point, as most applications store the e-mail folders somewhere on the hard disk. Although you can get around this by using IMAP4 as your mail access protocol, you cannot always guarantee that a user will specify this feature.

Finally, always be aware of configuration and license information. For the Mac OS, most serial numbers and preferences are stored in the Preferences folder of the System Folder. For Windows, the registry is often the key point, but many applications choose their own locations to store some information.

Once again, the decision comes down to how quickly you think you will need to get individual machines up and running. For a secretary or project manager's machine, time may not be an issue. However, for somebody in the accounts or sales departments, the speed with which you can bring their machines back online may make the difference of hundreds or even thousands of dollars in lost revenue.

Section II Writing CDs

Choosing When to Back Up

The decision about when to backup your machine and how frequently depends on your working patterns, how important the work is, and when it's most convenient. The frequency is the first problem you should tackle, as it will help to gel your ideas about all the other issues. The importance of your information is the driving force here—the more expensive it would be to reproduce the documents you intend to back up, the more frequent the backup should be, up until a practicality limit of once or twice a day—with CD-R, at least.

Backup Frequency

For home users who use their machines only on the weekend, then a daily backup is obviously a little excessive. Weekly should be fine, but do the backup at the end of the session, rather than at the beginning. If you leave your machine off all week, it's possible that you may have a problem the next time you switch it on, so make sure that your last operation is to back up your machine.

In a home office or office environment, where you probably work on your computer every day, then a daily schedule is the most obvious solution. Even if you do only minor work each day, a daily schedule can be a good idea, and it's unlikely to take more than a minute just to back up the files you have changed during that particular day.

Although you can back up more than once a day, it's probably not worth the hassle unless your information is so time and mission critical. I have for years backed up my most important documents twice a day with tape (at noon and midnight), timed to coincide with when I'm eating lunch and, hopefully, in bed. Even so the interruption can be quite annoying if I happen to still be at my desk at the time. On CD, it would become even more of a problem, as I would probably use one or more CDs a week just to keep up with all the changes.

There is nothing wrong, however, with using CD-R in packet-writing mode (using Roxio's directCD) in order to create a "running" backup of important files. In this instance, what you do is continually update the same file on the CD each time you want to ensure you have a backup. You don't get the history of the file as it was added to the backup as you would with a typical backup system, because the new version of the file overwrites the old version, but you are guaranteed a safe copy of your most important documents during the course of a day.

Convenience

You should back up your files based on the time they are least likely to be in use. Most people and companies sleep or shut down overnight, so it makes sense to make the backup process the last task you complete during the day. You can either do this manually, or you can choose to set up a schedule so that your machine will automatically start the backup during the night.

My only recommendation if you choose to do the backup overnight, either scheduled or just by leaving the process running, is to consider what may happen before, during, or after the backup process. Without trying to depress you, if your data is important, then what happens if your computer is stolen or is in a fire? Your backup will be stolen or burnt along with the computers you are trying to protect!

That's not to say that I recommend doing a backup during the day; just be aware of the issues. If you are using CD to do the backup, then it's unlikely that the process will take more than half an hour. Is half an hour really that much of a sacrifice compared to the possible alternative—eight or even twenty-four hours of extra work?

Backup Methodologies

The real trick is to make sure that you have at least two backups of everything you might need. They don't necessarily have to be made at the same time—one version that is a week old and another that is a day old will often be enough to get you up and running. The more specific you want to be when restoring the information, the more complex the backup system becomes.

There is really only one basic methodology used for backup systems: the Grandfather-Father-Son. Although there are other methods, they all use the same basic principles. We'll look at three systems—a simpler system I've called Father-Son, a more robust system called Father-Mother-Son-Daughter, and the full-blown Grandfather-Father-Son system.

Note that CD-R is not an ideal backup format for any of these methods, since they all rely on you reusing the CD at some later stage. For this reason, and others I've mentioned elsewhere in this chapter, CD-RW makes a much better backup medium than regular CD-R. That said, all of these can be modified to work with CD-R, which has the added advantage that you have a permanent historical record of everything you've ever done on your machine. Just be sure to have a lot of physical storage space for all those CDs!

Personally, I prefer to use CD-RW and reuse the discs while using the archiving techniques discussed later in this chapter to keep a more historical record of my work.

Father-Son

The Father-Son (FS) system is very easy to use, especially for people who don't need regular daily backups or those who use removable disks for backup storage. The method can be seen in Figure 7.1, and the instructions for using this method are as follows:

Figure 7.1
Using the Father-Son method for backing up your machine.

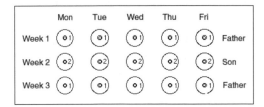

1. You start off by backing up all the information you want to store to CD on the first day. We'll call this CD-1.

2. You continue to use CD-1 all week—either Monday through Friday or Monday through Sunday. These backups will be "differential"—that is, you back up only the information that has changed since the previous day's backup.

3. On the last day, after the backup has been completed, put CD-1 in a safe place. CD-1 is now called the *Father*.

4. The second week, you use another CD, which we'll call CD-2. As before, CD-2 backs up everything on the first night, backing up only the differential information on the second, third, and subsequent days. CD-2 is called the *Son*.

5. On the last day, CD-2 becomes the Father.

6. The third week, we re-use CD-1, which is now the Son, and repeat the process.

This system is quite reliable and uses very few CDs for the backup. It also always ensures that you have two copies of the information—one will be a week old and one will be only a day old. That should be enough to cover you in the event of a failure or accidental deletion and certainly enough to get you back online quickly.

Father-Mother-Son-Daughter

A modification of the above system, Father-Mother-Son-Daughter uses four CDs. Two CDs cover your weekly backups, and another two cover your daily backups. You can see the basic structure of the system in Figure 7.2, and instructions on using the system are given below:

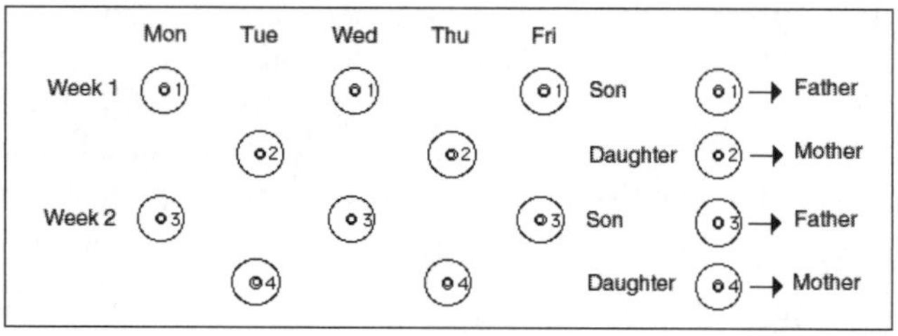

Figure 7.2
Using the Father-Mother-Son-Daughter method for backing up your machine.

1. On Mondays, Wednesdays, and Fridays, you back up to CD-1, the *Son*.

2. On Tuesdays and Thursdays, you backup to CD-2, the *Daughter*.

3. On the Friday of each week, the *Son* becomes the *Father*, and the *Daughter* becomes the *Mother*.

4. The following week, you use CD-3 and CD-4 as the new Son and Daughter CDs, respectively.

This system is much more robust than our Father-Son system and still uses only four CDs. You have full backups for the previous two weeks. If you need to, you can get the backup for both yesterday and the day before, which is useful if you modify a file and then find you need to go back to a version that is two days, rather than one day, old.

The only limitation is that we have no historical information—although it would be possible to store the *Son* CD from each week on a permanent basis. This would increase the number of CDs required. If you were using CD-RWs, you could reuse them after, say, four weeks, or even twenty-six weeks (six months) if you wanted to improve the restoration facilities, while still keeping the number of CDs required to a minimum.

Grandfather-Father-Son

The Grandfather-Father-Son (GFS) system is much more complex. The system usually works on a four-week rotation and provides the ability to go back to any backup on any day within the previous four weeks. Figure 7.3 outlines the basic process, with full instructions on the method given below:

Figure 7.3
Using the Grandfather-Father-Son method for backing up your machine.

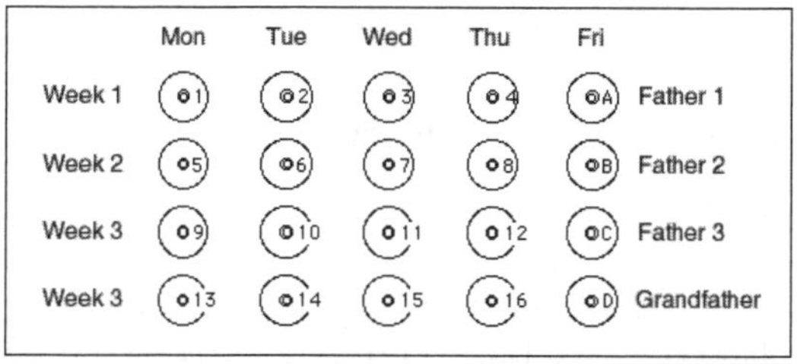

1. On Mondays through Thursdays, you back up to a different CD, one for each night of the four-week cycle (sixteen CDs). These are the *Sons*.

2. On Friday, you do a full backup, one per week (three CDs), each called the *Father*.

3. On the final Friday of the four-week rotation, you store the CD and call it the *Grandfather*. Unlike the *Sons* and *Fathers*, the *Grandfather* CD is not reused—it's stored permanently.

This system is probably the most practical if you want to have a permanent historical record of your files, without having to explicitly archive documents. Each Grandfather CD could be a CD-R, with the Father and Son backups using CD-RW.

I've employed this system at a client site for their accounting machines. Because we have a permanent weekly record of everything, we can not only go back to yesterday's backup, but also any backup from any day within the previous four weeks. In addition, we can go back to any week and, by extrapolation, any week of any year since the backup process began.

Media Storage

Many people make the mistake of creating backups and archives without ever testing them. If you are creating tapes, CDs, or other media that may go into storage for some time, it's always worth testing them first. Backup systems often include the ability to verify the information they have written, either during or after the backup process. Use it.

Worse still, some people make the mistake of archiving information to long-term storage without providing some form of secondary backup. CD-ROMs have a very high reliability level (some people will quote 100 years as a lifetime), but it doesn't take much to accidentally snap a CD or scratch it beyond repair. If that CD is your only copy, what would you do if it became damaged or lost?

The solution in both backup and archiving cases is to create a duplicate, or clone, of your backup. If you archive to CD, then consider backing up the CD to tape. If the tape fails, you've got the CD, and vice versa. For a really critical installation, creating two copies of the CD, and then two tape backups of the CD, is much more reliable.

Section II Writing CDs

Most backup software will also allow you to produce a backup clone during the process. Alternatively, with a good backup schedule and tape rotation system, you should be able to support a multiple-media configuration that offers the same level of protection.

In any of these cases, the storage and storage location of the media are as important as the information and methods you are using to create the backups. You should store the current backups and archive material in a safe and secure location. At the very least, store the CDs in a different part of your building, or better still, a different building—a garage or shed, for example—just to protect the CDs from a fire or theft. If you can, get a fireproof safe that's certified for media and paper storage with a combination *and* key lock.

For important information, many companies will offer pickup and drop-off services for your backup tapes. Bank safety-deposit boxes also offer a secure, fireproof storage location, and some banks will let you drop backup tapes into their night safe for storage. If worse comes to worst, give them to a neighbor or relative, or take the CDs from your company home with you at night to ensure that the information is kept offsite.

Also, keep in mind the physical security of your backups. If someone were to find and access your backups, they would almost instantly have access to all of your files, including ones that may be considered highly sensitive. Again, your backup software can come to the rescue by password protecting and optionally encrypting the data during the write process. But even with encryption, preventing physical access to your tapes is as important as ensuring that they are safe from corruption.

Cross-Platform Compatibility

Although it's not everybody's problem, it begins to affect more and more people over time—how to make backups (and archives) cross-platform compatible. Imagine a situation where your notebook PC has been stolen, but you need to get access to your backups from your daughter's iMac. Sounds unlikely, but how would you go about retrieving the information from the CD so that you can run off that report?

Some CD backup software writes the information as standard files, but other packages use a proprietary format for backing up the information. You'll need another PC with a CD drive and the backup software to be able to do the restoration, and then you may be limited by what you can restore.

If cross-platform compatibility is important, consider using something like Dantz's Retrospect backup software. This is Mac and Windows compatible, and a CD written on a PC or Mac should be readable and restorable on either platform irrespective of the source. We'll be looking in detail at Retrospect in Chapter 19.

Archiving

If you look at the files on a typical machine, you'll probably notice a lot of files and information that you no longer need to refer to daily, or perhaps even weekly. For example, when was the last time you needed to look at that letter to Grandma that you wrote for Christmas 1996? Do you really need it using up active space on your machine?

In all likelihood, the answer is no. Archiving solves this problem by allowing you to write infrequently used information to a CD that you can still insert into your machine and refer to, but without it using up valuable space on your machine. You also need to remember that once the information has been written to CD, you need to be able to find and locate that information again at a later stage with as much ease as possible.

You can use cataloging systems to make the process easier. Or, if you are backing up your CDs to another type of media—for example, tape (see "Protecting Your Archives" later in this chapter)—you can use the catalog generated by the process as the catalog for your archives. We'll be looking at cataloging systems in Chapter 19.

There's actually nothing special about archiving information to CD—although special software exists for the purpose, it's actually just a simple case of writing a CD with information you want to keep. What's different between archiving and writing a CD for a client, or creating a new audio compilation, is that you need to think about how, when, and what you will archive in order to protect the information you are trying to record.

In this section, we'll be looking at some strategies for archiving information and the layouts and methods for making the best use of the archiving process. Before we look at those specifics, I want to cover the issues surrounding the archiving process by having a look at the different storage levels that exist in any computing environment, from home computing to large-scale businesses.

Storage Levels

Everybody makes use of a number of different storage levels when they record information onto their computer, although they may not always be aware of the significance of the process. Although not everybody wants, or needs, to understand these different levels, they can help you to decide how you want to handle the backup, archiving, and restoration solution. We need to first take a look at the different levels of storage that need to be provided in most organizations. There are three types of physical storage: on-line, near-line, and off-line, which can be classified by the level of access they provide. To help you understand the different levels, see Figure 7.4.

Figure 7.4
A typical storage model for a project, from active (on-line) to completed (off-line).

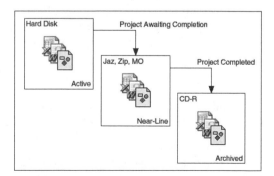

As well as the different levels, there is also a name for the control and operation of the different levels, called hierarchical storage management (HSM). Most people operate a manual HSM system, but you can also get software that will perform the removal of infrequently used information to near-line storage, and into a location ready for off-line or archiving.

On-line Storage

At the top level is on-line storage—storage that is available all of the time. For most users, this would be the hard disk on their computer, the storage on the computer network, and (for the servers in those networked environments), the disks and RAID subsystems used to store user files.

On-line storage is used to hold the information that you always need. This includes the operating system, the applications you use, and your current set of documents and files. On-line storage can be modified and is backed up each night in order to ensure that you have a backup of your "active" file system in the event of a failure. Eventually, information at this level will usually migrate to near-line storage and may eventually make it to off-line storage (archives).

For example, you would probably use on-line storage to hold an active project; everything from letters and documents to the project itself would be held on your hard disk or on the disk on a server for the duration of a project.

Near-Line Storage

The next level is near-line storage. This type is readily available, but not necessarily permanently available as with an on-line storage system. For example, if you have a Zip, Jaz, or CD-RW drive, you can modify the files on that disc, but in order to make the modification, you must put the removable disc into the drive.

Near-line storage is a great solution for those files that you don't expect to actively modify, but that you still may need to make modifications to at some time. Often, it's used as a stopgap location before the information is archived properly to off-line storage.

For example, going back to our active project example, imagine that active work on the project has finished, but you still have to write occasional letters and messages while the project is being completed and delivered to your customer. At this point, the files that make up the project are ideal for placing onto near-line storage. You don't need to keep the project files on your hard disk or network, but you do want to have a location for holding the project until all of the correspondence has been completed.

Off-line Storage

Off-line storage is the point at which the use of the information becomes rare or possibly even non-existent. You move projects to off-line storage once they have been completed and you no longer expect any related files to be included or associated with the project.

At the same time, you don't want to delete the project—you may want to use elements of the project in a future project, or perhaps you want to compare quotes and project plans between the old project and a new one.

CD-R is ideal for off-line storage (archiving), since you can easily store the files for a project onto a CD and make the information on that CD easy to find and recover when required. Because it's on CD, you don't have to worry about the project taking up disk space, and it's safely stored in a near-indestructible form so that you shouldn't ever accidentally overwrite or delete the project's documents.

Hierarchical Storage Management (HSM)

The amount of information stored, and the amount that users demand should be on-line, is increasing all the time. Unfortunately, the economics do not support this idea. Most of us cannot afford limitless amounts of hard disk (on-line) storage or RAM in order to store all of our information, as a majority of it won't be accessed at regular intervals.

The amount of information a company server stores, however, is many times larger. Once a project is finished, what happens to it? If it's a repeat project, it's possible that some of the information will be used in a future project, while a much larger chunk could be sent to the archive.

HSM is a system for creating a layered structure (hierarchy) for prioritizing your storage requirements. It creates a logical link between your data and access requirements and the facilities (size and speed) of your storage devices. By using an HSM tool, you can set policies that define the usage cycle and parameters for different types of data.

At the top level is the information that you access most often and that you need the quickest access to. This information should be stored on local hard drives, because they provide the fastest access times. As the information ages, medium-term information should be moved to a near-line storage facility. This will allow you ready access to the data without it using up valuable and expensive hard drive storage space.

Once the information gets beyond a certain age (i.e., after a prolonged period of disuse), it should be moved from near-line storage to off-line storage. The information will still be available, but probably on some form of removable media that requires physical intervention.

The use of an HSM system maximizes the cost benefit of any storage system by automatically moving short-, medium-, and long-term data onto suitable media. For the network user, it allows information to be almost instantaneously retrieved, while providing the network manager with the best solution for making the best use of the available storage systems on the network.

Choosing When to Archive

If you've followed the sequence of events within the previous section, you will have seen the basic sequence that a project takes during its life (see Figure 7.4 for a quick overview). As demonstrated, the sequence of usage that a project normally, but not always, follows is "active," "awaiting archive," and, finally, "archive." The project and its associated files are archived onto CD once the project has been completed.

Section II   Writing CDs

But not all files need or deserve this level of treatment. What do you do with a simple letter—it's not a project, but are you finished with it as soon as the letter has been sent, or do you wait until you have a reply?

There are three main triggers that you can use to decide when to archive material: project completion, date, and size.

Archiving By Project

We've already mentioned the archive by project system—as soon as a project has been completed, you collect all of the files, and then start archiving the material to CD. If possible, you should try to organize the contents logically—either the exact sequence and layout as used on your servers, or, if the material covers more than one CD, you can spread the individual folders over more than one CD.

For example, an ad agency might store manuscripts, illustrations, photo scans, and final page layout documents on separate CDs—or within suitably named directories on a single CD if it fits. See Figure 7.5 for a sample.

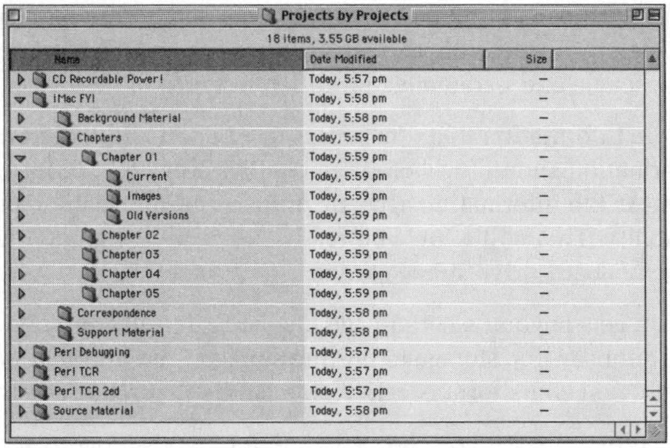

Figure 7.5
Organizing your
archive layouts
by project.

Archiving by Date

For files that are created on a regular schedule—for example, letters and other correspondence, or even regular articles or advert artwork—you can generally set up an archive to run weekly, monthly, or even yearly. With this system, the best organization is to follow your source layout or consider creating a system that allows you to locate information on the final CD by date.

If possible, you should organize the information according to your normal working patterns, but with the archive date in mind (see Figure 7.6 for a sample). I know companies that keep and work with daybooks, letters organized by client, and documents organized by project. If you decide that you want to archive by date, then organize your information using either explicit dates or by splitting the sub-directories into weekly, monthly, or quarterly blocks. Remember that you are trying to make the information as easily recoverable as possible!

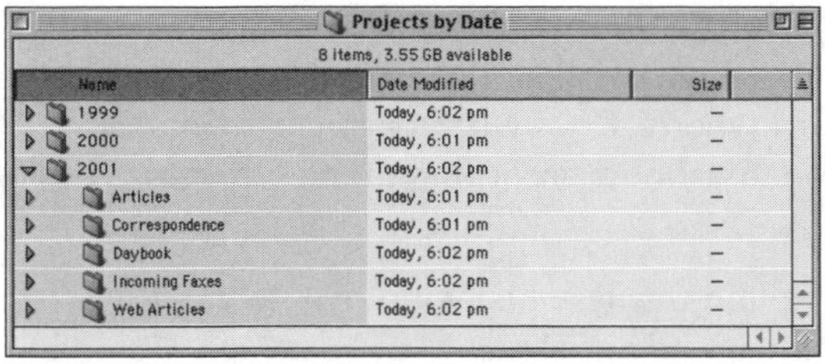

Figure 7.6
Organizing your
archive layouts
by date.

Archiving by Size

If you keep up to date with your operating system, software and game patches, updates, and service packs, you'll probably want to archive them onto CD so that in the event of some sort of failure, you can reinstall and reapply the patches and updates to get you back to the latest running system. There are also other types of files that fit into this category—that piece of downloadable software, shareware, or game demo should probably be kept as well.

This sort of information is not organized by project, and it's not really time sensitive, either. For this type of information, you need to archive only when the amount of information reaches the size of a CD. Until then, you can probably back up the information along with the rest of your files.

How you organize the information on your final CD is entirely up to you. I tend to organize these files first into the platform for which they apply, then into different directories according to the type of file—OS update, software patch, shareware, or demo. See Figure 7.7 for a sample.

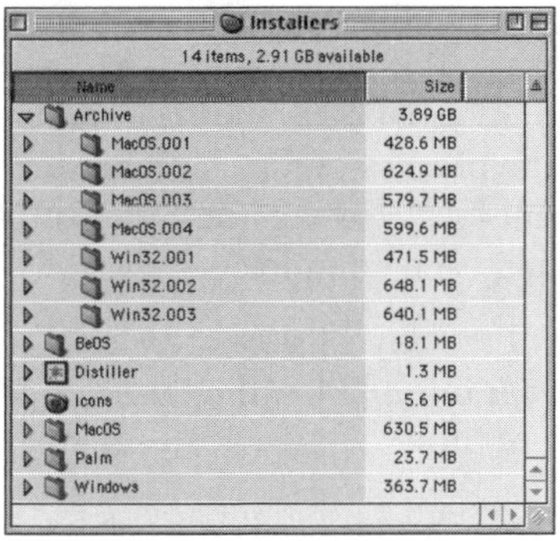

Figure 7.7
Organizing your
archive layouts
by size.

Other types of files can be archived in the same way. I put my photos onto CD based on the same basic criteria, although at the resolution I scan my photos, this generally equates to a single CD per film!

Choosing the Right Combination

It's unlikely that the above thresholds will suit everyone in every situation. There's no hard-and-fast rule that will work for everybody. Even within a single organization, it's likely that you'll use two or more of the above thresholds according to the different types of information you need to archive.

As an example, I'd like to explain the systems I employed while I was IT manager of an advertising agency that dealt with advertisements and catalogs. We had two main servers—the first contained administration and accounting information, invoices, correspondence, contracts, and all the source copy for the final artworked material

The second server stored all of the actual project material—the images, illustrations, and final artwork. A typical project would span one or more 2 GB partitions, depending on the size of the catalog and the number of languages and versions.

We needed to keep a copy of everything, just in case a future project required the same image or logo. However, with the project material taking up so much space, it became necessary to archive off as much material as possible in order to leave enough working space for current projects.

For the client-based administration material (letters, contracts, etc.), we basically archived yearly. Even with a team of twenty people and numerous clients, we never created more than a single CD's worth of information over the period of a year. Accounting information was archived monthly onto two CDs—the actual database was about 50 MB in size, and a copy was made on the server each night and sometimes during the day as well.

The incoming faxes were archived when they filled a CD, or I'd pick enough information from the "active" area to fill a CD. All of the project information would be kept until the final printed copies of the items were available, then the information would be archived onto as many CDs as required. Since some projects could be in the process of development for a year, with some being developed in up to twenty-six different localized versions, you can appreciate the sheer size of some of the project files once they had been completed.

In addition to all of this material was a small amount of separate files—installers, system updates, and a certain amount of nonessential information that was simply archived when we needed the space for more of the same sort of files

As you can see, there was no single policy we could use right across the organization. We chose different periods and systems according to the type and frequency of the information that needed to be archived.

Choosing What to Archive

What you archive is entirely dependent on your circumstances, and when you determine your need to archive information. If you don't produce a huge amount of information, then unless you are running seriously short of space, there probably isn't any need to archive any information. But, most modern companies, and many people who work at home, easily create a CD's worth of information over the course of a year.

What you archive, therefore, comes down to what you expect to need at some later date, and you'll need to be pretty ruthless about what you keep and what you ultimately throw away. For example, that letter to your bank three years ago about overcharging should be kept—just in case it's queried by the tax man—but that letter you sent to your milkman on the same day is probably wastebasket worthy!

Here are some specific examples of the sort of things you should archive and how they can be pruned to make the best use of the available space.

Letters, Correspondence

Most people should probably archive everything that is to an official body of some kind. For example, correspondence between suppliers and clients will need to be kept, especially if it relates to orders and payments. Any correspondence with utilities, banks and other companies should also be archived. With personal items, it's entirely up to you.

Projects

Irrespective of the type of project, you should archive everything required to reproduce the project, including any source material. For example, with a simple report, I'd store the final report, any revision I made to it, source spreadsheets, graphs, illustrations, images, and possibly even data sources and background information.

Files to avoid archiving include backups and temporary files (often created by Microsoft Word and other applications).

Images, Illustrations, Page Layouts

If you create advertisements, brochures, and other such materials, you need to archive not only the final version of the item, but also the source material. Always keep a copy of the original raw scan along with the cropped, modified, and pathed/cutout version you finally used. That allows you to go back and re-use the original image without having to re-scan the slide or photo. The same goes for any original scans you make at home.

Also, if you use Photoshop or a similar program to create image compositions, keep a copy of the Photoshop file in preference to a flattened TIFF or JPEG. Although it will take up more space, you will be able to re-create the file easily from the Photoshop source—recording the flattened image and not the Photoshop file will mean that you waste a lot of time recropping, adding paths, or making filters and modifications to the source scan. It also allows you to make changes or corrections to the image when you need the same basic component, but a different background, text, or other element.

You can prune the files that you may have saved as interim versions between the scan and the final photoshop image. If you are using an OPI (open prepress imaging) system, you'll also want to delete the layout files that are created by the server and used during the page layout process.

Section II Writing CDs

Installers, Updates, Service Packs

Any update, service pack, shareware, or other software or installable item should be archived onto CD. There is nothing worse than rebuilding your machine and finding that you are missing a critical service pack, driver, or other update. Furthermore, if you download software from the Internet from companies such as Digital River, the version downloaded may be your only opportunity to obtain the software without paying for it again. If you archive it to CD, you run a much smaller risk of losing it.

Audio and Video Material

Audio and video material is difficult to archive effectively onto CD, since it relies entirely on the source format and the sheer quantity. For example, if you've recorded raw WAV or AIFF files in order to build up your own compilations, you've probably recorded them from CDs anyway. In that case, when you record them onto CD, you effectively have your archive!

If you are using MP3s, the same rule applies—you've probably recorded them for use on CDs anyway. If you've downloaded them from the Internet, you can probably fit five or more albums onto a single CD.

For video it gets more difficult, although the same basic principles apply. You are unlikely to want to archive video to CD, as it's much easier to just write your final CD and use that as your archive. An hour's worth of camcorder video takes up about 2 GB of information, or three CDs worth. I'd recommend using DVD-RAM or tape (something like DAT, DLT, or OnStream, which have capacities upwards of 12 GB per tape).

E-mail

E-mail is no longer just a personal technology; it's used to place orders, agree on projects and schedules, and as a mechanism for exchanging ideas and decisions. If you use e-mail in this way, consider archiving your e-mail onto CD as well. I prefer to "save" my e-mail as text, creating one large file for each of my folders. That allows me to go back to a particular e-mail folder and time period and search my e-mail in my favorite text editor.

Software Source Code

I archive the "current" version of the source code, and any files in any source code revision system such as RCS (revision control system) or CVS (concurrent versioning system). That way, I can go back to the current version of the project and any previous version. It's also a good idea to use the same layout on your CD as you did for your original project—just use the project's source folder as the source folder for the CD.

Web Sites

Remember to archive not only the current version of the site, but also all of the material that goes with it. For example, past versions of the HTML files (I use CVS for my Web sites as well), illustration sources, and the full-size versions of photos and other images if you used a reduced version of them on the site.

Accounting Databases and Other Legal Requirements

Most countries have a policy of requiring companies to keep legally binding documents, including copies of their accounts, orders, invoices, and pay slips for a number of years. You'll need to archive the accounting database (if you use one) along with the other documents, just like correspondence. Just remember that it's a legal requirement to keep this information safe, so making a second copy, and perhaps even a tape backup, is always a good idea.

Databases

Most database software supports some form of data dump or backup-friendly solution to allow you to back up (or in this case archive) information for safe restoration at a later date. Where possible, I write the database files from Microsoft Access, Filemaker Pro, and Unix DBM databases straight to CD. For SQL databases, the best solution is to dump the information to a file, using either your database software or one of your own scripts, so that you can later read the dump direct into a new database.

I prefer the personal script method, which, in my case, always creates a list of SQL commands required to re-enter the data into the database. That means I then have a raw extract of the data in a format that can also be used directly on other sites and even on other platforms.

Whichever way you chose to go, you get the same result—you have a simple file that you can write to CD just like any other file.

Protecting your Archives

I've already mentioned this once when looking at the security of your backups, but it's important and worth repeating for archives:

CD lifetimes are long, but the CDs themselves are not indestructible. If the data is important to you, make two copies of all your archives (by duplicating the CD, rather than rewriting from the source—see Chapter 14 for the reasons why). If it's a legal requirement, or it would cost large sums of money to reproduce the information in its required format, then consider also writing the information to tape.

Section II Writing CDs

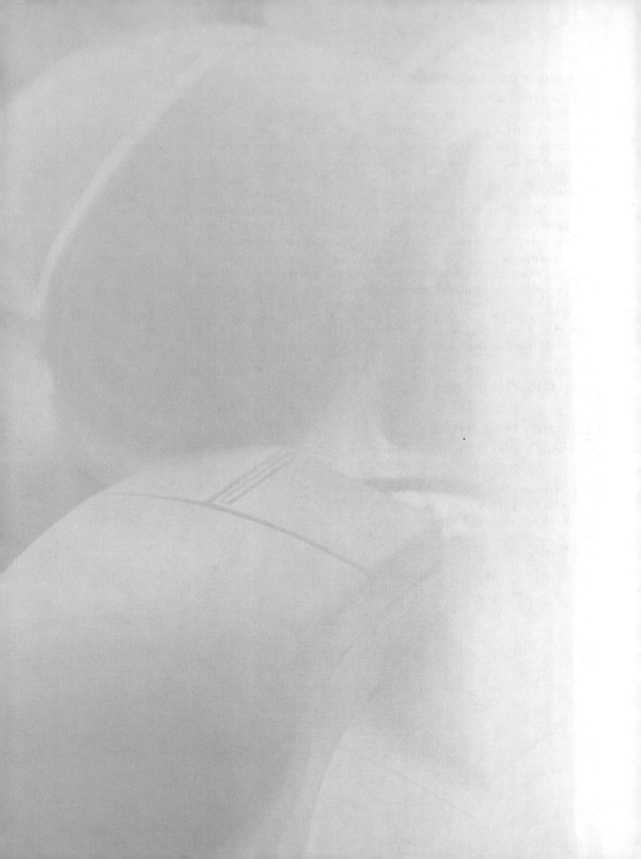

8

Creating Media Catalogs

Years ago, digital imaging was expensive. Getting an image from a slide or photo into your computer would cost you hundreds of dollars. And—if you could even get it— you'd need some very expensive hardware to actually use the image. Color printing was impossible without sending the image to a specialist. Images were also low quality, and the high-quality images used in magazines and brochures were the preserve of large companies that often had multimillion-dollar computer installations.

Nowadays, digital imaging is commonplace. You can buy digital cameras and some scanners for under $100. Even if you take photos with a traditional celluloid film camera, you can generally get the images immediately scanned and onto CD at the same time as you get your prints. We think nothing of working with large images, and most people can afford an inkjet color printer good enough to output photo-quality images, all from the comfort of their own home.

The problem with this advance in digital imaging is that it creates a lot of files that you somehow need to track. Archiving the information to CD is an obvious step, but what happens when you want to view all of the pictures that you've taken of Granny, or of your pet tortoise, or of the exhibition stand at the Expo that you want to feature in your latest product brochure? It's unlikely that you will collate all those images onto individual CDs. For example, how would you organize a set of pictures that featured multiple people—duplicate the images onto their own CD set?

The answer is to create a catalog of the images with not only a representation of the image itself, but also information about the image contents. Then, it doesn't matter if your family photos cross more than one film or more than one source (film, video, digital camera, etc.), you can always pick out the images you want just by searching the catalog. In this chapter, we're going to have a look at some of the techniques required to create media catalogs. Images—the most popular item stored in catalogs—will get a priority, of course, but the same principles can also be used for storing audio clips and even short pieces of video. We'll concentrate on using and making the best out of catalog software, as well as how to organize and layout your CDs. Finally, in case you just want to get a quick overview of the contents of an image CD without resorting to a full-blown catalog application, we'll look at ways of generating both on-disk and paper-based catalogs.

Image Sizes and File Formats

Before you start to store your images onto CD, you will need to make decisions about the file format, size, and, ultimately, the quality of the images you are storing. As I've said before, try to keep original scans of the images (or audio or video clips), so that when it comes to using the images again, you can work from the source material, not from an already doctored version.

Beyond that simple rule, the other points can be described as follows:

▶ **Choose a resolution comparable to how you expect to use the file.** If the images are used in print material such as catalogs and leaflets, use a resolution of at least 600 dpi for photos and 1200 or 2400 dpi for a negative source. If it's only for home use, you can probably get by with 600 dpi for nearly all shots.

▶ **Use a raw image format such as TIFF for professional scans.** TIFFs can be compressed to save space, without losing any of their quality. If you are not concerned about the overall quality and are storing photos, then use JPEG instead.

You can apply these rules to other file types. Movies can be compressed without loss of information using a number of different codecs (coder/decoders), and sounds can also be compressed (see Chapter 9 for more information).

Organizing the Media Structure

Your first problem when archiving photos and other information onto CD is how to layout the structure and name the files. If you are planning to create "stand-alone" CDs—that is, ones that will contain their own catalog and be useable by just about anybody just by inserting the CD into a machine—then your problems are relatively simple. All you need to worry about is giving each file on the CD a unique name, or using a structure that allows you to identify the contents very easily—we'll call this the "Single CD Catalog."

However, if you are creating a media library with a catalog program such as Extensis Portfolio or ImageAXS Pro, it's a good idea to ensure that the CDs have a unique name and, for clarity, that every file within the entire library has its own unique name. The reason for this is that cataloging software generally keeps its database of thumbnails and image details separate from the CDs. This system allows you to browse the catalog without needing the CDs. But once you've selected a file that you want to use, you need the CD—the software will ask for the CD by name and then look for the file.

Curiously, we can actually use the same basic process for both types of CDs—providing we retain consistency across all the CDs we are creating. The important thing to remember at all times is that the files must be accessible, and that requires careful file, directory, and CD naming. Depending on the source of the images, you'll want to make some simple decisions about the layout. We've already covered some of these issues in Chapter 6, but there are some additional issues that you should keep in mind:

▶ **Use directories to divide images by their film, type, location, or subject.** When storing the images scanned from digital or celluloid, or indeed any type of media gained from an external source, it's a good idea to split up the images by their film number (see the next point below). For images that you don't know the source of, divide them up by their content.

▶ **Name individual files within directories, or on the CD as a whole, according to their source.** For example, if you are archiving photos to CD from traditional celluloid film (rather than from a digital source), label each image according to its source film and frame number within that film. For 35 mm, 120, or large format images, you'll need to create your own film or plate numbering system, but APS films actually include their unique serial number stamped onto each film. For example, you might number frame 24 of an APS film 925-461.24.TIF.

If the images are from a digital camera, name them according to the date, time, and numerical sequence. For example, for an image taken at 10:30 on 12th January 2001, you would use a filename like 20010112.1030.1.

For video or audio sources, use the same numbering system, perhaps adding either by directory or file name the subject source—for example, "Brookside School 19981205.1215" or "Actor Bradshaw J 19990326.0908."

▶ **If you can't give the files a numerical reference according to their source, label them descriptively**—for example, "Family in front of Disneyland" or "Insulated Mug Shot 12."

▶ **Give individual CDs a sensible name.** Simply calling it "Images" is not good enough. Either label them according to their contents, such as "Horses and Mules,"or call the CDs "Image Archive," and in every case follow that with a three-or-more-digit number. For example, "Image Archive 001" to "Image Archive 999" gives you 1,000 CDs; that's enough for 1,000 rolls of 36-exposure 35 mm film.

If possible, try to include a catalog file (see "Manually Creating Catalogs" later in this chapter) or, at the very least, include a list of the contents as part of the CD label (see Chapter 20).

Using Catalog Software

Simply copying your images and photos to CD is not always productive. Even with a good naming system and printed or disk catalog, it can be difficult to find the precise image that you want. The solution is to use cataloging software.

Cataloging software does a lot more than provide you with a visual catalog of the files in your database. Most software records standard information such as the file size, resolution and modification and other dates. In addition, you can generally store key words and other field information along with your image. For example, you can see in Figure 8.1 that I've set up ImageAXS Pro to store a title, subject listing, location and a field that tells me on which Web site (or sites) the image is suitable for posting. In this case, it's a picture of one of my kittens for the family site.

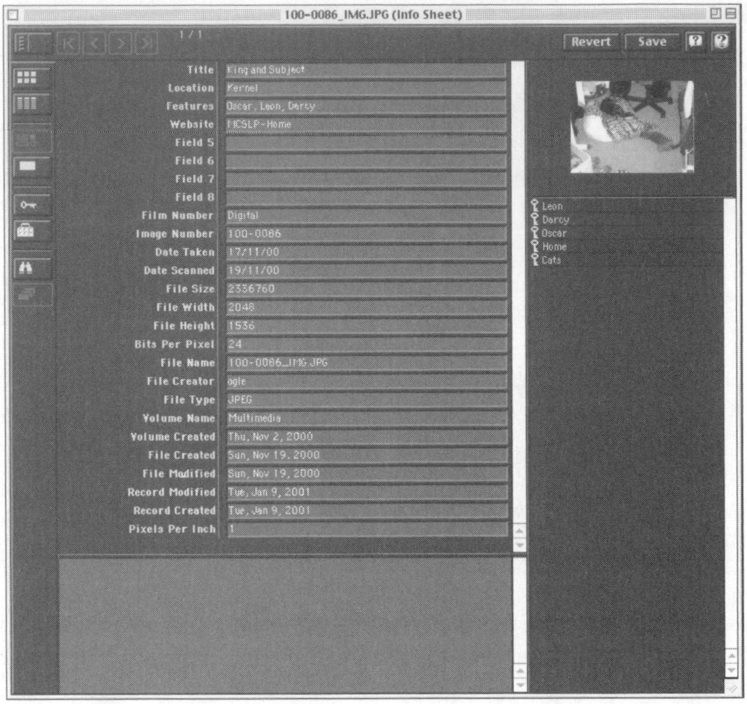

Figure 8.1
Image information
in an ImageAXS Pro.

Because the cataloging software stores this additional information, you can search for all of the matching images in the catalog according to your desired criteria. The process takes a little bit of time, as each time you add an image to the catalog you must update the information. However, once done, it makes it very easy to find all of the images featuring your cats, a particular product, or a location that you are looking for.

Most important of all, especially when it comes to archiving images onto CD, a cataloging system will keep a low-resolution version of the image available on disc, while leaving the full version on the CD. That allows you to browse the catalog "off-line" in order to find your files (see Figure 8.2). When you've found the image you're looking for, the cataloging software will ask you to insert the CD that contains the full image, which you can then open with Photoshop, Quark, or InDesign. To make the process easier, most catalog software includes plug-ins for the major packages so that you can access the catalog and immediately open the image right from within Photoshop or place the image straight into a Quark layout.

Figure 8.2
Browsing an
image catalog in
ImageAXS Pro.

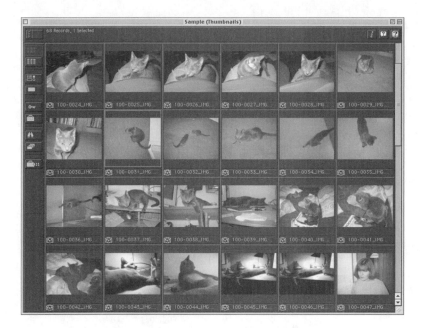

Manually Creating Catalogs

Not everybody wants or needs complex searchable catalogs that not only allow you to view the images but to search them for key words, features, and other information. Some simply want a way of knowing what images are on the disk without manually opening and examining them all. They just want a quick overview of the contents to see if it might possibly hold the image they are looking for.

There are different ways of doing this that will appeal to different people. Some of them still rely on having the original CD available—you can place a disk-based catalog onto the CD along with the rest of the images, or use the browsing facilities offered by the software to produce the catalog for you. You can also use different software to create an automatic slideshow of the images on the disk—not quite a catalog, but still a useful way of browsing through all of the images in a directory or on an entire disc.

Paper catalogs can also be useful—you could create paper versions of all the images on a disc and keep them in folders for people to browse, in much the same way that companies sell image books. For a designer, looking through samples, even low-resolution representations of samples, is generally more useful than seeing them on screen.

The last solution is to create a Web site from the images in your catalog. The Web-oriented method is one that will appeal to companies wanting to centralize their images or those people who want to share their images on a Web site—perhaps to show their latest kitten photos to the rest of the family.

Section II Writing CDs

On Disc

Creating a catalog on disc can be a useful means of providing a quick guide to the full CD content. Creating a physical catalog of the contents relies on using some software on your machine to create a catalog.

The process itself is also quite straightforward—all you need to do is load the image, create a thumbnail of the suitable size, and then arrange the thumbnails (along with the filename) into a new graphics file. This distinguishes the process from catalog programs proper, which store their catalogs in a proprietary format. Because the catalog is created and stored in a standard image file, you can open it with any suitable image viewer, without the need for a special catalog program.

Using Paint Shop Pro

Paint Shop Pro (PSP) supports a "browse" mode specially designed for browsing all of the images within a folder—you can see a sample in Figure 8.3. Double-clicking on any of the thumbnails opens the original file for editing.

Figure 8.3
Using Paint Shop
Pro's browser.

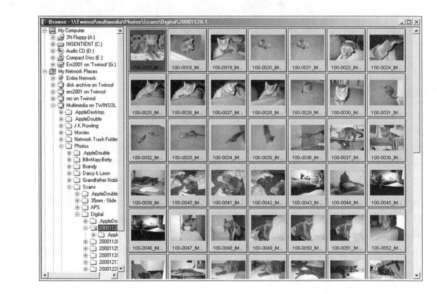

The feature works only for a single directory, so you'll need to go into each directory individually in order to create the browser file. To browse a folder in this way, choose File > Browse and then choose a directory to browse. It'll take a few minutes as PSP reads each file and creates a thumbnail for the image, but once completed, the information is stored in a file called pspbrowse.jbf. The next time you choose to browse the directory, PSP will look for this file and then update only images that have changed since the last browse.

If you use this method to create a browse file, and then write the images and browse file to CD, PSP will use the browse file without the need to update it.

Using GraphicConverter

GraphicConverter (GC) is a shareware package that offers much of the functionality provided by Photoshop. As well as the usual image viewing and editing capability, GC also supports numerous formats, both for reading and writing, and slideshow, browsing, and paper catalog facilities.

The browsing system works in a similar way to the browser in Paint Shop Pro—choose File > Browse and choose the directory that you want to view—then GC builds a thumbnail browser and displays the information in a window. You can see a sample in Figure 8.4. Selecting a thumbnail from the displayed list results in it being displayed in the right hand panel, while still allowing you to view the other images in the browser.

Figure 8.4
Using GraphicConverter's browse mode.

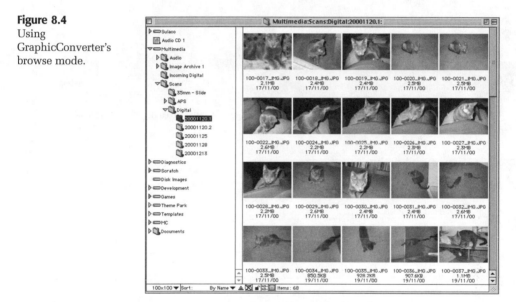

Note that unlike Paint Shop Pro, GC doesn't create a file that contains the thumbnails; it generates the information on the fly each time. Although this can lengthen the time taken to browse the images on disc, it does mean there is more space on the CD for the images themselves. Unfortunately, there is no way to create a catalog from within GC itself, although it will print catalogs for you—we'll see that process later in this chapter.

Section II Writing CDs

If you want to create a slideshow using GC, select File > Slideshow. Once again, you get to choose a directory. You can also configure other options, such as the delay between images and whether they are shown in a continuous sequence, or whether manual intervention is required to show the next image in the slideshow. However you decide to show the images, you'll get a controller, like the one in Figure 8.5.

Figure 8.5
GraphicConverter's
Slideshow Controller.

The buttons, from left to right are:

 Go back an image

 Go forward an image

 Play images (automatically displays the next image after mouse click or predetermined period)

 Pause the slideshow

 Stop the slideshow

 Delete the current file

 Create an alias of the file

Rename the file

Show the filenames with the controller (see Figure 8.6)

Figure 8.6
GraphicConverter's
Slideshow Controller
including filenames.

The GC slideshow is actually an excellent way to pick out images that you want and also as a way of filtering images before you finally place them onto the CD.

Using Photoshop

Photoshop allows you to create contact sheets. Contact sheets are used by designers and print houses to output a series of images to film and then onto paper. This ensures that colors coordinate and the images reproduce properly on paper before they are placed into the page layouts and output as part of the final job. Until recently, this had to be done manually by opening up Quark or PageMaker and placing each image.

The Photoshop contact sheet system automates the process by creating a thumbnail and file title into a standard Photoshop document of the physical size you specified—or multiple documents if you have that many images to create a contact sheet. To create a contact sheet, choose File > Automation > Contact Sheet II. You'll get a dialog box like the one shown in Figure 8.7.

Figure 8.7
Photoshop's Contact
Sheet II dialog box.

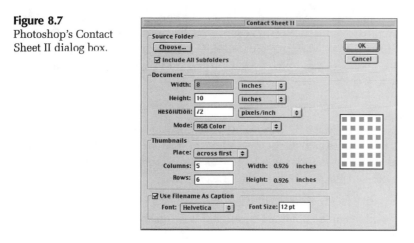

You can use this configuration window to control the size of the final image and the number of images on each sheet. As with other systems, the filename is given beneath each thumbnail image. You can see a sample of the final output in Figure 8.8.

Figure 8.8
A sample Photoshop
contact sheet.

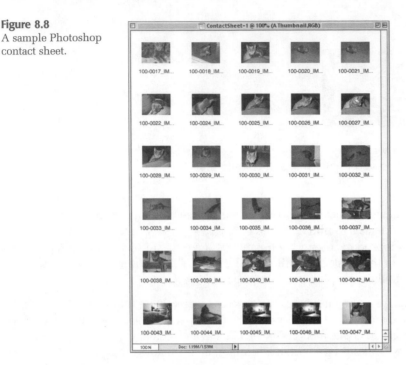

The result of the process is that a number of images containing the contact sheet information are produced. You'll need to manually save these files in order to record an on-disc catalog. Or you could print them out to produce a printed catalog. Aside from the obvious cataloging advantage, the Photoshop mechanism also allows you to output color controlled images to your printer, proofing device, or ultimately to film.

Using iContact

iContact is a freeware script written by Mark B. Hanson and designed for use under Unix. It uses Perl and the NetPBM toolkits to generate a contact sheet. The NetPBM toolkits support a lot of different file formats. You can also use the freely available JPEG packages for JPEG images and, if necessary, use GhostScript to convert PostScript files into image files.

To use iContact under Unix, you'll need to download iContact, NetPBM, Perl, and the JPEG and other graphics libraries (all of which can be obtained through **www.freshmeat.net**). You'll need to build NetPBM, the libraries, and Perl, and then make a simple modification to the iContact Perl script so that it points to your Perl interpreter. Once this is done, all you need to do is supply a list of files to the iContact script. For example, the command…

```
$ icontact *.gif
```

…produces an output similar to Figure 8.9.

Figure 8.9
A sample contact
sheet generated
by iContact.

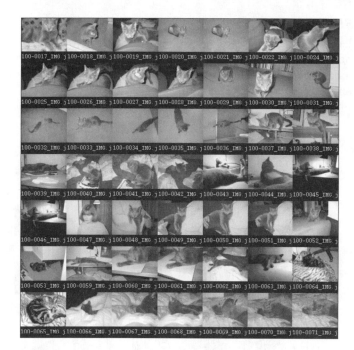

The above command will create one or more catalog images, by default called ic-###, in the
PPM format. By default, the filename of each file in the catalog is not included, but if you use
the -l command line option, the filename is added beneath each thumbnail.

On Paper

Although it may seem like a cumbersome method for finding information, the paper catalog does
have some advantages over a true media database or a simple disc catalog like the one we saw in
the last section. For a start, we can view the catalogs without needing a computer—it might
sound trivial, but sometimes you want to browse for images in the middle of a planning meeting,
or even while away from the office without access to the normal computerized resources.

The other advantage—and something that designers will appreciate—is that you can view the
images without having to manually step through each one on a computer screen. This means
that you can compare images and even select the exact image that you want from ten or twenty
possible samples without requiring a degree in advanced window control!

Creating a paper catalog is relatively easy with the right software—in fact, most of the tools that
we've already seen that produce on-disc catalogs and cataloging software can be used to produce
paper versions—you just print the files that were created or output a selection of the files direct
from the catalog software.

Using Paint Shop Pro

Once you've selected a directory to browse within Paint Shop Pro, you can print out the browse file in order to produce a catalog printout. The printout is identical to the browser display, consisting both of a thumbnail of the image—about an inch square—along with the file's name. You can see a sample of the printout in Figure 8.10.

Figure 8.10
A printed version of Paint Shop Pro's browse window.

Using GraphicConverter

GraphicConverter supports a browsing mode, as we have already seen, but it also includes a catalog mode that generates a printed catalog of a folder, in much the same way as Photoshop's contact sheet—except that the generated image is immediately sent to the printer.

To create a printed catalog in GC, choose File > Print Catalog. You'll be asked to choose a folder to use as the source material. You are then presented with a standard Print dialog. By choosing the GraphicConverter window from the popup menu, you'll get a window like that shown in Figure 8.11, which allows you to configure the format of the output.

Figure 8.11
Creating a printed
catalog from
GraphicConverter.

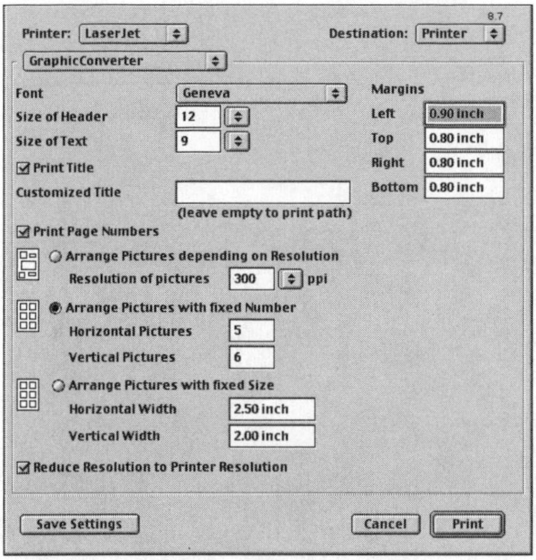

From this window, you can select the margins, number of images per page, and other details before you finally print the catalog to paper.

Using Photoshop

The contact sheet system that we have already looked at for Photoshop is actually designed to produce printed copies of images, rather than file copies. Once the images are produced, all you need to do is print them out.

Using iContact

Because iContact, like Photoshop, produces images, all you need to do is print out those images in order to produce our paper-based catalog.

On the Web

More and more people are developing their own Web sites for their families and homes, and it's a natural progression to want to display your family photos as part of the process. Wouldn't it be great to put up your latest kitten or children photos for the rest of the family to browse instead of sending copies of the photos to different people?

Producing a Web-based catalog is not an easy or straightforward task, and it's not a process that should be taken on lightly if you want to produce the catalog manually. You'll need to know HTML or how to use a package like Microsoft's FrontPage, FileMaker's Home Page, or HoTMeTaL Pro. You can produce the site manually if you know HTML, and if you have some Web programming expertise, you could easily create a complex searching and cataloging system.

Section II   Writing CDs

Another alternative is to use the facilities offered by some cataloging systems. Many different packages will perform the process for you—even including your own headers and footers into the final output. The examples below in Figures 8.12 and 8.13 show the browse window and an image display window produced by ImageAXS Pro. You can also get it to output the additional field information that you store along with each image.

Figure 8.12
A Web-based catalog browser window, as generated by ImageAXS Pro.

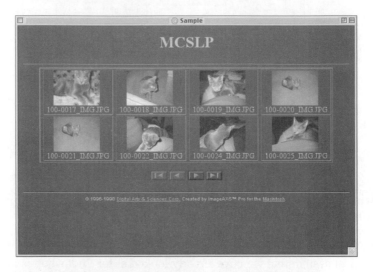

Figure 8.13
A Web-based catalog showing a full image, as generated by ImageAXS Pro.

In order to produce the Web images from ImageAXS Pro, choose File > Export > Web Pages. The configuration of the system is split into five different windows. The primary window configures the filenames and destination folder and allows you to preview the layout of the final pages before producing the entire catalog. Other pages then allow you to configure the layout of each page, including which template to use for the header, footer, and overall page layout.

You also have full control over the thumbnail and final image size and format—see Figure 8.14 for an example. From within this window, you can control whether to use JPEG versions of your images, regardless of their existing format, or a copy of the images you already have. The latter option is useful when you already have JPEG or GIF images in the library that you may have already prepared for the Web. If you elect to create JPEG copies, you also can control the final image size.

Figure 8.14
Controlling the Web pages generated by ImageAXS Pro.

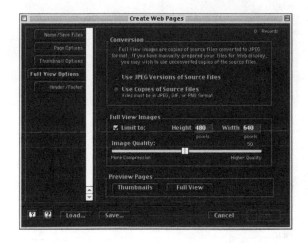

Other packages, including Extensis Portfolio, allow you to produce Web pages based on your existing catalog. There are also programs that will take a directory full of images and create Web pages with thumbnails without requiring a catalog program.

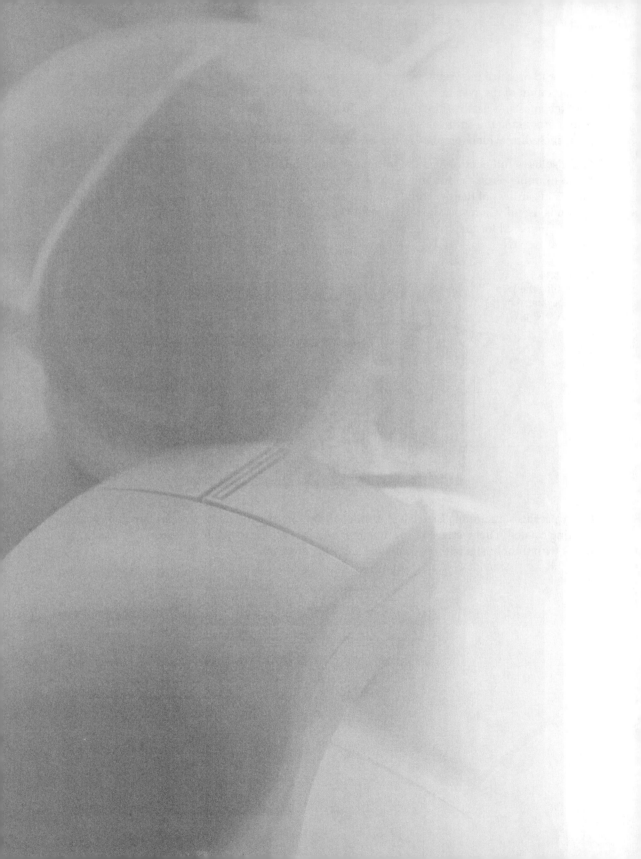

9
Audio CDs

Most people will have been exposed to audio CDs long before they were ever exposed to CD-ROMs, but one of the major complaints of consumers (and something seen as a major failure by some companies) was that the CD was never designed as a recordable technology.

As people started to buy CDs, it became apparent that they would still record their compilations and combinations onto tape and then use that in their cars and personal stereos. Then, CD player prices started to get cheaper and cheaper. It used to cost a few hundred dollars to get even a basic CD player—now, you can buy a portable CD player for significantly less than a hundred dollars, and multi-changer CD players are fitted as standard equipment in many cars.

The problem with CDs is that people still want to produce their own compilations, but they want to keep the quality and the accessibility of CD audio. MiniDisc (MD) is one solution. The other is to use the CD-R drive on your computer to create your own audio CDs!

Writing audio CDs is relatively easy—you just need to tell Toast, Easy CD Creator, or your favorite cdrecord front end that you want to record an audio CD, and it will do the rest. But before you get that far, you need to have sourced your audio files, either from existing CDs, the Internet, or from some analog source, get them into a format that is supported by your CD writing software, and, finally, write the CD. In this chapter, we'll look at the entire process, starting with selecting the right audio format for your CDs.

Audio File Formats

Before we start to look at how you can source and write audio information to CD, it's worth looking at the different audio formats available. Although there are many different audio formats, there are only three basic formats that we can use as sources for writing to CD. These formats are AIFF (Audio Interchange File Format) typically used on a Mac, WAV (Windows Wave audio) used on Windows, and the universally supported MP3 (MPEG 1 Audio Layer 3). Before we look at the specifics of each of these formats, we'll first look at the core CD digital audio standard used on all audio CDs.

CD Digital Audio

CD audio is recorded by taking a sound, "sampling" the level and frequency of the sound, and then repeating the process a number of times each second. The result is a stream of numbers that are expressed digitally. The binary stream is then written to an audio CD, and a CD player reads the binary data stream, converts the binary digits into real ones, and then into an analog form for playback through a normal amplifier and speaker setup.

Audio CDs use a sampling rate of 44.1 kHz—that means that 44,100 times every second the sample is taken, in the case of a CD using a 16-bit sample. The overall format is called PCM (pulse code modulation), which just relates to how the numbers that make up the sound are represented by a series of pulses (the zeroes and ones that make binary data). For a more technical overview of the audio settings used for digital audio on CD, and for reference to DVD-Audio, see Table 9.1.

Table 9.1
Technical specifications of CD and DVD-Audio

	CD Audio	DVD-Audio
Audio Format	PCM	PCM
Channels	2 (stereo)	Up to 6 (for 5.1 digital surround)
Frequency Response	5–20 kHz	0–96 kHz
Dynamic Range	96 db	144 db
Sampling Rate (stereo)	44.1 kHz	44.1, 88.2, 176.4kHz or 48, 96, 192 kHz
Sampling Rate (multichannel)	n/a	44.1, 88.2 kHz or 48, 96 kHz
Sample Size	16 bits	12, 16, 20, or 24 bits

The data stream on an audio CD is slightly more complicated than simple streams of PCM information; the actual data also include error correction information. The data is divided into blocks 2,352 bytes long. There are seventy-five of these for each second of music, making 176,400 bytes for each second of audio. Each of these blocks contains ninety-eight frames that in turn consist of twenty-four bytes of useful data: six 16-bit stereo samples. In addition, each frame has an associated subcode byte and eight additional redundancy bytes that are used for error correction. The subcode byte is used to store additional information, such as track locations and timings.

AIFF

The AIFF format was designed as a way of storing CD quality audio on disc, originally for use as sounds and samples for games and as alert sounds. It was adopted by Apple and others for use in Mac OS because the quality is so good. Although AIFF supports a number of different source formats, its primary format (stereo, 44.1 kHz/16 bits) has the same technical specifications as CD audio.

AIFF is also very practical as a file format because, just as with CD, you have a raw stream of information that you can optionally compress using a variety of different techniques (usually called AIFC or AIFF-C). The Mac OS QuickTime multimedia system comes with a number of codecs (coders/decoders) that will compress and decompress AIFF audio on the fly. It's possible with some codecs to achieve a 2:1, and even 4:1 compression ratio. For the sacrifice of some audio quality, you can even get a 6:1 compression ratio.

If you are "ripping" information from an existing CD to make a new compilation CD, AIFF is one of the best formats to use (on a Mac, PC, or Linux) because of its lossless CD quality. However, it's not a practical method of exchanging files over the Internet, as the size of a typical music track will be 65-80 MB.

WAV

The WAV (or Wave) audio format was developed by Microsoft as the standard audio format for sounds under Windows. The WAV format is similar in principle to AIFF, supporting a number of different sampling rates, bitsizes, and channels, making it ideal for recording CD audio into a file on your hard disk. WAV also supports the use of different codecs in order to compress the audio using either lossless or lossy techniques to achieve different compression ratios.

WAV should be your format of choice when ripping an audio CD on a PC—it doesn't offer any benefits of AIFF, but it is more likely to be supported under Windows and Linux. WAV files are also directly playable by Windows Media Player, any QuickTime enabled player, and much of the audio software available on the Mac.

MP3

MP3 has only recently come to the fore. Originally an audio layer with the MPEG video digitizing standard, MP3 has rapidly become a standard for exchanging audio on the Internet. The primary reason for this is that the size of the audio files created is significantly smaller than the raw source from a typical CD. Many people are now "ripping" their audio CDs into MP3 files and then creating playlists to play their CDs direct from their hard disk.

The MP3 files are small, with a typical seventy-four minute CD shrinking from 650 MB of information to about 80 MB when using the highest quality settings, significantly less if you lower the quality. That's a reduction to about an eighth of the original size. Using a modest 20 GB hard drive, you could store 256 albums in MP3 format—that's more than thirteen days of music without ever having to get up and physically change the CD. It's easy to see why the MP3 format has become so popular, especially with programmers, college IT graduates, and general Internet users.

MP3 has exploded in use, but it's also become a subversive way of sharing what is legally copyrighted information. With files that are so small, and the gradual increase in Internet connectivity speed, people have begun exchanging MP3 files over the Internet, allowing users to pick up "free" copies of tracks and even entire albums without paying the artist, producers, record company, or anybody else any of the money that would normally be obtained through sales of the CD.

Companies like MP3.com and Napster have perpetuated the process and ended up in court over the issue. Napster went one step further and provided a simple way for you to share MP3 files that you had ripped from CD with other users on the Net without the need to upload the files to a server. The issues raised have now mostly been resolved, but people are still illegally exchanging MP3 files without ever paying for them, and it's a problem that is not going to go away any time soon.

Regardless of the legal implications, MP3 (or a successor—see the "Future Formats" section) is here to stay. For music purists (including myself), there are fundamental issues with the MP3 format that make it unappealing for most uses. MP3's biggest problem is the quality of the audio that is produced. The important term to remember when dealing with MP3s is that it produces "near CD-quality audio," but doesn't actually produce CD quality audio. If you want to use MP3 as a temporary format to create CD compilations, you *will* lose quality—try using AIFF or WAV files, which store raw audio data, not a compressed version.

MP3 uses a number of different tricks in order to squeeze so much information into such a small space. Although normal compression techniques used in applications like WinZip and StuffIt are used, the most significant decrease is achieved by reducing the amount of audio information that is actually stored. The different compression techniques employed by the MP3 audio standard can be summarized like this:

▶ **Lowers the audio range**—The CD audio format will have a tonal range of between 5 Hz and 20 KHz. In order to save space, the MP3 format will reduce that range, thereby removing some of the low and high end of the audio source. This reduces the amount of bass and treble stored in the MP3, which makes some tracks lose punch and clarity, especially rock, rap and classical pieces.

▶ **Lowers the overall bitrate**—Connected to the sampling rate, the bitrate is the combination of sample size (16 bits on CD) and sample rate (44.1 kHz). This gives us a bitrate of 88.2 KBps; because the signal is in stereo, it doubles this again to 176.4 KBps. MP3's maximum rate is 160 KBps, with typical standard rates running between 64 KBps and 128 KBps. Because not all music requires such a rate, the MP3 format also allows for a variable bitrate that will automatically adjust during the recording and playback to give the best possible combination of quality and size. In order to achieve these changes, MP3 lowers the sampling rate—the number of samples taken each second. The downside is that this can lead to drops in audio quality and also to unnatural changes between sound levels as the sample rate of the MP3 skips one or more of the samples contained in the source audio.

To get an idea of the configurable parameters available to you when converting existing CD tracks to MP3, see Figure 9.1, which shows the recording settings for MusicMatch, an MP3 encoder and player.

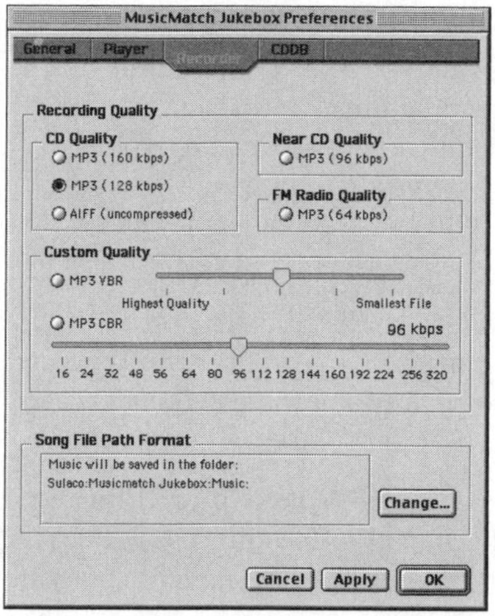

Figure 9.1
Configuring the
recording quality when
ripping CD tracks.

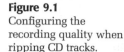

The combination of these two factors allows the MP3 format to reduce the overall size of the audio files it creates, all ultimately at the expense of the quality of the audio recorded. Although fanatics will tell you that the MP3 format only removes the sounds we supposedly "can't hear," in truth this information is important to our perception of the music, providing you can hear it in the first place. Herein lies one of the main problems when comparing MP3 and CD sources— different people have different perceptions of music and vastly different levels of hearing.

To add to the perception problem, many people listen to MP3 music on their computer speakers, which are often not up to the same quality standards as even a low-end stereo system. Some people, even on the highest quality stereo system and the best MP3 source, would be unable to distinguish the difference between MP3 and CD. Others are able to tell the difference simply by listening to the two sources on their computers.

MP3 has its place—I use MP3s on my machines, not for music, but to record books on tape. Now, when a title takes eight or more hours and up to ten CDs, I can listen to the entire book without interruption and without having to physically change any media.

Most CD writing software will convert MP3 files into the raw digital audio on the fly into the audio tracks on a CD. Primarily, this is to allow you to create audio CDs from MP3 sources such as the Internet, but MP3 should be avoided if you are recording and creating your own compilation CDs from existing audio CDs, as the loss of information will be noticeable on the final CD. If all you want to do is produce a CD with a number of different albums in MP3 format, then just write a CD.

Future Formats

MP3 seems to be the favorite technology and buzzword at the moment, and its effects on the music industry are undeniable. Downloading music from the Internet will ultimately become just another way of obtaining music, in the same way that we would buy music on vinyl, tape, or CD from our local store. However, as we've already seen, MP3 suffers from a quality problem that, although ignored by most people, will cause problems for audio purists.

The other problem with downloadable music is that like any computer file, it can be easily copied. Because it can be copied, it can also be distributed, potentially freely, just as you would with any document. Being just an ordinary file, we can't rely on the same "activation" code techniques employed by some software packages or the use of a CD to act as a "key" to allow you to play the music.

Many would argue that the same process was possible with traditional formats. CDs, tapes, and vinyl can all be recorded onto tapes of different forms and distributed, but compare the ease of distributing an entire book physically to that of distributing a file over the Internet!

There are a number of possible ways in which companies can restrict access to protect their investments. Technologies such as SCMS (serial copy management system) embed signals into the digital stream that are then identified by a music player. Attempts to copy the music to another source—for example, CD to MD and then MD to another MD—will fail, but this works only when copying between traditional music media. The SDMI (Secure Digital Music Initiative) system is being pushed by a group of record and music companies and will hopefully allow an individual to play music he or she has downloaded, but not allow the music to be shared with another party.

Integrating this information with a better quality audio stream will require a different audio standard, and I've listed below some of the up and coming standards that may replace MP3. Whichever audio standard is chosen, you can guarantee that we'll be seeing more of the digital music debate for years to come.

ATRAC (Adaptive Transform Acoustic Coding)

The ATRAC system was designed by Sony and is currently in use with the MiniDisc format. MiniDiscs are similar to CDs, but they store information using a compression system onto optical media that stores only 160 MB. The ATRAC system uses a compression system not entirely different from that of MP3, but specially designed by Sony engineers to produce an audio stream that sounds so close to CD as to be virtually undistinguishable.

Because the MiniDisc medium provides ATRAC with potentially twice as much space as even the highest quality MP3, Sony can extend the tonal range and make the best use of the available data rate. It does, however, still pay some attention to what the Sony engineers consider to be audible information. ATRAC concentrates less on reducing the raw audio information and more on compressing the digital stream using fairly ordinary block-based compression algorithms.

At the moment, ATRAC is in its third version, which now supports up to eighty minutes on a single MD and up to 320 minutes of stereo audio at a much lower quality (ideal for spoken word audio presentations). Although ATRAC has a number of advantages over MP3, it seems unlikely that Sony will make the move from ATRAC as an MD-only technology to a more general audio format that could be easily used on computers.

TwinVQ (VQF)

The TwinVQ standard was development by NTT (Nippon Telecom) for Yamaha. It uses a different approach to MP3 and ATRAC called "Time-domain weighted vector interleave quantization," which results in high-quality audio with much lower data rates. TwinVQ can achieve compression ratios of 18:1 (compared to 12:1 for MP3), but it has very slow encoders, making it impractical as a public solution when some software can encode MP3 at four or six times the speed of the source.

AAC (Advanced Audio Coding)

AAC is an extension of MPEG-2 Layer 3 and can encode with better quality and lower datarate than MP3. In addition to improved quality, AAC also supports multichannel audio such as that used in surround systems, including the Dolby AC3 standard used in many movie theaters (and pioneered by *Star Wars Episode 1: The Phantom Menace*) and on some DVDs. AAC is therefore seen as a suitable method for the digital distribution of sound and movies over broadband services like DSL (digital subscriber line).

MP4

Although it owes nothing to either MP3 or, indeed, any of the MPEG standards, MP4 is seen as the next step from MP3. Unlike MP3, which supports only a single encoding and compression methodology, MP4 is actually a collection of a number of different audio codecs, including text-to-speech, MIDI, and the TwinVQ and AAC techniques discussed here.

MP4 is therefore a more general-purpose standard that will allow producers to select the right codec according to the type of audio stream they are encoding. Speech and MIDI do not require the same level of compression or indeed provide the same amount of raw data, while music and surround sound have different needs. The MP4 standard is also expected to include SDMI or similar technology for upholding copyright, although how the whole system will work is still undetermined.

Audio Sources

However you decide to write your CD, and from whichever format, you'll need to source the information in the first place. There are lots of different ways in which you can obtain files for putting onto a true audio CD. For those people with large vinyl and tape collections that they want to transfer over to CD, there's a special section later in this chapter ("Digitizing Analog Audio") that deals with all the different issues.

If, on the other hand, you want to create some new compilations from a collection of existing CDs, you need to know how to rip information from the CD into a suitable file. Another alternative is to download an album or selected tracks from the Internet and use those files to create the CD.

Ripping from an Audio CD

You probably already know that you can get your computer's CD-ROM drive to play audio CDs for you through your speakers. CD-ROM drives will operate as CD players just by sending them suitable commands. Most machines work by asking the CD drive to do all the work. It's the drive that extracts the digital audio, converts it into an analog sound, and then sends that over normal copper cables to your sound card, which supplies it, undoctored, to your speakers.

Modern Macs (most iMacs, and all the G3 and G4 machines) and some PCs take a different approach—they read the digital files straight from the CD, run the digital stream through their own DSP (digital signal processor), and then output the sound through the speakers. If you have USB speakers, the digital audio stream is not converted until it reaches the speakers themselves, resulting in crisper sound.

The latter method can be used to extract digital files straight from the CD ready for re-recording onto your own CDs. The process is called ripping or, more formally, DAE, digital audio extraction. The resultant files can be encoded in AIFF, WAV, or MP3 format, depending on what you expect to use them for.

The MP3 wave has created a whole mini-industry devoted to creating software that rips information from a CD digitally and saves it in either raw (AIFF/WAV) or MP3 format for you. My own personal favorite is MusicMatch, which is available for both Macs and PCs—you can see a sample of the application under Windows in Figure 9.2 and under Mac OS in Figure 9.3.

Figure 9.2
Ripping a CD with MusicMatch under Windows.

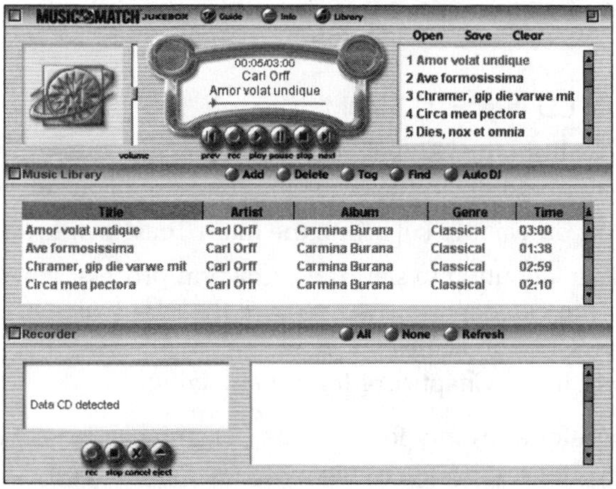

Figure 9.3
Playing your favorite
MP3 encoded CD
with MusicMatch
under Mac OS.

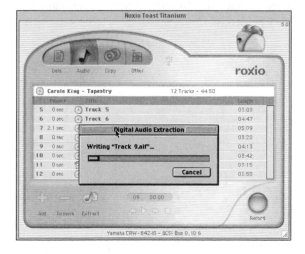

Like most packages, MusicMatch uses the CDDB, an online database that contains the artist, title, and track numbers of millions of CDs, saving you the trouble of typing the information yourself. When you rip the CD, it automatically saves the individual tracks using track titles as filenames and a directory structure that splits up artists and album titles. Although you can't write this information to the CD (well, not in a form that many CD players understand), you can use the information to populate your CD and jewel case insert labels. See Chapter 20 for more information.

Using Toast (Mac)

Toast 5.0 Titanium includes a tool called Toast Audio Extractor which prepares music tracks for audio CDs. It takes the digital files on the CD and saves them to disk so you can copy them to a compilation CD. It supports a number of different application formats and sound quality settings, up to and including the now familiar 44.1 kHz/16bit stereo supported by CD. You can see an extraction in progress in Figure 9.4.

Figure 9.4
Using Toast
Audio Extractor.

To extract a series of tracks from an audio CD and save them to disk:

1.   Open Toast.

2.   Insert the audio CD in your CD-ROM drive.

3.   Select the tracks from the CD that you want to record—use the Shift key to select a range of tracks or hold down the Apple button while you select individual tracks.

4.   Drag the tracks you want to copy into the main Toast window.

5.   Click on the Extract button to start the extraction process; you'll get a standard file dialog so that you can choose where to save the file. Toast will recognize these files as audio tracks. Once your files are extracted, you can burn your CD by clicking on the Record button (see Chapter 14 for more details).

Now, just leave it running—for a seventy-four minute CD, you can expect it to take anywhere from the standard seventy-four minutes to as few as ten, depending on the speed of your machine and the CD-ROM drive.

Using iTunes (Mac)

iTunes was released by Apple as part of the MacWorld Expo Keynote in January 2001. The application is free and can be downloaded direct from the Apple iTunes site (**www.apple.com/itunes/**). iTunes has been designed to take the place of a traditional audio collection manager and player, a streaming audio player (allowing you to listen to Internet radio stations), a CD/MP3 audio encoder, and even a CD writer. This means that we can use iTunes for creating compilation CDs (from ripping the audio from a CD through to writing it back) as well as a central hub for all of your audio playing. As if that weren't enough, iTunes will also upload your playlists and tunes to a number of the portable MP3 players on the market, including the Creative Labs NOMAD II series and SONICBlue/S3 Rio series.

The central hub for iTunes is the Library screen, which keeps a catalog and record of all the tunes the software knows about. You can add any MP3 tracks during software installation or by choosing File > Add to Library… and selecting the folder that you want searched. iTunes then records the location of the tracks and adds the header and/or filename information to the library. You can see a sample Library screen in Figure 9.5.

Figure 9.5
The iTunes
Library window.

To rip the contents of a CD to MP3 files, all you need to do is insert your audio CD into the CD drive of your Mac—the Source panel on the left-hand side of the window will change to show the information about the CD (as identified by CDDB), and then display the list of tracks in the main panel, as shown in Figure 9.6.

Figure 9.6
Playing/ripping an
audio CD with iTunes.

Section II Writing CDs

You can play the CD directly from here, but to convert to MP3, you must click on the Import button at the top right of the window. This will start the process using the settings configured in the application—to change these settings, choose Edit > Preferences and change to the Advanced tab (shown in Figure 9.7). From here you can select one of the present MP3 audio rates, or you can select Custom from the popup and make more specific selections about the MP3 settings. You can see a sample of the custom settings window in Figure 9.8.

Figure 9.7
Changing the
preferences in iTunes.

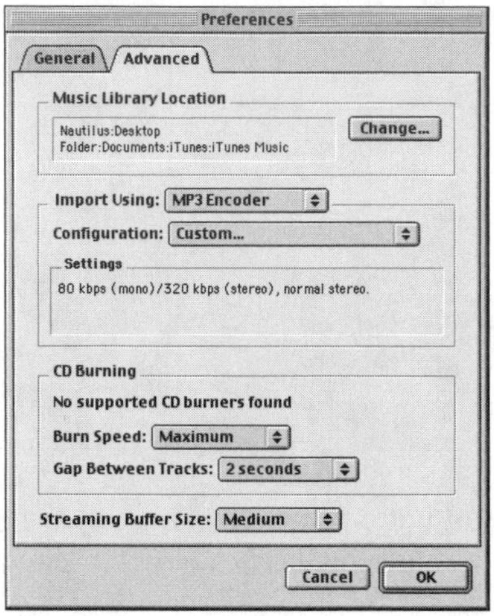

Figure 9.8
Configuring a
custom MP3 format.

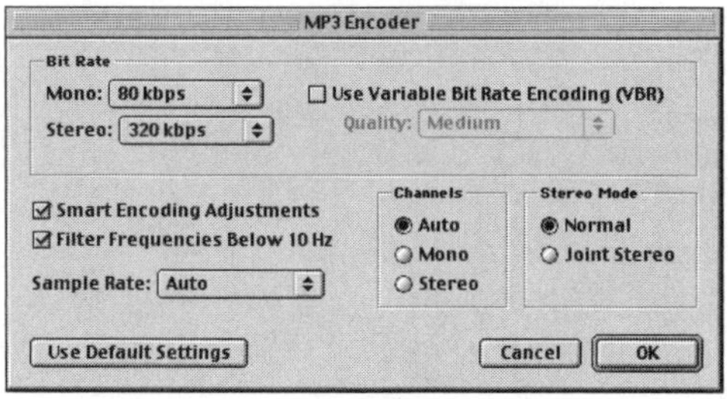

When you click on the Import button, iTunes starts the import process, writing files into a directory structure within the folder configured in the preferences. The folder structure creates a folder for each unique artist and another folder within that for the album title, with the individual tracks within the album folder. Tracks are named according to what you've created or those identified by CDDB. If your machine is fast enough, iTunes will even play the CD you are ripping at the same time as it rips the audio!

When it comes to writing a CD with iTunes, I have to admit to not being able to try it, since iTunes was released as the book was going through the final stages of production. Compatibility of iTunes with CD-R/RW drives is currently patchy, with some makes and models working better than others. It's inevitable that the CD-R/RW and DVD-R drives fitted to the new Macs will work and support for other drives will follow in due course. Look out for updates on this book's Web site (**www.mcwords.com/projects/books/cdr/**) about writing CDs with iTunes.

Using SoundStream (PC)

Easy CD Creator Deluxe used to be supplied with a product called CD Spin Doctor, which allowed you to record audio both from existing CDs and also from external analog sources. With the release of Easy CD Creator 5.0, this has been replaced with SoundStream. SoundStream does everything and more than CD Spin Doctor. (You can also use Music CD Project in Easy CD Creator 5.0; however this section concentrates on SoundStream only.)

SoundStream is a general-purpose program that can be used with CD and analog sources in order to produce file-based versions of the audio. It can also be used to record digital audio streams into AIFF or MP3 format straight from CD (otherwise called ripping). It also comes with an extension, called Spin Doctor, which can record from an analog source to an AIFF or MP3 file for you. In addition to all this, SoundStream can also be used to clean analog audio sources to remove crackles and to make modifications using a graphic equalizer to either digital or analog sources.

To rip audio tracks digitally from a CD, follow these steps:

1. Open the Roxio Easy CD Creator 5 > Project Selector application from the Start menu.

2. Click on Make a Music CD.

3. Click on SoundStream—you should get a window like the one shown in Figure 9.9.

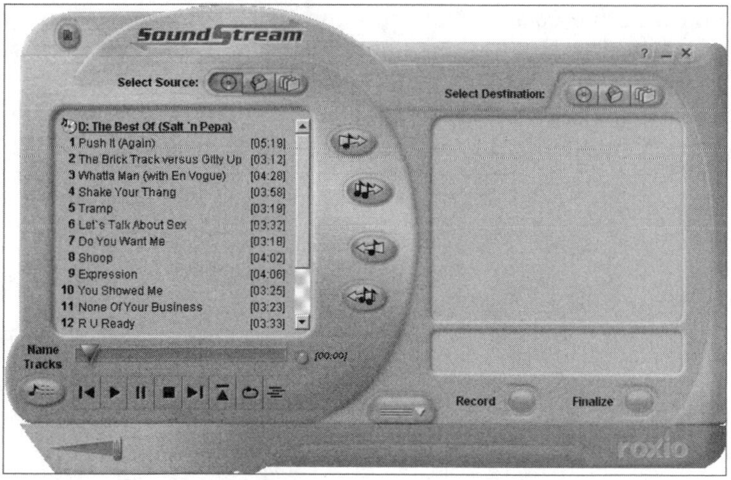

Figure 9.9
Using SoundStream
to record audio tracks
from a CD.

4. Insert the audio CD that you want to rip tracks from into the CD drive of your machine.

5. Click on the CD icon on the left-hand panel, and then click on the multiple folders icon on the right-hand panel—you'll be asked to choose a location for the files you want to save and the format in which you want them recorded.

6. Now select the tracks you want to rip from the CD and click on the top, single-noted button between the two panels. To select all of the files, click on the second-from-top, double-noted button.

7. Once you are happy with the track list, click on the Record button. You'll be prompted with the window (shown in Figure 9.10). Click on the Record button to start the process.

Figure 9.10
Starting the recording process.

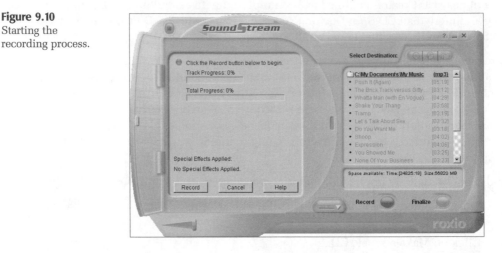

Note that SoundStream allows you to apply special effects to the tracks as they are being lifted from the CD—you can use the graphic equalizer to adjust the levels of different frequencies (just as you would with the equalizer on your sound system), or you can clean the audio of pops and crackles (rarely needed when reading from CD). To configure these options, click on the large button in the middle at the bottom of the window—the window will extend, as shown in Figure 9.11, to show the graphic equalizer panel. You must click on the checkbox on the left to actually make the equalizer settings apply to the sounds you are recording. To set the effects, click on the Effects button.

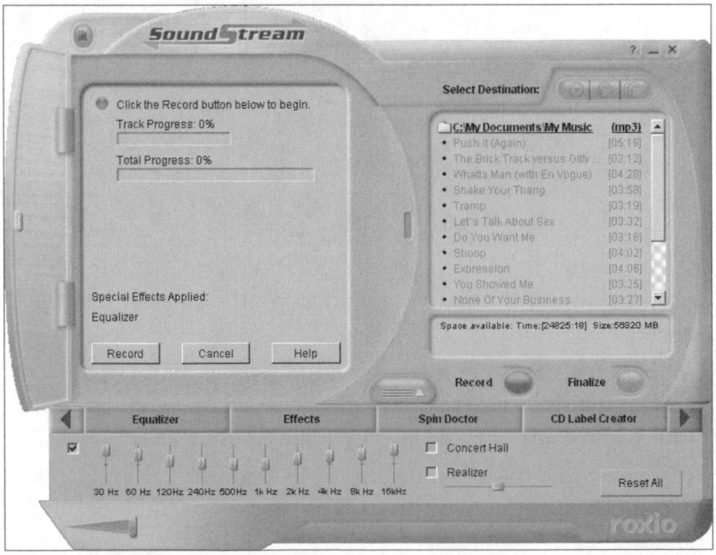

Figure 9.11
Configuring the graphic equalizer.

Using CDR Toaster

The CDR Toaster application is our preferred front end to the cdrecord application under Unix and Linux. CDR Toaster also interfaces to cdparanoia, an application that rips information from CD into individual files. The cdparanoia application enables you to store the tracks from a CD in WAV (the default), AIFF/AIFC (a compressed form of AIFF), or raw PCM encoded (identical to that used on CD).

To extract tracks from a CD using CDR Toaster and cdparanoia:

1. Open CDR Toaster, usually by typing **cdrtoaster** at X terminal prompt.

2. Click Do Tricks > Read audio tracks from CDROM, which will bring up the configuration window shown in Figure 9.12.

Figure 9.12
Configuring the audio properties or the files you rip.

3. First, select the source drive's device file by clicking on the top Peruse button—you'll probably need to choose /dev/cdrom or /dev/cdrom1.

4. Select the destination for the files you are ripping by clicking on the bottom Peruse button—it defaults to your home directory.

5. Choose the tracks you want to extract, select all of the tracks, or provide cdparanoia with a custom list of arguments. You'll need to use this last option if you want to change the default format from WAV to AIFF, AIFC, or raw.

6. Click Do It and let cdparanoia get on with it.

You'll end up with a series of files in the current directory containing the extracted tracks.

Alternatively, if you prefer to use cdparanoia directly, you can get away with:

```
$ cdparanoia -B '1-'
```

…if you want to record all the tracks, or:

```
$ cdparanoia -B '2-3'
```

…if you want only tracks 2 and 3. If you want to change the output format, use **-p** for raw format, **-w** for WAV format, **-f** for AIFF and **-a** for AIFC. For example, to create an AIFC version of track 2, you would use the following:

```
$ cdparanoia -Ba '2'
```

Note that the -B option ensures that the tracks are divided up properly into individual files. Without this option, you will simply end up with one very big file!

Section II Writing CDs

Downloading from the Internet

The MP3 explosion that I've already described has led to numerous files being made available on the Internet, both officially and subversively. Some bands have even embraced the digital revolution and started to release their new albums only in MP3 format, downloadable from the Web. They Might Be Giants (one of my favorites, and often pioneers in the field of new technology music distribution) were one of the first to do this, with their *Long Tall Weekend* album.

There are numerous Web sites you can try, and I've listed some of the more popular sites below. Note, however, that for many of these sites, the operations and charging structure (if any) were under investigation or adjustment at the time of this writing. You'll need to check the following sites for information on the cost of downloading albums and individual tracks from the Internet:

▶ **EMusic.com**—one of the original pioneers of selling digital music over the Internet as MP3 files. It has 150,00 tracks in 12,500 albums available from the site, from free samples right up to full-cost titles.

▶ **MP3.com**—the major proponent of MP3 files and distribution on the Internet, although it originally started simply as a site of information on MP3 encoders and players. The site now charges either per-title or subscription prices for downloading audio content from the Web.

▶ **Napster.com**—provides a software package that allows you to search for MP3 files across a number of "end user" machines over the Internet. Each user is effectively sharing the music files directly from his or her computer over the Internet. Like MP3.com, it charges individual and subscription prices for downloading content.

▶ **Liquidaudio.com**—supports a network for song artists to distribute their work and end-users to download it. Often used by a number of new groups to provide digital-only versions of their music.

Once you've download the files, you can either play them using Windows Media Player, QuickTime Player, or many other MP3 tools, or you can use your CD writing software to write the MP3 files as an audio CD.

Digitizing Analog Audio

Although most people will probably be creating CD compilations based on tracks from their existing CD collections, many people are also using their computers to convert their existing vinyl and tape collections into CDs. For some, this is the only way they can preserve their collections, as a large number of vinyl and tape albums have never been officially released as CDs. There is also the issue of cost—if you've bought an album once on vinyl, is it really worth buying it on CD as well?

Vinyl, tape and, indeed, any source that is supplied through a microphone, headphone, or line jack is an analog source. The sounds are made up of a variable rate electric signal, which is what your amplifier increases in order to make the sound louder. CD, as we know, is a digital format, so we need some way of converting your analog signal into the digital format required by CD. When you play a CD, the digital signal is converted to analog format before being boosted by your amplifier and sent to your speakers. You can see a simple diagram of a typical stereo system in Figure 9.13.

Figure 9.13
A typical stereo system setup showing digital and analog devices.

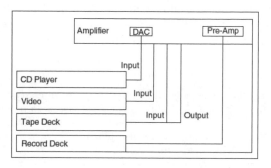

The conversion of an analog signal to a digital format is handled by an ADC—an analog to digital converter—which converts an analog signal into a digital data stream using the same technique used to produce audio CDs. An ADC is generally combined with a DAC (digital to analog converter), which is what your computer uses to generate sounds on your computer speakers. The whole system is combined into an overall DSP (digital signal processing) chip, which performs ADC and DAC as well as containing the code to generate its own sounds and even to simulate different instruments. The layout of a computer's sound system, including external inputs and ADC/DAC devices is shown in Figure 9.14.

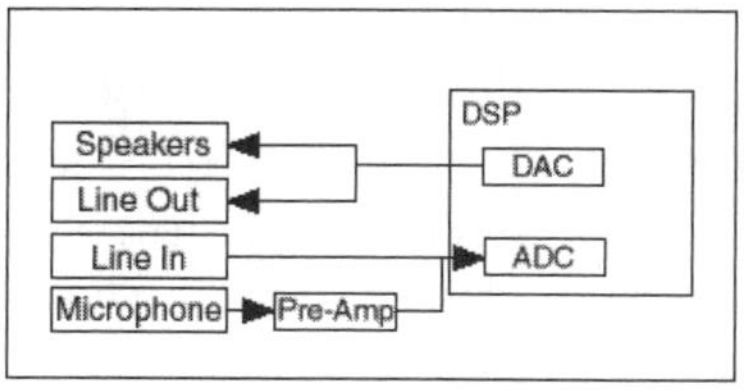

Figure 9.14
The electronic layout of a computer sound system.

Checking your Machine's Hardware

Before you start, you need to know if you can record sound on your PC from an external source. If you have a PC, you will need to have an audio card such as a Creative SoundBlaster, Turtle Beach, or similar. The sound card contains the DSP and the necessary connections to output sound, take sound input, and simulate instruments. If your computer already is connected to a pair of speakers, it's highly likely that you also have a sound input jack on the back of your computer.

Even the most basic of sound cards supports CD-quality sound recording in stereo, so if you have a sound card, you should be able to handle digital recording. However, be aware that some sound cards rely on the power of the PC's CPU to supply some of the computational ability required when recording audio. We'll have a look at ways of preparing your machine later in this chapter.

Macs (Quadra, Centris, or any PowerPC-based machine) have their own DSP on the motherboard. The Mac DSP is capable both of outputting sound or recording it, both at CD quality, but it's up to QuickTime, the multimedia component of the Mac OS, to support the instrument emulation normally built into PC audio cards. We're not worried about instrument emulation—you just need to know that you can record sound on most Macs.

NOTE

The iBook and the new Titanium Powerbooks are the only exceptions to the rule when it comes to audio input ability. Neither machine includes the ability to take sound from the outside, aside from the CD/DVD drive and the built-in microphone on the PowerBook. However, you can get USB devices that will digitize audio for you. See Macintouch's USB device guide (**www.macintouch.com**) for more information on the available products.

Analog Recording Steps

There are a number of different steps required to take your analog audio source and convert it into a digital file that can then be written to CD. The entire process, from start to finish, works like this:

▶ **Connect your analog source to your sound card**—Depending on what you are recording from, you may need some additional hardware to connect your record player, tape deck, or other analog source.

▶ **Record the audio to a file**—You'll probably want to record the information straight to an AIFF or WAV file to get the best overall quality source.

▶ **Filter the audio**—One of the problems with analog sources, particularly vinyl, is that they can contain hiss and pops and crackles. Although accepted in their original formats, the effects will be quite noticeable once the source is on CD.

▶ **Trim/split the audio**—Because you are recording from a manual source, there are no "physical" breaks between individual tracks and you'll have lead in and out at the start and end of the source. You'll need to manually break up tracks and trim the "empty" or "white" noise.

▶ **Organize and then write the CD**—This is the easiest part of the process, as you just need to tell the CD writing software to write the audio files as an audio CD.

We'll have a look at each stage below in more detail. Before then, however, it's worth looking at the different packages available. Although there are many ways to record audio on all three platforms, not all of the available tools allow you to filter and trim the audio—a required stage if you want to produce a professional-sounding CD. Under both Windows and Mac OS, the tool to use is CD Spin Doctor—if you have Easy CD Creator 5.0 under Windows, then use the Spin Doctor extension to the new SoundStream application. Although the applications share the same name, they don't work in entirely the same way. On Windows, you configure everything about your source, including any filtering and identification options before you start recording, and then let Spin Doctor make all the decisions and do all the work during the process of recording.

Under CD Spin Doctor on the Mac, you record a raw audio file and then use the filtering and other mechanisms within the application to post-process the file to get rid of the hiss and crackles. In order to make the best of the process, you therefore need to record the files to disc, make a copy, and then post-process them to remove any unwanted information. In all other ways, the applications are more or less identical.

Suitable software on Unix/Linux is more difficult to come by, although a quick search of the Internet will find all sorts of solutions for you. Typically, the software is provided free, though the level of product support and features is not always up to the same level as that offered in the commercial Mac OS and Windows packages. That's not to say the software is substandard, but I've yet to find an audio recording package that will also support the filtering technology provided by CD Spin Doctor. Unix/Linux-based recording does have one major advantage—it's much more able to keep up with recording from an analog source while your machine is doing other things. I record analog audio on my Solaris server, which also handles all my file, Web, and mail services, without any loss in quality or performance.

Connecting your Analog Source

For most analog sources, all you have to do is connect the output from the device into a 3.5-millimeter stereo jack that you then plug into your sound card or microphone input (if using a Mac). There are some exceptions to this rule, so to help you choose which solution to use, I've listed the top audio sources and how you should attach them:

▶ **Tape Deck**—You can connect the audio output of the tape deck (usually phono/RCA jacks) through a cable to the input of your sound card. Most will take line output directly without requiring amplification. If you don't have phono/RCA jacks on the back of your tape deck, either use the headphone output (and follow the instructions for tape-based personal stereos) or, if you have spare phono/RCA outputs on your amplifier, use them—they are usually marked "tape out" or "monitor out."

▶ **Personal Stereo (tape)**—Get a 3.5-millimeter jack-to-3.5-millimeter jack cable and connect the personal stereo to the audio input. Now, adjust the volume until it's about 10 to 15 percent below maximum; that should give you the best quality input without affecting the sound input levels. You may have to adjust the levels for your equipment, as it varies from machine to machine.

> **Personal Stereo (MD)**—If you've recorded the MiniDisc from CD, use the CD original and the digital audio extraction techniques we discussed earlier. If you don't have the CD, follow the steps for tape-based personal stereos above.

> **Video**—If your video has phone/RCA jacks *out,* use those in combination with an adaptor cable to supply the input.

> **Record player (vinyl)**—Record players do not provide the same level of output as other analog devices, so you will need a special record player preamp. Many amplifiers have the preamp built in, which is why you have special record deck inputs on the amplifier. If you don't have an amplifier, you can buy preamps to bring the levels up to the same as other devices. In either case, you'll get a phono/RCA output from the preamp or the tape/monitor out on your amplifier, which you can use with a suitable cable to provide the input.

In all cases, connect the input to the "line" in, rather than "microphone" in—check your sound card documentation for more information. Under Mac OS, don't worry—there is only one input, and that takes line input unless a special microphone connector is attached, so you should automatically be using line input.

For a quick overview of how to connect all the different types of equipment, see Figure 9.15.

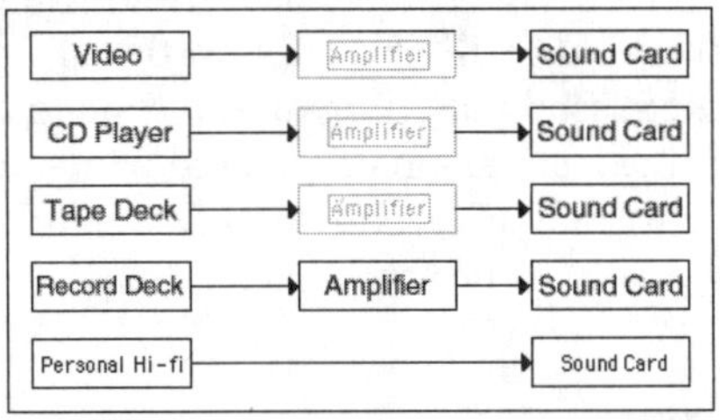

Figure 9.15
How to connect different pieces of personal stereo equipment to your machine for analog recording.

With all analog sources, it's a good idea to check the input level before you start recording—with SoundStream (which incorporates the Spin Doctor extensions for recording analog audio), you can check this by looking at the VU (volume unit) meter; this shows the audio input level. Under Windows, this is shown once you've selected an analog source in the main window—a close-up of the meter is given in Figure 9.16.

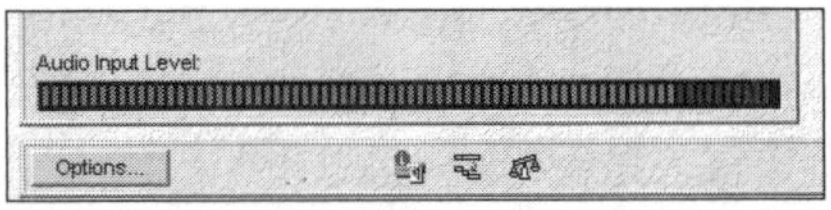

Figure 9.16
The VU meter under Spin Doctor/ SoundStream (Windows).

In CD Spin Doctor on the Mac, a VU meter is shown between the control buttons and the option buttons at the top right of the window. See Figure 9.17 for a close-up.

Figure 9.17
The VU meter under CD Spin Doctor (Mac OS).

Whichever tool you use, try to adjust the input volume (from a personal stereo or headphone output) so that the sound uses the full range of the VU meter, but only occasionally touches the top (usually red) mark. Although this may introduce some low-level hiss, we can filter that out more easily than we can increase the overall volume range.

If you are using a fixed input source—for example, direct phono/RCA from the back of a tape deck or video—you can adjust the input levels through software. Under Windows, open the Sounds and Multimedia control panel and click the Volume button—you'll see a window like the one shown here in Figure 9.18. The window allows you to control the levels of all the different inputs on your machine—in this case, because I'm using a SoundBlaster Live! Card, there are four analog input volumes—make sure you change the line input control.

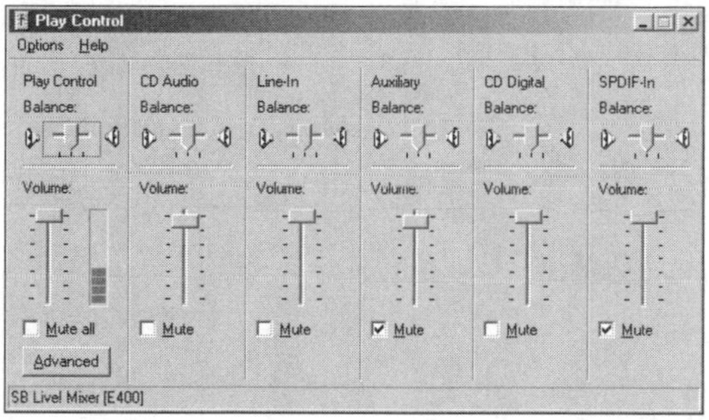

Figure 9.18
Checking the input level using the volume properties in Windows.

Play Control	CD Audio	Line-In	Auxiliary	CD Digital	SPDIF-In

On the Mac, you control the input level from the software you are using. We'll see how to do this in the next section.

Under Linux, check the documentation for the software you are using. Products like sox and ecasound have their own methods for adjusting the input levels.

Recording the Audio to a File

Now that you are connected, you need to set up your software and actually record the information to the disc. Irrespective of the software you are using, the basic process is:

1. Set up your software with your desired options and configuration.
2. Get your analog source ready—for tape, MiniDisc, or video, use pause on your decks if supported; for record decks, lift the arm and place it over the record at the position you want to start.

3. Start the recording process on your PC.

4. Start the source playing.

Now, you just need to wait until the source finishes and you can tell the software to stop recording. There will probably be some post-processing that you need to conduct before the files are finally ready, but we'll cover that later.

Recording from an Analog Source using SoundStream

To record from an analog audio source to a file using SoundStream under Windows:

1. Choose Start > Roxio Easy CD Creator 5.0 > Project Selector, click Audio Project and then SoundStream in the next two windows. You should get the SoundStream window (as seen earlier in Figure 9.8). To get to Spin Doctor, you must click on the big button in the center and bottom of the SoundStream window—the window will extend as shown earlier in Figure 9.11.

2. Click on the Spin Doctor button to bring up the Spin Doctor window, shown in Figure 9.19.

3. Select the source that you want to record from—a suitable source should have automatically been selected for you.

Figure 9.19
The main Spin Doctor window as part of SoundStream.

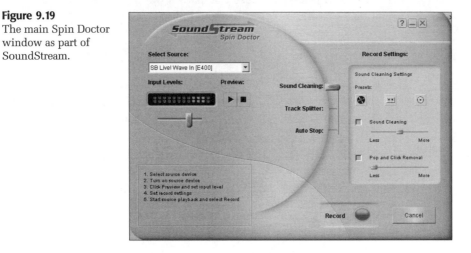

4. Configure the sound cleaning settings—you can either manually adjust the sound cleaning and pop and click removal settings or use a predefined setting by clicking on the button at the top of the settings panel. Pre-configured settings are supplied for vinyl, tape, and analog CD input.

5.   Configure the track-splitting options using the panel shown in Figure 9.20. In general, you should choose the last option and split the track based on the "blank" gap between tracks.

Figure 9.20
Configuring the track-splitting options on recorded audio.

6.   Configure the auto-stop settings—use manual unless you want to leave the recording process unattended.

7.   Once you are ready, click the Record button—you'll be prompted with the window shown here in Figure 9.21. Set the file name and specify whether you want to record to a file (recommended) or straight to CD. The latter option will automatically start writing a CD with the file or files you have recorded once the process has finished. When you are ready, click the Start Recording button.

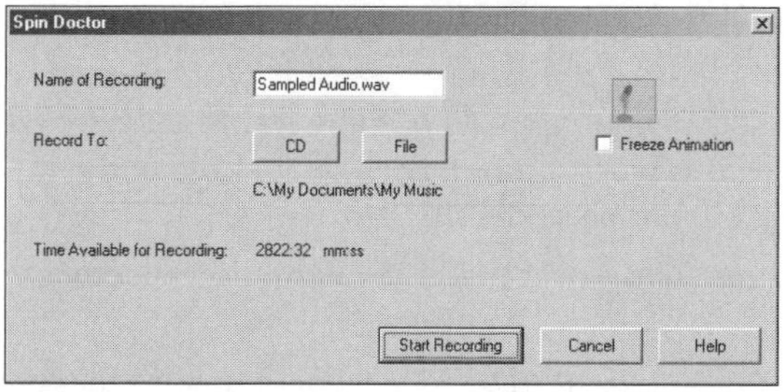

Figure 9.21
Setting the name and destination for the recorded audio.

Recording From an Analog Source Using CD Spin Doctor

To record an audio file using CD Spin Doctor under Mac OS:

NOTE
CD Spin Doctor will not work if you have virtual memory switched on. To switch off virtual memory, open the Memory control panel, click the Off radio button under Virtual Memory, and then restart your machine.

1. Open CD Spin Doctor—you'll find it in the CD Spin Doctor, which is itself within the main Toast Deluxe folder. You'll get a window like the one shown in Figure 9.22.

Figure 9.22
The main CD Spin Doctor (Mac OS) window.

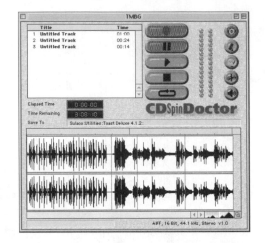

2. The track section at the top lists the tracks you've already recorded in this session—it should be empty at the start. The top right contains the normal recording/playback controls, a VU level meter that shows the signal strength of the incoming audio, and the option buttons for controlling the input levels and filtering.

3. Click on the Inputs menu and choose the input source. The microphone and Sound In options usually refer to the same physical input, but the input gain is adjusted to cope with the microphone input. Choose Sound In for the best results. You can check the currently selected input device by looking at the Input panel in the Sound control panel—it should be set to "Built-in."

4. Choose File > Save To to select the drive and folder where you want the sound files saved.

5. Click the Record button (with the red circle), then start playing your source material.

6. When you've finished recording, press the Stop button (the black square). You'll be prompted for a filename. If you want to divide up the tracks, you'll have to do this after the recording has been completed and saved. See "Filtering the Audio" later in this chapter for more information on cleaning the audio, and "Trimming/Splitting the Audio" for details on how to turn one big track into individual tracks.

The resulting files will be in AIFF format, perfect for recording instantly onto CD.

Recording from an Analog source using sox

To record an audio file under Unix or Unix/Linux, you need to have installed some suitable software. I've been using sox for years, although there are a number of other products out and a number of front ends which you can use. To record a WAV file using sox, you need to supply the input device, and output filename. The sox application uses the extension of the filename to identify the output file format. For example:

```
$ sox -t ossdsp –b –u –c 2 –r 44100 /dev/dsp myfile.wav
```

The command line sample above records from the sound card (/dev/dsp) in stereo, at CD quality, to the WAV file myfile.wav. The moment you press Enter, sound is recorded, so you will need to start your source material immediately. Once the source has finished, press Ctrl+C to cancel the recording process. Unfortunately, there is no silence detection in sox, so you will have to split the file manually into the individual tracks.

Filtering the Audio

Analog sources tend to contain a lot of hiss and occasional pops because of the way the information is stored, either on tape or on vinyl. Especially with vinyl, crackles and noise occur because dust has gotten into the grooves that make up the album. The needle identifies the "bumps" from the dust as just another sound. You can avoid these effects by making sure your needle, vinyl, and tapes are as clean as possible. Use a new needle if you can, and clean the vinyl with a special cleaning fluid or bar—remember to clean along the line of the grooves, from the outside in.

For tape, use an alcohol-based cleaner and a cotton swab to clean the heads *and* pinch rollers—you'll need to turn the tape deck on to get the best results. Avoid at all costs any form of abrasive cleaner, including the "dry" tape cleaners that can often do more harm than good because all they do is wear down the head rather than actually cleaning it.

Even with all this preparation, you'll probably still end up with the occasional pop or crackle and some background hiss, especially between tracks and at the lead in and out of the record or tape side. Some software, including CD Spin Doctor (Mac) and SoundStream (with Spin Doctor, PC) can normally identify the blank portions and treat them as a track break, but to really get rid of the hiss, you need to use one of the special filters built into the software.

There are a number of different effects that you can apply to the tracks that you record:

▶ **Cleaning**—This removes the telltale hiss and crackle from the source. You can set the amount of hiss and crackle that is removed using a sliding scale, but you need to take care, as the higher the level, the more likely you are to lose information from the source material. Making the decision about where to draw the line is entirely up to you.

▶ **Morphing**—You can add echo, reverb, and many other effects to the sound as it is recorded. Unless you have special needs on the input, however, you probably want to avoid these, as they will not produce an identical digital copy of the analog source.

▶ **Silence Detection**—By "listening" to incoming sound, it's possible to identify where there is no music and, therefore, where there is a track split. On some sources, these tracks can be annoying—for example, when recording a talking book or video, silence is a natural part of the "sound," but for music, it means you can automatically split a single recording session into individual tracks. This is especially useful when recording music from tape or vinyl.

Section II Writing CDs

▶ **Balancing**—Not all audio sources are recorded at the same volume level. Spin Doctor on the PC will allow you to balance the incoming audio signal to a standard volume level, overriding the manual input level settings. Unless you have a specific need to record at a given gain level, you should use this option to ensure the clearest sound.

Window's Spin Doctor performs all of these filters for you automatically on the sound as it is recorded.

Post-processing Audio with CD Spin Doctor

On the Mac, you can perform only a selection of the filters, but only *after* the sound has been recorded to disk. To perform the cleaning process:

1. Open CD Spin Doctor.

2. Find the track that you just recorded and make a copy of it—the filter process changes the file itself without any ability to undo the process, so you need to make a backup.

3. Select the track that you have just recorded and click on the filter button (second one up from the bottom).

4. You'll be asked to configure the different filters (see Figure 9.23)—the Noise and Pop filters are used for cleaning, the Realizer adjusts the tone of the sound, and the Output Level can help to balance the overall volume of the track.

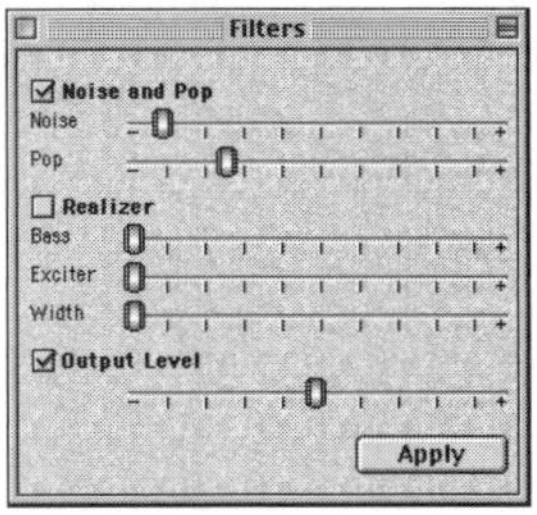

Figure 9.23
Setting the filter options in CD Spin Doctor (Mac OS).

5. Once you've configured the settings, click the Apply button. You'll be warned that the process will permanently alter the file. Click OK to continue.

6. Your machine will now apply the filters and re-save the file.

7. Press the Play button and listen to the new version of the track to make sure you are happy with it.

Filtering the Audio Under Unix/Linux

Under Unix/Linux, things are not quite so straightforward. The sox application can apply a number of different filters and effects to a sound file and convert a file between different formats, but none of them are really targeted at removing the normal crackles, hiss, and pops that originate on analog recordings.

Trimming/Splitting the Audio Under Windows

The Windows version of Spin Doctor attempts to split up the source audio for you automatically. If you need to make any sort of modification after that, you will need to open Sound Editor, which comes as part of the Easy CD Creator package. Sound Editor lets you open a raw audio file, perform a number of different operations such as equalization, and offers the ability to trim and split audio. The basic operation of trimming audio is as follows:

1. Open Sound Editor.
2. Use File > Open to open the sound file.
3. Play the file, and then determine the point at which you want the trimming to occur. Because the sound is displayed graphically, you can usually identify blank spots by a low signal line.
4. Click and hold the mouse to select the area you want cut from the file.
5. Select Edit > Cut or the Cut button on the toolbar—this will delete the portion you highlighted.

If you want to split a file into smaller components, then instead of highlighting and cutting the tracks individually from the file, use copy and then create a new sound file and paste the copied portion into it.

Trimming/Splitting the Audio Under Mac OS

CD Spin Doctor on the Mac supports file trimming and splitting directly on the file you have just saved or on a previous one that you have opened. It can autosplit the file, but only after the recording has taken place. To use the autosplit feature, open the file you want to work on and select Tracks > Auto-Define Tracks. CD Spin Doctor will identify the blank portions of the recorded track and try to identify each of the individual tracks.

Alternatively, you can define your own tracks, which solves both the trimming and track splitting problem—just click and hold a mouse button to highlight the area of the track and then choose Tracks > Define Track.

Trimming/Splitting the Audio under Unix/Linux

You'll need to use an application like ecawave or ecasound or one of the many other tools to edit the sound into individual files under Linux.

Writing an Audio CD

Once you've recorded, filtered, and trimmed the audio, you need to go into Toast, Easy CD Creator, or CDR Toaster and tell it to write an audio CD. We'll look at these tools in more detail in chapters 15, 16 and 17, respectively, so we'll leave the CD writing process to those chapters.

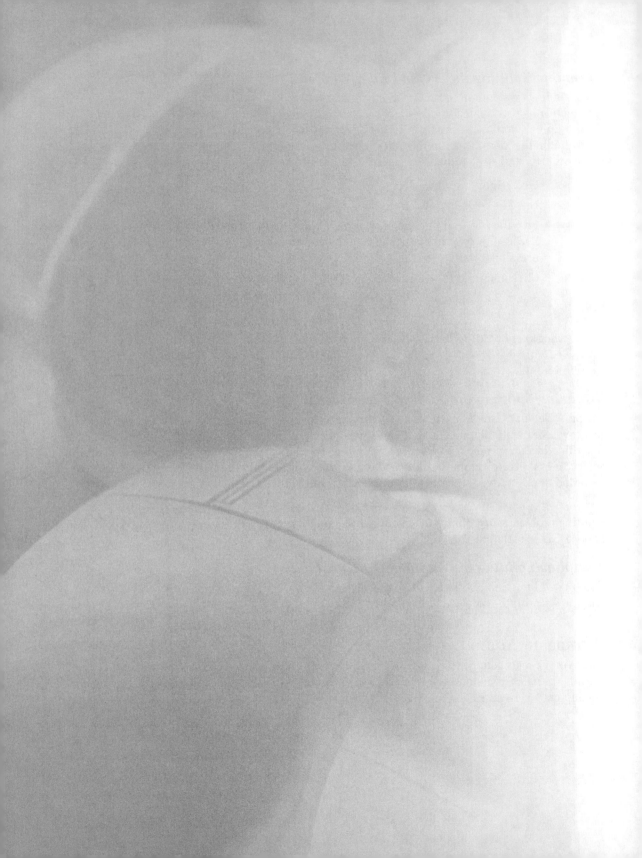

10

Diagnostic, Installer, and Autolaunch CDs

It's happened to the best of us at some point or another. You've just booted your machine and now it won't start again properly. On a Mac, you can try starting up without extensions (by holding down the Shift key), and on a Windows PC, you can try starting Windows in safe mode. Under Unix, it depends entirely on which system you are using. Linux generally uses a bootable floppy "rescue" disk, while others allow you to boot up in single-user mode.

The approach is always the same—you just want to get the machine booting again so you can check that the disks don't have any problems and, if necessary, back up the data and start all over again. The problem is that most solutions require you to boot up from a different disk so that you have complete, unencumbered access to the hard drive—you can't normally make changes or fix the drive running either the current operating system or a diagnostic application like Norton Utilities or Disk First Aid.

The solution is to create a CD with everything you need already on it. All Macs and most PCs support the ability to boot up from CD; in fact, most machines now come with the operating system on bootable CD that you must insert before the machine is ready to use.

In this chapter, we'll look at the methods and tricks you can use to create a bootable CD and the sort of software and programs you can add to the CD. While we're examining the process, we'll also look at how to create a CD that automatically starts a particular application when the CD is inserted. Although it's not as useful a method as a bootable CD, it can be useful when you are writing CDs that install software or support applications that you have written.

Creating Bootable Diagnostic CDs

Creating a bootable CD is quite straightforward, but there are limitations as to what you can do with it. First and foremost, a bootable CD is (of course) read-only, which means you can't enable virtual memory. Under Windows, this also means you can't install Windows onto a CD—you can install DOS, but not a full Windows operating system. Similarly, with Linux it's actually very difficult to recreate a full Unix system onto a CD. However, a reduced Unix system, good enough to boot and run tools such as fsck, is possible.

The Mac is actually the easiest platform for which to create a bootable CD, because a Mac can boot from any volume and from just about any type of removable or fixed device (except tape). Once you've installed the operating system onto a suitable partition or temporary volume, you can then add other files including installers, diagnostics software, and other elements. Because we can write the contents of a volume, including its operating system and boot compatibility, onto CD, we can quickly create a bootable CD to help diagnose, fix, and update a machine without needing to access the hard drive.

Installing the Operating System

Both Windows and Linux base their bootable CDs on an existing bootable floppy disk. In the case of Windows, you can create a suitable floppy through the Add/Remove Programs control panel. Under Linux, it's probably easier to use one of the bootable floppy disks that came with your RedHat, Suse, or other Linux distribution. You can then use these bootable floppies as the bootable components of a CD. However, you are limited to a DOS-based interface and tools, which usually means reduced or restricted versions of disk tools and anti-virus utilities.

It's not possible in any way to install a Windows tool and use it successfully under DOS, which severely limits the usefulness of a bootable CD in the first place. Under Unix or Linux, although you can install full operating systems and most of the software and even X Windows, it's always easier to use one of the bootable floppies or CDs from one of the distribution houses.

Unfortunately, all of these limitations make creating bootable CDs for diagnostic and software installations under Windows and Linux virtually impossible or, at the very least, impractical. See Chapter 16 for information on creating a bootable CD with Easy CD Creator.

Under Mac OS, the situation is quite different. Any Mac volume, from a floppy to Zip, Jaz, CD, and, of course, hard disk partitions can be made bootable, and there is no limitation or configuration required to get your Mac to boot from your desired volume. Because it's not considered good practice to update your operating system while it's running, you could boot up from this partition to install an update onto your main drive.

For your source volume, the best recommendation is to use a separate partition on your hard drive or a removable disc that you can boot from. Not all removable devices are boot-compatible with all machines, so choose carefully. If you have your hard disk split into a number partitions, choose one of the partitions to work with. If you can't support any of these, use a disk image instead—see Chapter 13 for information on how to create a disk image using Disk Copy.

The reason why an existing partition or other bootable device is a good idea is that once the operating system has been installed, we can test it, configure certain portions of the operating system, and add and update diagnostic software—things we can't do to an unbootable partition such as one created with Disk Copy. Make sure that whatever partition, removable disk, or disk image you decide to use has recently been formatted so that it is completely blank.

To install the operating system onto your new volume:

1. Find the Software Install disk that came with your Mac and insert it into your machine. Alternatively, if you've ordered a "full install" version of a later operating system, put that into your CD-ROM drive instead.

2. Double click on the Install Macintosh Software icon on the CD; you'll be presented with a window similar to that in Figure 10.1.

Figure 10.1
Selecting the country for your operating system installation.

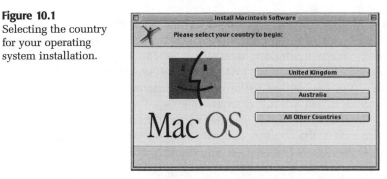

3. Click on the desired country. You'll be prompted with the main Welcome screen, shown in Figure 10.2. Click Continue to move to the next window.

Figure 10.2
Starting the installation process.

4. The window in Figure 10.3 controls where you want to install the operating system. Click on the popup and choose the partition, removable disk, or disk image volume that you want to use as the source for your disk. Click Select to choose where to install the operating system.

Figure 10.3
Choosing a disk for installation.

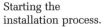

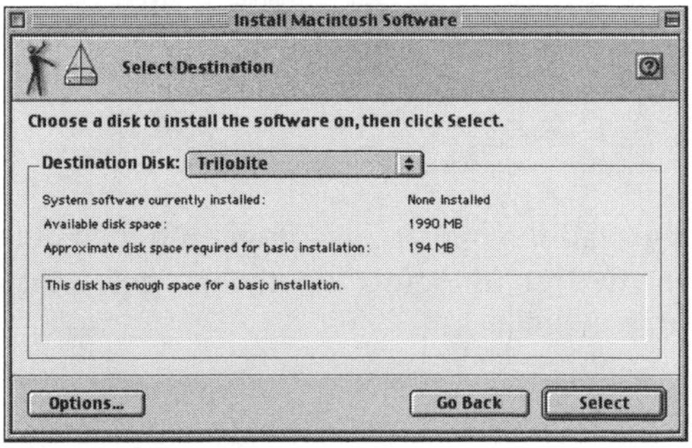

5.   The next few screens prepare you for the process—you can just click Continue to move through each screen. Remember to click Agree when prompted to agree to the software license.

6.   Once you are past the license screen, you should be prompted with the window seen here in Figure 10.4. Before you go further, click on the Customize button, which will bring up a slightly different window, shown in Figure 10.5. The window allows you to select which parts of the operating system to install and to what level. Since we are creating a disk only for booting, installing, and diagnosing, many of the features are not required. In fact, installing anything except the core operating system, networking (including AirPort, if you use it), and Internet access is a waste of space and will also reduce the memory and speed of your machine when you boot from CD. Use the checkboxes to deselect everything but the core items and then click Start.

Figure 10.4
The final stage of
the process.

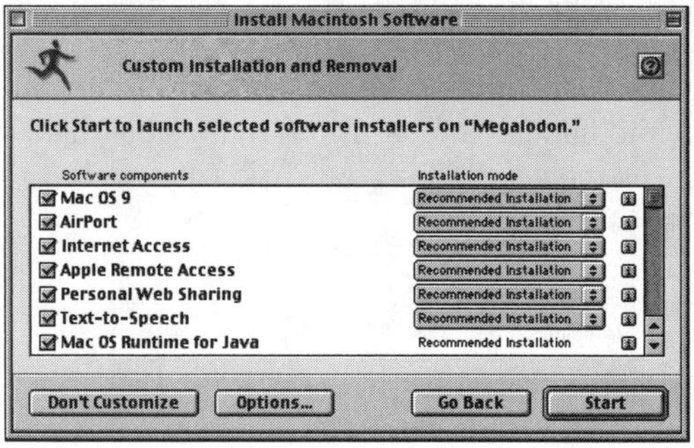

Figure 10.5
Customizing
your installation
components.

The installer software will now install the operating system onto the volume you selected. The process can take a long time; you can see in Figure 10.6 that it's going to take fourteen minutes to install the OS onto the partition Trilobite.

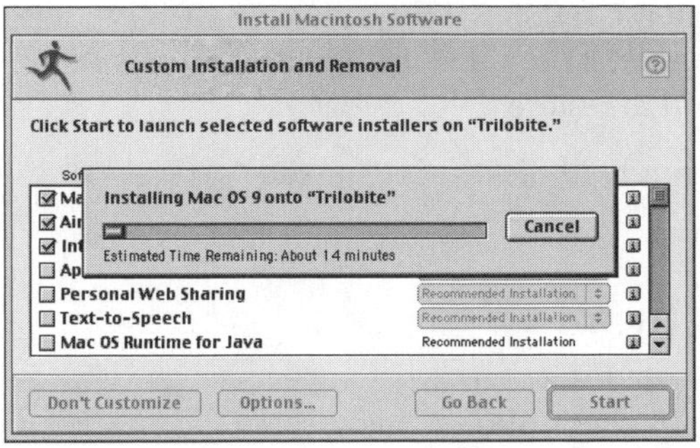

Figure 10.6
Monitoring the
progress of the
installation.

Once the operating system has been installed, repeat the process with any critical system updates. For example, if your machine came with 8.6, make sure you put 8.6.1 on the CD and, similarly, if your machine came with 9.0.4, update it to 9.1 if you have the updaters handy. This will ensure that your new volume, and the CD it will be used to create, is the latest possible version.

Once the operating system is installed, and providing your temporary volume supports it, reboot your Mac and boot using your new volume. You can set the startup volume using the Startup Disk control panel (shown in Figure 10.7). Once booted on the new volume, make the following changes to the system:

Figure 10.7
Configuring your new
operating system
configuration for
running from CD.

Section II Writing CDs

▶ **Configure your network settings**—Having access to a network disk during a diagnostic session can be handy, as you can use it as a backup location or even as the source for installers and updates. Use the AppleTalk control panel to select your preferred network device (probably Ethernet).

▶ **Configure your TCP/IP settings**—Most networks now use TCP/IP instead of AppleTalk for communication, so make sure your TCP/IP settings are correct. If your network supports DHCP or BOOTP (check with your system administrator), then use it, rather than manually setting numbers. A conflict on the network will render the CD unusable.

▶ **Disable virtual memory**—You cannot use virtual memory on CD, because the swap file needs to be written to. Disable it in the Memory control panel to ensure that your operating system doesn't try to use VM on boot up.

▶ **Configure a RAM disk**—If you have the RAM available, configure a RAM disk. Even a small one of 5 to 10 MB may give you enough space for creating small backups of files or allowing you to restore deleted files.

Now, reboot back onto your main hard disk (using the Startup Disk control panel again if necessary).

Adding Diagnostic Software

Because under Mac OS we are not limited by what appears on the CD or what we can run from the CD, it's a good idea to take the opportunity to add some diagnostic tools to the CD volume during preparation. The Mac OS install will have added Disk First Aid and Drive Setup utilities to the disk automatically. Here's a list of other tools that can be useful when diagnosing and fixing a Mac when booted from CD:

▶ **Anti-Virus software**—Useful for scanning your machine without fear of infecting the disk from which you are scanning. McAfee VirusScan or Norton Anti-Virus are the best products, but even Disinfectant, a free tool available from **www.macupdate.com**, can be handy.

▶ **Disk Diagnostics**—Norton Disk Doctor or any one of a number of similar packages can help you to find and fix problems on your disk, as well as allow you to recover files that you may have accidentally deleted.

▶ **Disk Defragmenter**—Speed Disk, part of Norton Disk Doctor, will defragment your drive and speed up your machine by a small amount during the process. The only way to reliably run the software on a volume is while booted from another, as it needs to take the disk entirely off-line during the process.

▶ **Backup software**—Retrospect, or something similar, can be very useful if you need to do a complete upgrade. You can boot up on CD, start Retrospect, back up the drive, reformat the hard drive, and recover, all without the hassle of rebooting.

NOTE
You'll need to use Retrospect 4.1 or later, as earlier versions don't allow you to run Retrospect from a read-only partition.

▶ **Disk formatting/partitioning software**—Drive Setup will work only a restricted set of drives, so if you have USB, FireWire, or an unsupported IDE or SCSI drive, you will need different software. I've been using FWB's Hard Disk Toolkit for as long as I can remember and never had a problem with it.

▶ **Text Editor**—A simple editor such as BBEdit that allows you to open files larger than 16 KB, a limit on SimpleText, can be useful for opening documents in a pinch.

▶ **ResEdit or FileTyper**—Great tools for changing the type and creator code of a file on the fly.

Whatever you decide to add to your disk, the most important thing to remember is to install the latest versions. If you are adding anti-virus software, it's vital that you include the latest version of the virus definitions to ensure that you are fully protected from all the latest viruses.

Adding Software Installers

Because booting up from CD leaves the hard disk alone, it's a great way of installing software without worrying about upsetting the system already on the machine. Which installers you include is entirely up to you and what you expect to use the CD for. As a general rule, you should try to include everything that you would need to bring your machine back up to a usable state.

Here's a list of what I usually include on a CD ready for installation elsewhere:

▶ **Operating System**—I always include the current full operating system or, if not possible, the previous version plus any updaters to bring it up to the latest version.

▶ **OS Updates**—Updates to the OS, including updates to the Software Update, graphics, QuickTime, and other major components are a good idea. Also, include Mac OS ROM and firmware updates for any machines that you own.

▶ **Anti-Virus Software**—Installing AV software from another disk is always a good idea, but make sure you also include the latest updater.

▶ **"Standard" control panels/extensions**—If you always install a standard set of control panels and extensions, include those on the CD.

▶ **Internet Explorer/Outlook Express/Netscape**—It's always useful to have these in installer form on disk, as it makes the process of installation much easier.

The things to avoid including on a bootable diagnostic CD include any third-party software installers (browser/e-mail client excepted). Normally, these come on their own CD and will want to install components into the currently running System Folder, which, of course, is on the CD. Wait until you have the main hard drive up and running again before trying to install third-party extensions and software.

Creating a Bootable CD

Once you've installed the operating system onto a volume or partition, as described above, creating a bootable CD is simply a matter of marking the correct checkbox when creating a CD under Toast. See Chapter 14 for more information.

Booting from CD

You can boot from any CD on a Quadra or later machine just by inserting the CD and holding down the "C" key during the boot process. Assuming your CD has been created correctly, it should boot from the CD and startup more or less as normal.

Installer CDs

Although it's not possible to create a bootable installer CD under Windows or Unix for installing software onto your machine, there is nothing to stop you from creating a CD onto which you put installers for upgrading your machine.

http://www.muskalipman.com

Section II Writing CDs

In fact, one of the biggest uses for the CD is as a method for distributing software, and the reasons are obvious. Its size makes it practical for even large software packages, and because you can't delete the contents, you cannot accidentally ruin the software by deleting the wrong file.

Creating Personal Installer CDs

Writing your own installer CDs is even more important now that so much software is distributed over the Internet. Over the years I've collected fourteen CDs worth of shareware, game demos, and Unix source code that I've downloaded from the Internet. Now, when I need to rebuild a machine or install a new one, it's simply a matter of inserting the CD with the software I need and double-clicking.

To create a CD with different installers on it, just copy the installers and other files to a directory and write that directory to disk. You can see in Figure 10.8 that I've got a disk full of different installers under Mac, and Figure 10.9 shows a similar disk under Windows.

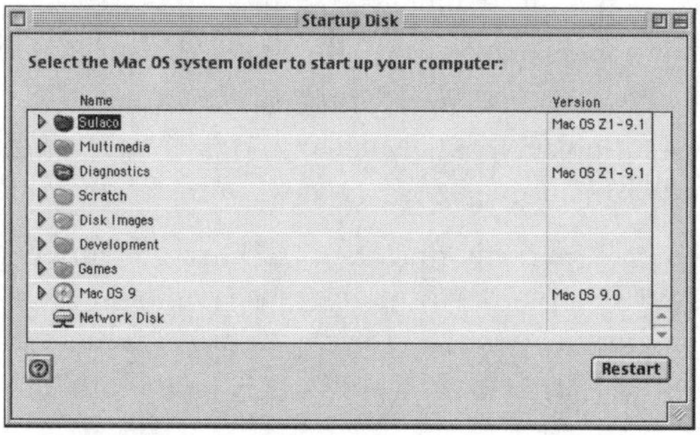

Figure 10.8
An installer CD under Mac OS.

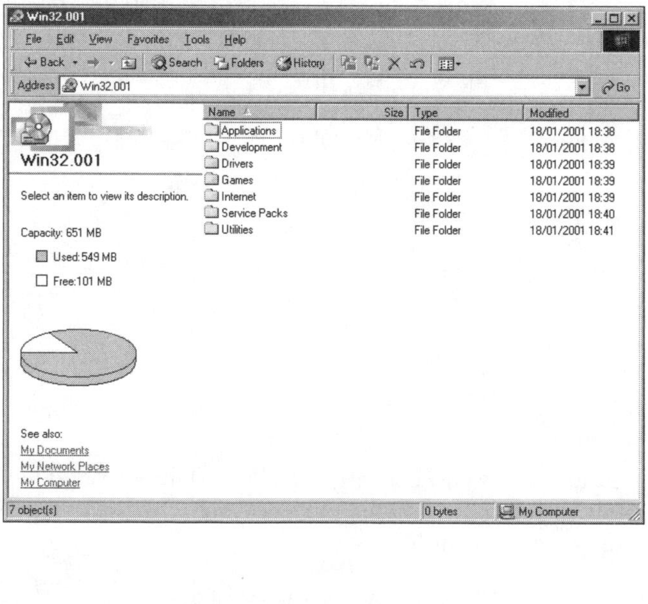

Figure 10.9
An installer CD under Windows.

Here are some tips for creating good installer CDs:

▶ **Use a suitable layout**—You'll need to be able to find the installers after you've copied them to CD. I always change the filename of an update that I downloaded from the Internet, as it's usually fairly company centric, and then put it into a folder that names the content type. For example, today I downloaded the file SP8126.EXE, which happens to be the filename of the diagnostic software required for Compaq Deskpro 2000 machines. The file was renamed to Compaq Diag 1_26.exe. The 1_26 is the version number, which is important to keep a record of so I don't waste time double downloading the file. Then, I place it into a directory called Diagnostic Tools, to help me find it later.

▶ **Compress the files**—You can save a lot of space by compressing the files using PKZip, StuffIt, or **gzip/bzip2**. Most installers that you download will arrive compressed anyway, others will automatically be extracted. In the case of Unix installers, including source code, it's generally compressed using **compress** or **gzip**. I prefer **bzip2**, which can save you an extra 10 to 15 percent over **gzip**. Whatever tool you decide to use, make sure you include a copy of the tool on the CD, in case it's not already installed when you need it. PKZip, WinZip, and StuffIt are supplied as stand-alone installer applications. For **gzip** or **bzip2**, supply an uncompressed **tar** archive of the source instead.

▶ **Keep a "current" set**—If you find you have a lot of CDs containing software, you might find that the CD you need is never the one you have in your hand. Over time, it's possible to collect installers, demos, and shareware packages that, although you want to keep, you don't want or need on an "active" CD. If possible, keep all the installers that you would need in a pinch on a single CD, or on a multi-CD set, while storing all of the nonessential installers onto a different set. CD-RW is perfect for the active CD, as you can easily update the contents without wasting and recreating the CD.

Creating CDs for Installing your own Software

If you write your own software and want to release it on CD, you have a different set of issues to resolve. Your primary concern is actually writing the installer software, which is beyond the scope of this book. Depending on which installer (and platform) you are using, you will have different requirements, and it's best to check the instructions for the software before going any further. However, some other points are worth noting:

▶ **Consider using an autolaunch system**—We'll cover the details in the next section, but autolaunch allows you to automatically start the installation software or, more often, a wrapper around it each time the CD is inserted. It makes the process of installing the software much easier.

▶ **Name the installer "Setup" or "Installer"**—If you don't use autolaunch, or the user has the autolaunch system switched off, there is nothing worse than being unable to find the installer or having trouble finding it. Naming it Setup or Installer makes it obvious what the user needs to install.

Virus check before you write—Always make sure that your virus software is up to date and that you check your machine and the CD after it's been written before it goes to duplication.

Autolaunchers

The autolaunch facility is part of Windows 95 and beyond and an extension to the Mac OS that comes as part of the QuickTime system. In both cases, the effect is the same—when you insert a CD that has the autolaunch system installed, a file or, more often, an application is automatically started.

Most companies use this system as an easy way of allowing their users to install software or run an application or game each time the CD is used, without asking them to search manually on the CD for the application or resort to the Start menu. You can see in Figure 10.10 the autolaunch screen from Maxis' The Sims game, which allows you to install or run the game, as well as some demos.

Figure 10.10
The Sims autolaunch screen.

Benefits

The main benefit of either autolaunch is that it makes running software from a CD, especially installers and diagnostic tools, so much easier for the user. There is nothing worse than opening up a piece of software and then having to search for the installation or diagnostic tool on the CD. It may seem fairly minor, but think about how many CDs you insert into your machine when first installing the machine and software, or when playing games. How many times do you just click on the Play or Install button on a window that pops up, and how many times do you have to search for the installer or game?

Dangers

There are a few dangers to watch out for:

▶ **Autolaunch can be disabled**—Under Windows, you can control the autolaunch system by setting the properties for the device in the System control panel. Mac OS can disable its AutoPlay system through the QuickTime Settings control panel.

▶ **Autolaunch CDs can spread viruses**—If you create an autolaunch CD that contains a virus, the virus may well be loaded and spread as soon as the CD is inserted. This is, in fact, the main reason that people switch the autolaunch system off. Providing you check your system for viruses before writing a CD, there shouldn't be any problems. But be aware.

▶ **Autolaunch CDs can cause crashes**—Although it's very rare, it is possible that automatically starting a program through an autolaunch will cause the machine to crash. If the software is bad, or if there's a conflict with an existing package, autolaunch can cause all sorts of problems.

Creating an Autolaunch CD

Creating a CD that automatically starts a program when you insert the CD is actually not as difficult as it sounds. Although Unix does not support a standard method of starting an application when a CD is inserted, even through the volume management system, both Windows and Mac OS support the option. We'll look at both systems below.

Windows

The Windows autolaunch system is called AutoRun or AutoPlay, depending on which piece of documentation you read. Creating a CD that automatically runs an application is actually very straightforward. All you need to do is create a text file called AUTORUN.INF in the root directory of the CD that you create. The contents of the file are a simple header and a series of options, written in the standard Windows INI file format. For example, the file below would automatically open the SETUP.EXE application:

```
[autorun]
open=SETUP.EXE
```

The [autorun] is a header and is required for Windows to identify the rest of the configuration; the only other required line is the "open" option, which defines the path to the application or file that should be opened. Another common option is the "icon" option, which specifies which icon should be used for the CD-ROM as a whole. You need to specify the file that contains the icon and the icon number within that file. For example…

```
[autorun]
open=SETUP.EXE
icon=SETUP.EXE,1
```

Section II Writing CDs

…would use icon 1 in the SETUP.EXE file. Alternatively, you can specify an icon file:

```
[autorun]
open=SETUP.EXE
icon=setup.ico
```

For more detailed information on the format of the file, and some of the more advanced options, see the Microsoft Web site: **http://msdn.microsoft.com/library/psdk/shellcc/shell/Shell_basics/ Autoplay_works.htm**.

Mac OS

Under Mac OS, the autolaunch system is called AutoPlay and is part of the QuickTime multimedia extensions. AutoPlay is configured as part of the information written to the CD rather than the existence of a special file, as used by Windows. As such, the configuration of opening a file or application is controlled during the writing process. Under Toast, you set the file that you want to open automatically by clicking on the AutoPlay button when configuring the information written to a data CD. You can set any file to be opened; it doesn't have to be an application, but it does have some restrictions:

► The file or application must exist at the root of the CD; it cannot be contained within any folder on the CD.

► The file or application must be real—aliases to an application or file somewhere else on the disc are not allowed.

► The file or application must have no more than eleven characters.

See Chapter 14 for complete details on how to create an AutoPlay CD under Toast.

Section III
Writing CDs for Business

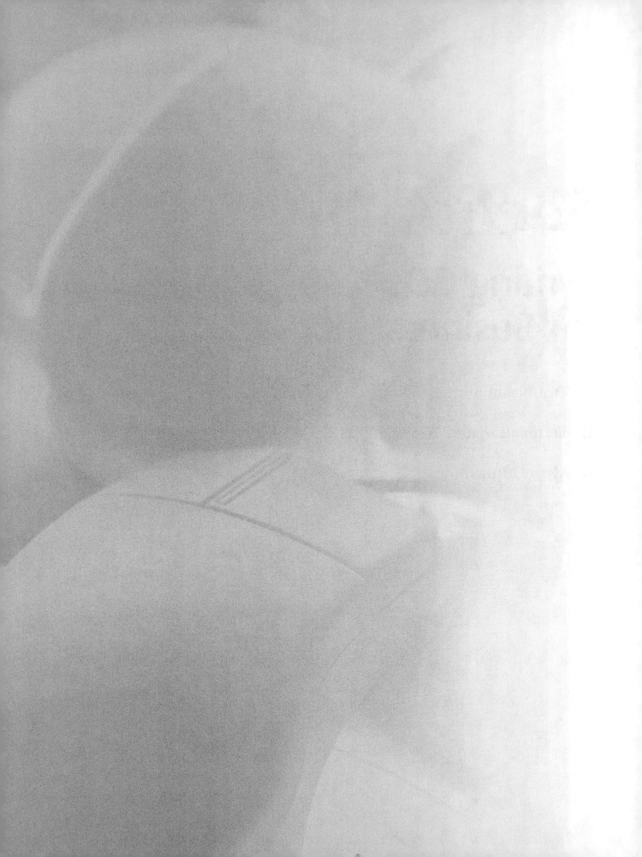

11

Troubleshooting

When writing CDs, it's an unfortunate fact that you can still run into problems. Some of the time these are easily resolved and relate to what you are trying to write, but some occur during the writing process and force you to throw away the partially written CD and start all over again. In this chapter, we'll look both at the reasons for failure and how to resolve the problems so that they don't cause trouble again.

Problems Before Writing

If you've copied all the files into the right places and are ready to write the CD, but then get an odd error message from your CD software, then it's probably just a minor configuration or software problem. If, when you put the blank disc into the machine, you get an error about "lack of space," "wrong media type," or "non-empty disc," then check the following before continuing.

Media

You might think that you'd never be so stupid as to use the wrong media in your drive, but it does happen, even to professionals. Most of the time the problem will be that you are using the wrong media in your drive, but there are others. When looking at the media, remember:

▶ **You cannot use CD-RW media for producing a CD-R**—Some drives will allow you to continue (since the two types are basically identical), others will refuse, even if they support CD-RW media.

▶ **You cannot use CD-RW media in a CD-R only drive**—Although the basic technology is the same, the dyes are different and the lasers used in each case also differ.

▶ **Throw away discs that failed during the write process**—You can't "reuse" CD-R media; if something goes wrong during the writing process, the disc is better off in the garbage.

▶ **Some media are bad**—Although it rarely happens, you can get a piece of blank media that was faulty before you started. Take it back to where you bought it and ask for a replacement.

Space

If you are writing a new CD, then you've probably just selected too much material. A standard CD-R can hold only 650 MB of data, or seventy-four minutes of music. You can get eighty-minute (700 MB) discs, but these aren't compatible with all drives. Easy CD Creator will show you how much space you've selected to write using the bar at the bottom of the window. Toast shows you the time and MB that you have selected. Under Unix, use **du-sk** to check that the directory you are trying to write does not exceed the size of the medium you are using. All three environments will refuse to write a CD if the data size exceeds the space on the medium. If you are using a CD-R disc that you have previously used to write individual sessions to, it may be that the amount of data you are trying to store just won't fit. Again, use the features of the software (or operating system) to check the space against that available on the CD.

If you are using a CD-RW that you think is empty, check it first, and if you think you can reuse it, reformat (or erase) the disc before continuing. CD-RW media must also be formatted before you can write anything to them.

Software

When you load the software, does it report any errors? If so, then you might have installed the software incorrectly, the software might not have completed installing, or what has been installed has been corrupted. There are a few things you can try before actually reinstalling the software.

Under Windows, you need to go into the Device Manager, which is part of the System applet in Control Panels (accessible through the Start menu), and then check that your computer can see the CD-R drive in the device list, an example of which is shown in Figure 11.1. If the drive isn't listed, it may mean the drive is not connected properly; switch off your machine and then check all the connections before continuing. If the drive has a red cross through its name, it means the drive has been disabled in the current configuration. Right-click on the drive with your mouse and make sure that the device has not been disabled for the current hardware profile.

Figure 11.1
The Windows System
Control Panel.

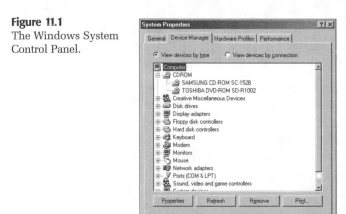

If the device has a yellow exclamation mark (!), the drivers have not been installed properly or the wrong drivers have been installed for the device. Right-click on the device and select Properties > Update Drivers and follow the instructions to install new drivers for the device using the discs or CD-ROM that came with your machine. Alternatively, if this doesn't fix the problem, right-click and delete the device from the system and then restart—Windows should automatically detect the new drive and search or ask for suitable drivers for it. If you're still having problems, contact your supplier. Remember that the drivers for devices are often updated regularly, and it's not uncommon for the drivers on the disk that came with your device to be out of date. Check the manufacturer's Web site for an updated set of drivers or try using Windows Update (accessible through the Start menu under Windows 98 and Me).

On a Mac, open the Apple System Profiler (available under Mac OS 8.x and later) and change to the devices tab. Your drive should be listed among the devices, either as an IDE or SCSI device, or as one of the devices connected to either the USB or FireWire ports on your machine. For example, you can see in Figure 11.2 that I have a CD-R drive connected to the FireWire port on my Mac. If you don't see your CD-R device listed, check the connections to ensure that the device is on before continuing. If the device is either IDE- or SCSI-based, remember to switch off your machine before checking the connections.

Figure 11.2
Using the Apple
System Profiler to find
your CD-R device.

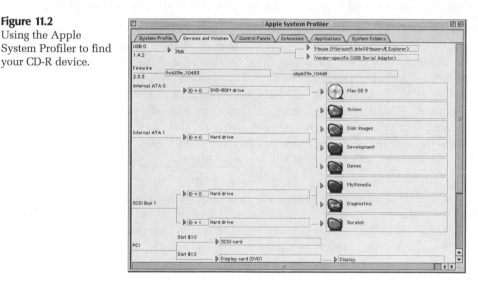

When using an IDE or SCSI device, you shouldn't need any additional drivers to be able to use the drive from your CD-R software. However, if the drive is connected to your machine using USB or FireWire, you must ensure that the drivers that came with your drive are installed. Try unplugging and reconnecting the device—your Mac should identify the device and attempt to load the drivers. If it can't find them, you should get an error message—such as the one shown in Figure 11.3—telling you that the drivers are missing. Click Cancel and then re-install the drivers from the CD.

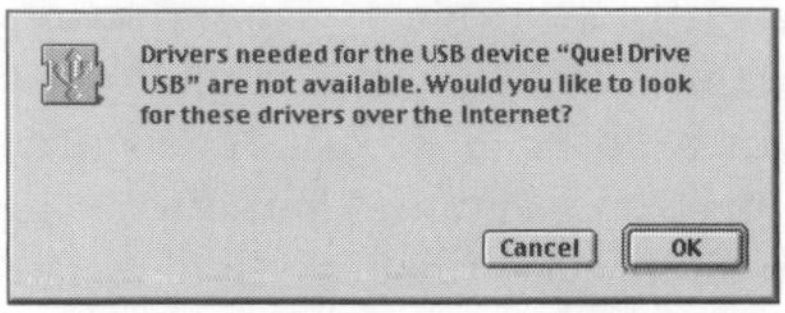

Figure 11.3
Notification of
a missing USB/
FireWire Driver.

> Drivers needed for the USB device "Que! Drive USB" are not available. Would you like to look for these drivers over the Internet?
>
> [Cancel] [OK]

Under Unix/Linux, you'll need to determine whether the drive was detected during boot up. Check the **messages** file, generally found under /var/log/messages or /var/adm/messages. For example, you can see below that the SCSI Plextor drive installed here in a Linux box has been identified and the device name is /dev/sr0:

```
Nov 21 19:31:39 penguin kernel: (scsi0:0:5:0) Synchronous at 10.0 Mbyte/sec, offset 8.
Nov 21 19:31:39 penguin kernel: Vendor: PLEXTOR  Model: CD-R  PX-R820T  Rev: 1.03
Nov 21 19:31:39 penguin kernel:  Type:  CD-ROM    ANSI SCSI revision: 02
Nov 21 19:31:39 penguin kernel: Detected scsi CD-ROM sr0 at scsi0, channel 0, id 5, lun 0
Nov 21 19:31:39 penguin kernel: sr0: scsi3-mmc drive: 20x/20x writer cd/rw xa/form2 cdda tray
```

The name you use to access your drive is also important, as the CD-R drive won't be automatically identified for you. Most of the "can't find device" problems actually relate to specifying the wrong device, rather than an actual problem with the device's connectivity.

Under Linux, drives are given sequential names according to the order in which they were found, and these are generally simpler to use than the explicit addresses that are outlined later in this chapter. Linux creates aliases for IDE drives first, then in order of the primary/secondary IDE controller and master/slave priorities, followed by SCSI drives according to the SCSI channel and ID number. Therefore, if you have two CD-ROM drives in your machine attached as slave devices on the first two IDE channels, the primary IDE/slave will be /dev/cdrom, and the secondary/ slave will be /dev/cdrom1. If you have an IDE and SCSI CD-ROM, the IDE drive will be /dev/cdrom and the SCSI /dev/cdrom1. Lastly, if you have two SCSI CD-ROM drives at IDs 1 and 6, then ID 1 will be /dev/cdrom and ID 6 will be /dev/cdrom1.

Under most SVR4based Unix flavors, including Solaris and HP-UX (and Linux, if you prefer), drives are accessible instead by a direct reference number device description according to the controller, target, and disk number—for example, /dev/dsk/c0t0d0. If your machine has an IDE controller, it would be controller zero (0), primary channel is target zero (0), and secondary is one (1). Finally, the master disk is disk zero (0) and the slave is one (1), thus to access the slave on the secondary channel you would use /dev/dsk/c0t1d1.

The same basic rules apply for SCSI devices, except that target is the device's SCSI ID number, and disk is the individual disk within that device in order to support drive arrays—for single drives, the last number is always zero. For example, /dev/dsk/c0t0d0 refers to the first controller and the first physical drive.

You can get cdrecord to scan all of the available devices to determine which are CD-R capable by using the **-scanbus** command-line argument, for example:

```
$ cdrecord -scanbus
Cdrecord 1.10a05 (i686-pc-linux-gnu) Copyright © 1995-2000 Jörg Schilling
Linux sg driver version: 2.1.36
Using libscg version 'schily-0.4'
scsibus0:
    0,0,0   0) 'IBM  ' 'DNES-309170  ' 'SA30' Disk
    0,1,0   1) 'IBM  ' 'DNES-309170  ' 'SA30' Disk
    0,2,0   2) *
    0,3,0   3) *
    0,4,0   4) *
    0,5,0   5) 'PLEXTOR ' 'CD-R  PX-R820T ' '1.03' Removable CD-ROM
    0,6,0   6) *
    0,7,0   7) *
```

Here, you can see that the CD-R drive is installed as target 5 on controller 0. Luckily, we can use this information directly with cdrecord—to specify the drive in this case, we just need to specify the device as 0,5,0 to cdrecord or one of its front ends.

If, after checking all of this, you still cannot see your drive, you may need to build support for either IDE or SCSI devices into your kernel. You should check the documentation that came with your machine for information on adding new features to your kernel.

Drive "Not Ready"

If your drive is reporting that it is not yet ready to start recording, the problem could be related to one of the following situations:

▶ **Mounting**—When you insert a disc into your CD recorder, it will take some time to identify the disc and determine whether the disc is of the correct type for the drive and whether you have inserted a blank disc or a prerecorded one. Different drives take different amounts of time to determine this information, so check the activity light on front of the drive to determine whether it is ready to start recording. The light should be constant—whether on or off; a flashing light will always indicate a busy drive.

▶ **Finishing**—Just after the data has been written to the disc, your drive will need to "close" the session, whether it's writing a single session or an entire disc. Not all software displays this process, so trying to eject the disc before the drive has completed will be impossible.

▶ **SCSI Termination**—If you have a SCSI drive, make sure that the SCSI chain has been terminated properly and that no devices have conflicting ID numbers. If there is no termination or an ID conflict, your drive may never receive the "are you ready" request.

If, after all this, you still have the same problem, try rebooting the machine; it may just be that your drive got confused. Finally, try reinstalling the software and drivers; it's possible that your computer is not talking properly to your drive.

Dealing with "Buffer Underrun"

Once you've got everything set up and you press the "Record" or "Write CD" button, nearly all of the problems reported during the actual process of writing will be related to what is called the "Buffer Underrun." When you write a CD, the information is taken from your hard disk and sent to the CD recorder. Built into the CD-R driver is a buffer that holds the information that needs to be written in preparation for translating the information onto the surface of the disc itself.

Buffer underrun occurs when the computer can't supply the drive with information fast enough to keep the buffer full. In these situations, the buffer "empties" and the CD-R drive runs out of information to write to the disc, so the entire process fails because there is no way for the CD-R drive to recover from where the error took place. This means that you end up with a half-written CD-R that cannot, unfortunately, be used for anything—except a rather stylish coaster!

Different CD-R drives have different sized buffers, and, in theory, the larger the buffer, the less prone you should be to buffer underruns. There are some things that you can do to improve your chances of writing a good CD-R the first time. All of them rely on improving the rate at which you supply the drive with information so that it matches the capability of your system. If you look back at Table 3.4 in Chapter 3 you'll see that to write at 8x we need to push 1200 KB/s of data to the CD-R drive. Although in computer terms that's not a lot, in reality there are a number of things that affect the speed at which information can be sent to a device, and in the case of CD writers, the information rate needs to be constant.

Many of the problems can actually be traced back to interruptions on your machine while you are writing. These include background software like virus checkers, but you should also avoid running other software while using your CD-R software. The effects of transfer-speed problems can also be reduced by either improving the speed at which the information is read from the source or reducing the rate at which it needs to be written.

Here are some hot tips for getting the best performance and reliability out of your CD writing attempts:

Record at a Lower Speed

Buffer underrun occurs because you can't supply a constant stream of information to the CD-R drive. Lowering the recording speed reduces the rate at which you need to supply information. For example, lowering the speed from 8x to 4x reduces the transfer rate by half and lowers the transfer speed to just 600KB/s.

Most software allows you to burn a CD in "test" mode in order to determine whether the write speed you have selected is suitable for your machine and drive combination. Writing an entire CD in test mode will obviously double the time it takes to write the CD. However, after you've checked the speed once, you shouldn't need to adjust it again unless you are concerned about a particular CD.

With Easy CD Creator, click on the Advanced button when you choose to write the CD and choose either the Test Only or Test and Create CD options. In the former mode, Easy CD Creator will go through all the motions but won't actually write the CD, while in the latter mode, it'll run through a test and (providing it succeeds) will then repeat the process while actually writing the information.

Using Toast, you can test the overall writing speed of your system by using the Check Speed button in the main interface panel. This will test the file source compared to the writing speed that you have selected.

Record from an Image

Most software will allow you to record a CD from an "image," an exact copy of the disc about to be written stored in a single file on your machine. Usually, the software will have tried to write the image in one contiguous space on your disc, although this isn't always necessary. It improves the speed by letting the software and OS know where to read the next block of information, instead of having to hunt for the information.

On a PC using Easy CD Creator, set up your CD as normal and then choose Create CD Image from the File menu. this will write all of the files into a single CD image that you can then use to produce the final CD. To actually create a CD from an image, use the Create CD from CD Image option from the File menu.

Using Toast, select the Save as Disc Image option from the File menu. You have the benefit under the Mac that you can "mount" the disc image just as if you had written it to CD, allowing you to change and, if necessary, tweak the files before writing the final version.

CD images aren't generally required under Linux (see the next section for an explanation), but you can duplicate CDs by creating an image from an existing CD and then writing that image. See Chapter 13 for more information on CD duplication, and Chapter 16 for information on writing CDs under Linux.

> **TIP**
> Using a CD Image is a great way of setting up a CD so that it can be written a number of times. I've used this in the past as a way of setting up standard CDs for prospective clients. Because the CD is already created in an image, I know that it works and it can't be modified in any way, so I always know that what I've selected to write will be written perfectly every time.

Defragment your Drive

When you ask your software to load files from the disk, it has to ask the operating system to get the files, and in turn the operating system has to look up the location of the files before it can supply any data back to your CD recording software. On most disks, this won't be a problem, but your hard disk can exhibit what is called *fragmentation*. This is where your disk has a lot of files that are spread across two or more physical locations on the disk. Instead of reading the file in one big chunk, the file is read in little pieces as the OS searches around the disk for the different pieces of the file.

When you defragment your drive, you correct the fragmentation and put the files back into single contiguous streams. Defragmenting doesn't only improve the speed and reliability of writing CDs; it can also help to improve the overall speed of your machine.

Section III Writing CDs for Business

To defragment your machine under Windows, go to the Start menu and choose Programs >
Accessories > System Tools > Disk Defragmenter. The process will take a long time and you can
improve the speed of the process by booting Windows in "Safe Mode." Check the online help
for information on how to boot into Safe Mode. You can see a sample of the defragmentation
process in Figure 11.4.

Figure 11.4
Defragmenting a
Windows disk.

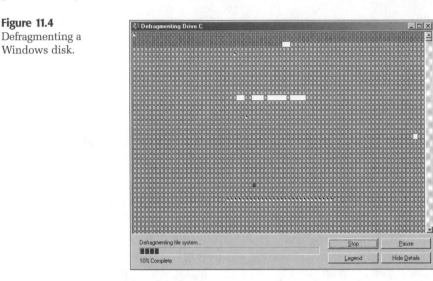

Under Mac OS, you will need a separate piece of software to defragment your hard drive. I
recommend Norton Utilities, which also comes with a number of other tools to help diagnose
and fix problems on your machine and is well worth the investment. You can see a sample in
Figure 11.5. Alternatively, check out Alsoft's DiskExpress Pro™ or PlusOptimizer™
(**www.alsoft.com**).

Figure 11.5
Defragmenting a
Mac disk using
Speed Disk (part of
Norton Utilities).

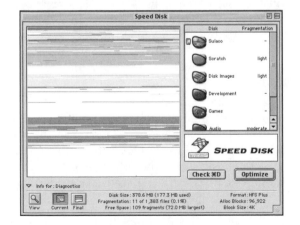

There is no way on the Mac to optimize the actual writing process; you can optimize only the layout of the final CD. However, if you can't defragment your drive, try creating a disc image of the CD and then writing that. Alternatively, you can use Disk Tools to create a disk image—see Chapter 10 for more information.

Under Unix/Linux you shouldn't have to worry—the file system under Linux does a certain amount of defragmentation on the fly. Even on a heavily fragmented disk, the problems of fragmentation are not experienced so much because of the file system architecture. After fifteen years, I've yet to run into a defragmentation problem under any flavor of Unix!

Shut Down Unnecessary Applications

Although, in theory, your computer should be able to write a CD and continue to run your word processor or e-mail program with no problems, the reality is that running other programs while writing a CD is probably a bad idea. If you have problems writing a CD, make sure you shut all open applications and any background applications that might be interrupting the writing process. On a PC, this often includes the items in the system tray, such as virus checkers, printer monitors, and even the System Scheduler, if you are using it to run programs at regular intervals. To shut these down, right-click on each item in the system tray and choose the "Disable" or "Exit" option that appears. Once you've written your CD, the quickest way to get back and running properly is probably just to restart.

On the Mac, there are a number of background processes that you cannot easily stop, but you can shut down software that you are not using and the background processes that may be causing problems. These include file sharing (use the File Sharing control panel), anti-virus software, and Norton Filesaver, if you have it installed. If you still have problems, use the Extensions Manager (in Control Panels) and create a startup set that includes only the Apple standard extensions plus those required for your CD-R drive, then reboot and try again.

Under Unix, there are many things that could potentially cause a problem. Running busy NFS, e-mail (including POP3 and IMAP), Web, or FTP services on your machine are all good examples of demons that slow down your machine. However, if your machine is not a dedicated server and used fairly lightly as a home or desktop Unix machine, then most daemons are well-behaved and shouldn't suddenly start using resources in the middle of a CD writing process. You should also avoid running any compilation process while you are writing. If your machine is used only on the desktop, you should be OK, but try to avoid any CPU-intensive processes while the CD is writing.

Problems Reading What You've Written

Even if everything goes according to plan, you can still experience problems with the final disc that you produce. Often, the problem is related to the drive you are trying to use to read the disc, but it can also point to a problem with the writing process itself. Included below are some examples of the problems you can encounter and some solutions or suggestions for resolving them.

Reading Problems with Individual Drives

Some older CD mechanisms used both in computers and stereo systems have trouble reading both CD-R and CD-RW media. If a disc works fine in many drives, but not in one specific drive, then it's probably due to the age of the drive itself rather than the disc you have written. You might try an alternative medium that uses a different dye combination, but this is not guaranteed to work.

Reading a CD-R/RW in Another CD-R/RW Drive

Because of the different dyes used in the CD-R/RW media from different manufacturers, you can come across an incompatibility reading a CD-R/RW disk recorded in one drive when it is read in different CD-R/RW drive. This may be the case even though the disc works fine in a standard CD-ROM drive. There's nothing you can do about this except try changing to a different media—the green/gold combination is one of the most compatible, although I had few problems with the blue/gold combinations used by TDK and Verbatim.

Disc Isn't Recognized

If the disc is not recognized at all by your CD-ROM drive, it could be due to a number of factors:

▶ **Cleanliness**—Make sure that the CD-R is clean and free from grease and dust. See Chapter 4 for information on handling and cleaning CDs.

▶ **Wrong format**—If you have recorded files in Mac format and try to read the disc in a PC, the disc will be unreadable. Try recording the disc again using ISO9660 format. Similarly, not all Unix variants support the Joliet extensions. Also, remember that Unix is case-sensitive, so if the problem is reading a specific file as part of a documentation or software product, consider converting all of the files to uppercase to ensure compatibility.

▶ **Open session**—If you've written a session to a disc, make sure the session has been closed. A standard CD-ROM drive will be unable to read an "open" session.

Truncated Filenames

A disc that contains filenames in the 8.3 format instead of the long filenames you expected has been recorded in ISO9660 format, when it should have been recorded using the Joliet or Mac extensions. Check your settings and re-record the disc.

Audio Imperfections

If you get clicks between the tracks on an audio disc, you've recorded the disc using the track-at-once writing mode. This is known to cause unpleasant clicks on some audio CD players because the laser shuts off between individual tracks and it's this "blank" space that causes the clicks. Try recording the disc using the disc-at-once writing mode, which should eliminate the problem. Unfortunately, this is only supported on some CD writers, although most new models support disk-at-once mode. Fuzzy music or truncated tracks could be due to problems caused while generating, or "ripping," the audio from a CD or from corrupted or interrupted files that you have downloaded from the Internet. Try listening to MP3, AIFF, or other audio format files using Windows Media Player or QuickTime before writing to the CD to make sure that the file is suitable. If the file sounds fine, then try adjusting the speed at which you write the audio CD and use the disc-at-once mode.

Mixed-mode Discs Show Only One Session

This is probably a problem with the CD-ROM drive you are using to read the disc. Many older drives are unable to read the CDExtra format required when reading mixed-mode discs. If other mixed-mode discs are OK, check the CD-R again to ensure that the disc and sessions have been properly closed.

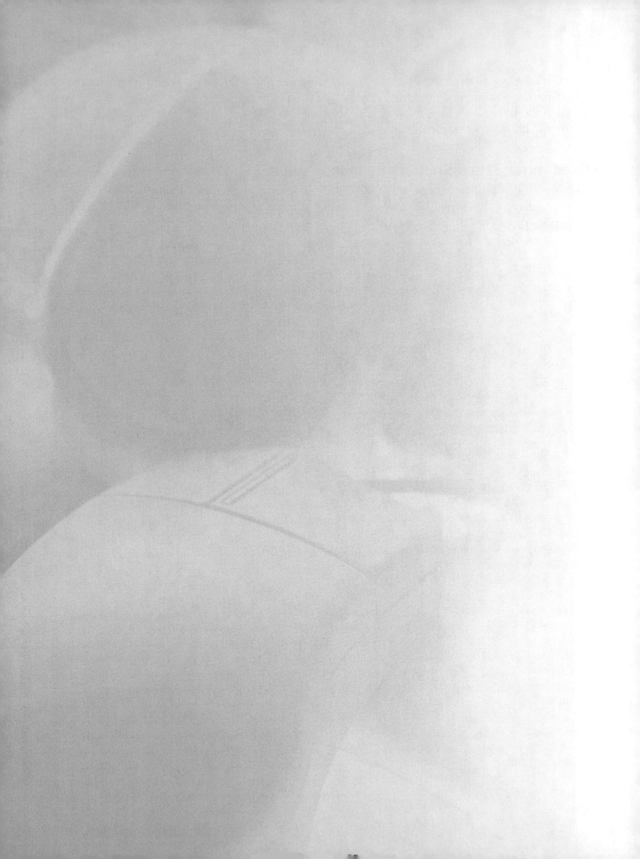

12

Verification and Testing

Once you've actually created your CD, you'll need to make sure that what you've written now exists on the CD properly. After all, it would be a real shame if the CD reached your client and didn't work. Worse, if it's an archive CD, you won't want to insert it into your machine in a year's time and find that you hadn't archived everything properly.

Bad CDs are actually a rare occurrence, but they are not completely impossible. As a general rule, if your CD writes okay and you don't have any problems, then the contents are probably okay. But if the information (and the client) is important to you, then you need to be aware of the potential pitfalls and what you can do to verify that what is on the CD is readable.

There are, in fact, two parts to checking a CD: The first is to check the contents, and the second is to check the CD as a whole. When checking contents, you need to verify the files, audio tracks, and other information that you've written. For some data, it's simply a case of opening the files—for others, it requires more work. With a CD using HTML, for example, you need to check that the HTML opens properly in the browser and displays the graphics and links necessary for you to navigate through the site.

You also need to think about the environment under which your CD will be used. It does no good, for example, to distribute a Word document that uses some special fonts that aren't supplied as standard with the operating system. For that reason, we'll also have a look at the basics of creating a test machine that can be used only for testing CDs, both in terms of their readability and their content.

Creating a Test Machine

If producing CDs is a core part of your business, then you should think about setting up at least one machine that is devoted entirely to the testing of the CDs that you write. It doesn't have to be an expensive machine (quite the opposite), but it should be a separate machine from the one that you use to write CDs. Remember that this machine is for testing CDs—not for testing the software on those CDs. For that, you should have a separate suite of machines.

When selecting and setting up this machine, keep the following in mind:

▶ **Hardware**—Make the hardware as basic and simple as possible. It doesn't need much memory, or disc space, and it won't need anything more than a 14-inch monitor. Unless you specifically need it to be connected to your network for Internet access, I wouldn't bother installing a network card or modem. This machine needs to be as separate from your own personal network as possible—just like the end user's machine would be. If you can, install more than one CD drive, but make sure that each drive is from a different manufacturer.

▶ **Operating system**—Install an OS with the basic features that you'll need. Choose standard fonts and avoid installing additional extensions and applications that you don't need. Try to use the previous OS revision if possible. For example, on a Windows machine, install Windows 98 or NT instead of Windows Me or 2000. On the Mac, install Mac OS 8.6 if your system allows it (most modern machines support only 9.x or above). This isn't as necessary under Unix, since upgrades tend to happen more frequently and it's impossible to decide which patches are the right ones to choose.

▶ **Applications**—Unless you are testing application-specific data, try to avoid installing any applications at all. If you do need applications on the machine, then do a basic installation—don't install everything. That way, you'll know if there's something on the CD that relies on an extension or feature somebody doesn't have. Also, if you can, install the version previous to the current one—not everybody upgrades to the latest version when it comes out.

In an ideal world, you'd have a number of these machines running different combinations of applications and operating systems, and all using different hardware. This is probably overkill, but if you do need this level of testing, consider talking to one of the many software testing houses or even a CD duplicator and manufacturer. They generally have these facilities to test the different CDs that they are producing in house.

Verifying the Contents

Your first job should be to check that the files you have written on your CD work as expected. This means more than checking the filenames and layout—you really need to look at the documents closely to ensure that everything works properly. Exactly how you perform the test is entirely dependent on the type of files that you have written to the CD.

Your primary concern is, of course, ensuring that the contents are correct. If you've written a CD with the works of Shakespeare, you don't want to find out that it's transmogrified into the works of Dickens!

Beyond something as simple as checking that the file sizes match, you also need to think about file formats, compatibility—especially if you are creating a CD that might be used on a number of different platforms—and any files that are required to make up the content of the other files on the CD (HTML for example).

The trick is not to check every file, unless it's really important and you have loads of time. Instead, you should concentrate on trying to verify all the different file types that you can, while spot-checking the remainder of the CD for other problems. The tests we cover in "Testing the CD" later in this chapter should help to highlight more specific areas on which you might want to concentrate.

The following sections examine some of the more common formats and the problems that you face when verifying CD contents.

Text

There are few things that can go wrong with text files—or so you might think. Text files are the most basic form of any document, but you need to check them and ensure that they are readable. Check the line wrapping (the point at which a new line is created), and also the line termination. Line termination can be a problem if you expect to use a text file on a number of platforms.

Windows uses both the carriage return and newline character for terminating each line in a text document. Mac OS uses only a carriage return, and Unix uses only a newline character. This means that when reading a text document created on a Mac on a Unix box (or vice versa), you end up with concatenated lines and it becomes almost impossible to determine where lines are supposed to start and end.

If you are creating a text file that you want to be readable on all platforms, save it in Windows format, as this will be displayed properly on all three platforms. Alternatively, consider creating three files, one in each format.

When checking a text file, try it in all the platforms that you expect to read the document. If you can, try using the standard editors or display mechanisms to do the checking. Under Windows, you should use Notepad or WordPad; Mac OS uses SimpleText, and Unix uses either the more (or less) command or the vi or emacs editors.

Application Specific Documents

Storing application specific documents on a CD can cause all sorts of problems. Although it often can't be avoided, there are some things you can test to make sure that the process has worked correctly. For example, if it's a Word document, you need to open it and ensure there's no corruption anywhere. You should also check the following:

▶ **Fonts**—Using nonstandard fonts can cause display problems on other machines if the fonts are not available. Either supply the fonts on the CD or consider using a font-independent format such as Adobe's Acrobat PDF (Portable Document Format).

▶ **Linked Files**—It's possible in most applications now to link in a document from another application. For example, you can embed Excel spreadsheets and graphs straight into Word documents and reports. Other applications, like QuarkXpress and Macromedia Director, also allow you to place images and even movies that are sourced from external files. You need to check that these files are on the CD, and that the version of the document on the CD uses this file and not your original.

▶ **HTML**—When using an HTML document, you must check that the links to other documents and images work correctly from the CD. You must do this on a different machine—preferably one isolated from the Internet—so that you can check the CD properly.

▶ **Platform Compatibility**—This is an issue only if you are creating a CD that you expect will be used on multiple platforms. Most modern applications are compatible across platforms—you shouldn't have difficulty opening a Windows Word document using Word for the Mac, for example—but you should check that your Windows, Mac, or Linux files can be opened using a compatible application on another platform.

Images

You should open graphic images using different packages on your machine and, if possible, different machines and platforms. Some formats are better than others at being used on different platforms. The GIF and JPEG formats are the most compatible, but these have some limitations. The TIFF (Tagged Image File Format) file is a purer image format, but there are also Windows and Mac OS versions of the format. See Chapter 9 for more information on the different image formats that are available and which, ideally, you should be using.

Audio CDs

The easiest way to check an audio CD is to play it in an audio CD player. Don't use the CD-R or CD-ROM drive in your machine, as these may give seemingly perfect reproductions, even from a badly recorded CD. Try it on your stereo system and perhaps the CD player in your car or a portable. These will be more susceptible to any problems that exist. Unfortunately, you can't do "spot" checks on an audio CD. You need to listen to the entire contents to check for audio aberrations and the telltale clicks between tracks.

Video CDs

You'll need to check a video CD in its entirety as well. Because of the way in which compressed video works, spot checking a video stream every five minutes may not locate a problem, even if it's there. You need to watch and concentrate on the video to make sure that there is no corruption between frames.

Testing the CD

Beyond looking at the structure and contents of individual files, you also need to look at the overall quality and validity of the CD that has been created. This means checking that all of the files that you wanted to write onto the CD have actually been written and comparing the number of files and their sizes to the source material. Although it's fairly rare nowadays, it's also worth checking the readability of the disk—is it identified when you insert it into a different CD drive?

Checking the Directory Structure

It's a good idea to make sure that the directory structure you wanted on the final CD matches that on the CD that you've written. The easiest way to do this is to simply insert the CD into a CD-ROM drive and check the root directory contents. If you want to go deeper, you'll need to check the CD-ROM with Windows Explorer (accessible by right-clicking and selecting Explore from the pop-up menu) or view the CD in list mode under Mac OS (choose View > as List). You can see examples of both in Figures 12.1 and 12.2.

Figure 12.1
Viewing a directory tree in Mac OS.

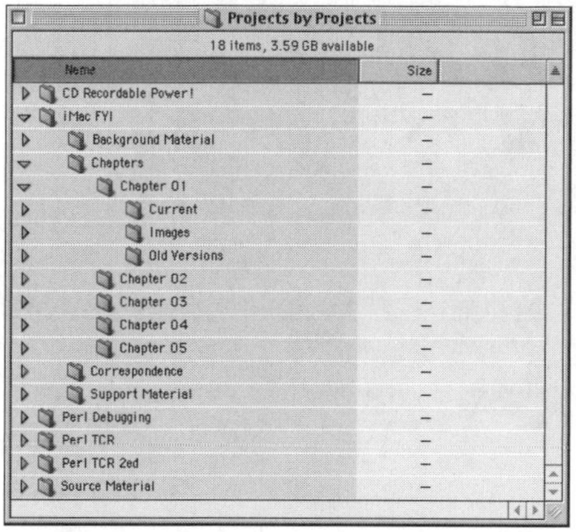

Figure 12.2
Viewing a directory tree using Windows Explorer.

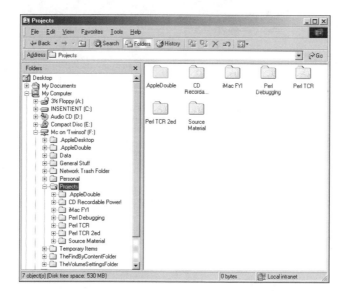

Section III Writing CDs for Business

Under Unix, use find to show the directory structure within a terminal window or use the browsing systems of your X Windows window manager—you can see examples of both in Figures 12.3 and 12.4—the file manager shown in this figure is part of the KDE system, although other systems will support similar functionality.

Figure 12.3
Viewing a directory
tree using find.

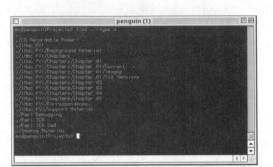

Figure 12.4
Viewing a directory
tree using KDE.

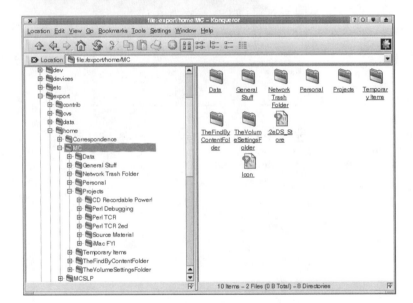

It's unlikely that you'll find anything missing with this method, but you might spot a problem with the layout that you hadn't expected.

Checking Files and Sizes

If you compare the number of files and their total size on a disc, this should give you a good idea about how well the CD has been written. For example, if you check the source folder and find 10,000 files using 625.4 MB and a CD that contains 10,000 files using 625.4 MB, it's a pretty good bet that the CD and source contents match.

However, there are slight differences that are safe to ignore. For example, a minor discrepancy of a few KB, perhaps even a MB, on a full CD is not too much to worry about if the number of files matches. The rule is to be sensible—strict matches are not required, but you shouldn't be too lax or you might miss something. It's also worth remembering that some systems compress the information on the disk (even at file level under Windows NT and 2000), and it's written to CD in an uncompressed format.

Windows

To compare the number of files and their total size under Windows, select the CD and press Alt-Return or right-click on the CD and choose Properties. You'll get a window like the one shown in Figure 12.5. The important items in this window to check are the number of files and the bytes used.

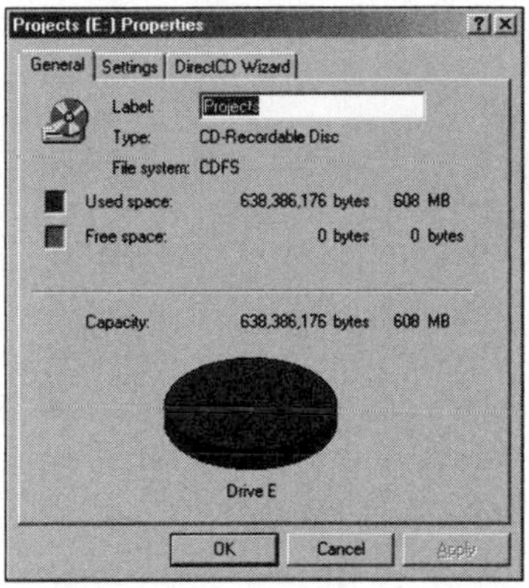

Figure 12.5
Checking CD volume
sizes under Windows.

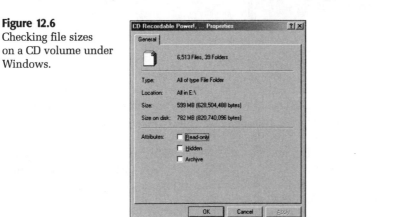

For example, in the figure you can see that we have a CD that uses up 640 MB. Note that it only shows the volume detail—we don't get a list of files or other details. This, unfortunately, includes the information and areas used as lead in and lead out for the tracks on the CD and the general volume information and file system. To get information on the files and the space they use, you need to open the CD, select everything, and choose Properties using one of the methods outlined above. This will now show you the number of files and their sizes within your selection in one easy window. You can see a sample in Figure 12.6.

Figure 12.6
Checking file sizes
on a CD volume under
Windows.

Section III Writing CDs for Business

If we now compare this to our source folder, shown here in Figure 12.7, you can see that the number of files/folders and size information matches—looks like our CD is OK!

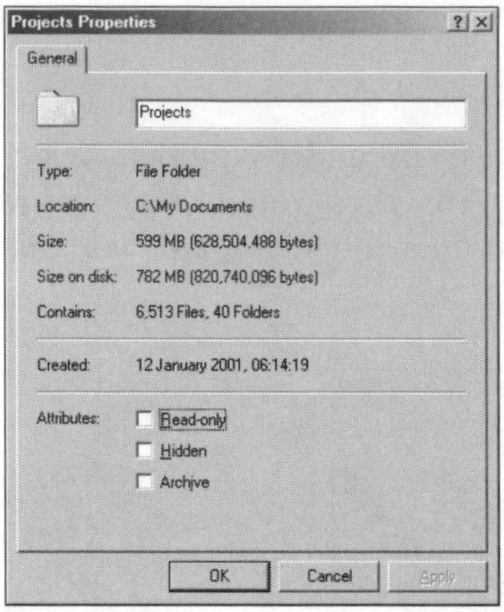

Figure 12.7
The file size information for the source folder.

Mac OS

Under Mac OS, all you need to do is select the CD and choose Edit > Get Info. The information shown is slightly different to that under Windows and needs to be interpreted differently. Look at Figure 12.8, taken here from one of my archive CDs for a sample.

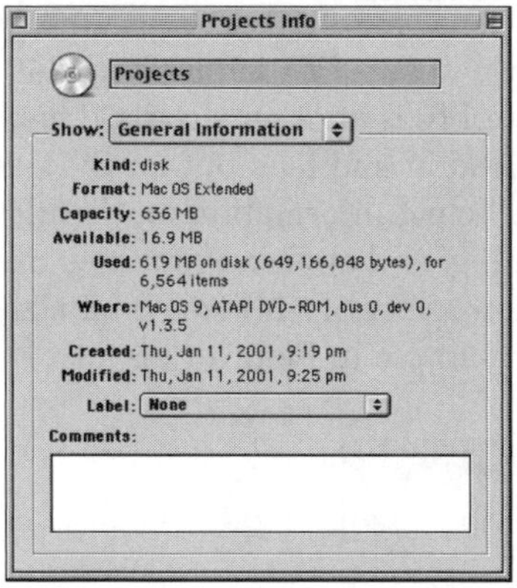

Figure 12.8
Getting the volume information for a CD.

The Capacity field is the total size of the track (or volume) written on the disc. This won't necessarily match the total amount used. The Used field contains a summary value before the words "on disk"—this is the total *space* used on the disc. The figure is based on the number of blocks used—not the actual total size of all of the files—and may be substantially higher than the actual file size. This number is also subject to change on different discs, so comparing this figure against your source folder is not a good way of verifying the space usage. Instead, use the figure given in brackets as the total size of all of the files. You can see in Figure 12.9 the source folder—here showing a discrepancy compared to our CD volume.

Figure 12.9
Information on our
source CD folder.

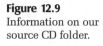

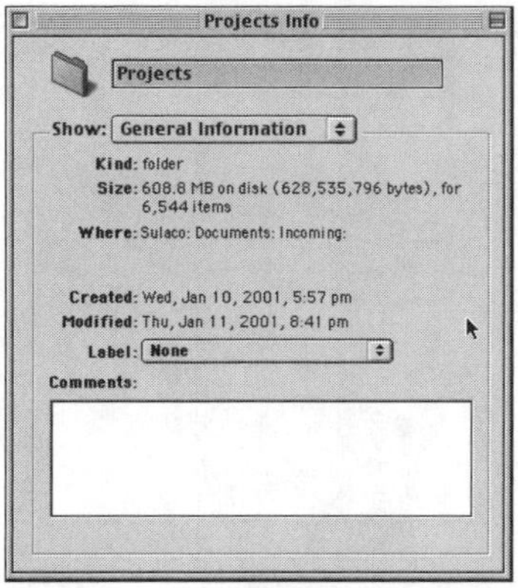

Checking the information, you can see that we have two more files on the CD volume compared to our source folder and a not insignificant size increase on the CD. This is because of the desktop database on the CD—it's required on all volumes but won't appear in our source folder. Unless you've recorded from another volume—including a disk image—the size of the CD will always be larger by two files and up to 10 percent of the source folder size. This is perfectly normal, and nothing to worry about. If you have written an ISO9660 disk, then the difference will be more significant, as some of the hidden files that are written to a Mac CD are not written to ISO9660 disks. Files that are not written to an ISO9660 CD include the two desktop files written to all Mac volumes, and the custom icons used on some folders and files.

However, if the size and file numbers reported on the CD are lower than the source folder, you need to worry. Here, it's best to check on a folder-by-folder basis. Open the CD and the source folder and view in list mode. Then, in the View Options window—accessible from the View menu and shown in Figure 12.10—make sure you check the Calculate Folder Sizes checkbox.

Figure 12.10
Setting the view
options for a folder.

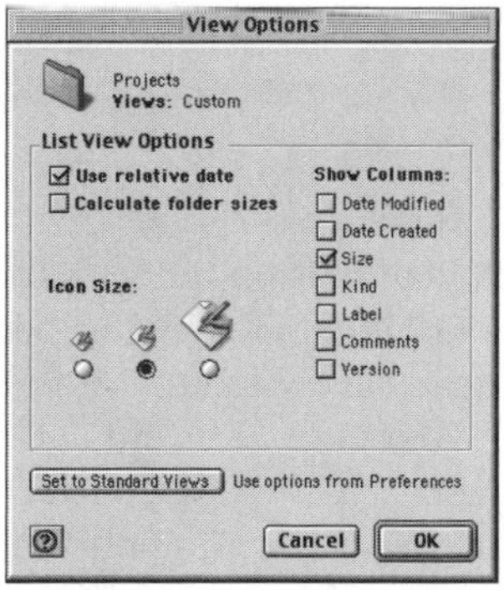

Once selected, you get a list showing the folder sizes, like the one shown in Figure 12.11. You can use the triangle tabs to display further levels of the folder structure and have the size information displayed.

Figure 12.11
Viewing a folder
with subfolder
summary sizes.

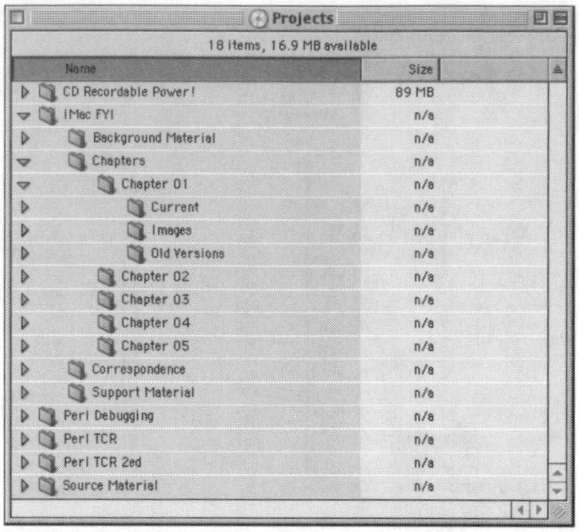

Unix

You need to use the find and **du** (disk usage) to compare file sizes from the source folder and the final volume under Unix. I use the following command to get a report on the number of files:

```
$ find /cdrom -print | wc -l
```

This works out the number of files in a directory by counting the number of lines output by find.

To compare sizes, use the du command:

```
$ du -sk /cdrom
```

The **-sk** options show a summary for the entire folder and give the information in kilobytes instead of in blocks. If you need to check subfolders, use a wildcard to select the files and folders in the base directory:

```
$ du -sk /cdrom/*
```

Try a Different Machine

I can't stress enough how important it is to check your CDs on more than one machine, and preferably more than one make of machine and/or CD-ROM drive. Just because the CD you wrote works in your own computer doesn't automatically mean that it will work in everybody else's machines. Remember as well that although your current machine may read the CDs, your next machine might not. It's *very* unlikely with modern CD-ROM drives and CD-R writers, but if your data is important to you—for example, your kid's christening photos/video or the accounts and sales information for the past year—then you must do everything you can to verify the CD.

Furthermore, you should try to test the CD in different types of drive if you can. For example, try your CD in a CD-ROM, CD-R, CD-RW, and DVD drive if you have them available—remember that some types of drive don't like CD-R or CD-RW media.

If you are really worried about your CDs, you might want to create a duplicate of your original, so that you have two, and even back up that CD on tape. See Chapter 8 for more information on the best way of archiving and backing up to CD.

Try a Different Platform

Even if you are not producing a cross-platform CD but are using a cross-platform compatible file system (such as ISO9660), try your CD in a Mac, Windows, or Unix machine if you have one handy. It's amazing to note that some platforms are remarkably tolerant of problems with discs specifically formatted for them, whereas a machine that supports the same format may not be. In the past, I've written Windows CDs that seemed to work fine in a PC but reported errors under Mac OS—it wasn't until I tried accessing one of the files from within an application that I realized something was wrong with the CD.

Final Note on Verification

Verification of your CD should be a vital step—especially for critical information—in your CD writing process. While I've mentioned some of the more common techniques, I don't want it to sound as if CD writing is an error-prone process that commonly writes bad CDs. In over a thousand CDs that I've written, I've had problems with only about ten, and most of those were problems during the writing process, not after the CD had been written.

Section III Writing CDs for Business

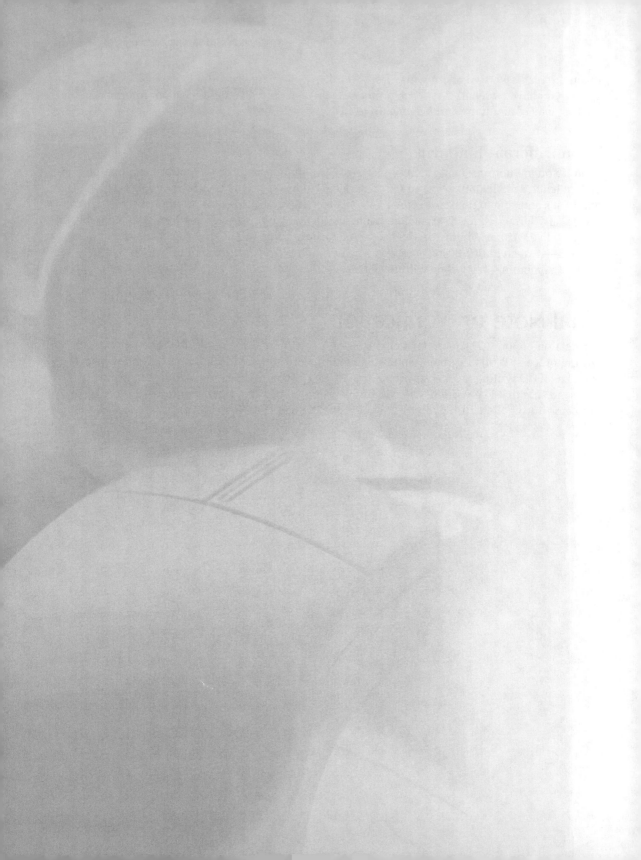

13

Mass Duplication

Although it's not everybody's reason for using a CD-R drive, more and more companies are turning to mass-duplication processes, even for relatively short runs of CDs. With the explosion of CDs as the format of choice over floppy disks, companies are using CDs for everything from cover discs (as placed on the front covers of magazines) to simple electronic catalogs of their products.

Although the method by which single and mass-duplicated CDs are produced is no different, there are some changes in the creation and verification process that warrant additional attention. While we look at those differences, we'll also take a more in-depth look at the mass-duplication process, from creating the master through to the presses, and at how you should go about producing your own master. The last section in this chapter looks at the different methods you can use for creating a number of identical CDs using a standard CD-R drive.

The Mass-Duplication Process

We've already looked at the specifics of the different CD writing formats, including the mass-produced CDs that you get software and music on, but I'd like to take a slightly more detailed look at the process, with specific regard to how it differs from the CD-R and CD-RW processes that we have so far been discussing.

The basic process for duplicating a CD in a production environment is to create a physical representation of the pits that make up the digital data stream, rather than burning away or changing the nature of a dye. This means that mass-produced CDs are actually *pressed*, just like an old vinyl album.

Because it's a physical process, we need to "press" only the image into a piece of plastic. Unlike CD-R/RW, this means that the production time for a single CD is calculated in seconds, rather than minutes, and we can produce hundreds, if not thousands, of CDs during the course of a few hours.

Section III Writing CDs for Business

The full process is shown in Figure 13.1.

Figure 13.1

The process behind mass-producing a CD, from source material to final CD.

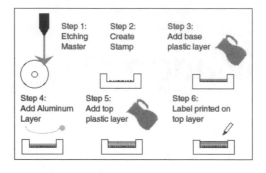

The process involves several stages, and details of each step shown in Figure 13.1 are included below. Although in this instance we've dealt with only a single master and stamp, it's quite possible to create more than one stamp from a glass master in order to generate a number of copies of the same CD simultaneously.

1. A glass "master" is made by using a laser to etch the pits into a photo-resistive layer on a piece of glass. This is similar in principle to writing a CD-R—a laser burns the data into the layer on the glass. This represents the pattern of pits on the final disc.

2. The master disc is used to create a metal "stamp," which will make the physical impressions in the polycarbonate disc.

3. The plastic is injected into the mold, creating a plastic disc that has an identical physical layout of pits to the original glass master. The resulting disc has two sides— the pitted layer is actually the top of the final disc, and the flat side is the bottom of the disc that will sit in the CD tray.

4. A layer of aluminum is placed over the pitted layer—this is the reflective surface that will be "read" by the laser.

5. A layer of polycarbonate is placed over the aluminum to create the flat top of the final CD.

6. The label is screen-printed or bonded to the top layer.

The process can be quite expensive, as producing a glass master and stamp is a costly business. In the '80s and early '90s, the cost could be as high as $5,000 for a master and stamp, but with costs of 10 to 25 cents per CD. However, market forces have lowered the overall cost, and many companies now waive the mastering fee, charging a slightly higher price for the individual CDs. The effect is that the cost of duplicating 500 CDs is now as low as $175, which is 35 cents per CD. Turnaround time is an issue—the actual time for duplicating those 500 CDs is probably less than an hour, but you will ultimately be placed into a queue of other people wanting to have their CDs duplicated, so it could take one or two weeks before you get your CDs back. Of course, if you have them professionally duplicated you can also have jewel cases, CD inserts, and other labels professionally printed along with the rest of the job.

Compare that to the cost of a CD-R—you can buy 100 good quality CD-Rs for about $45, so it would cost $450 for the media, but it would also take you, even at 12x, more than six minutes to write each CD. For 1,000 CDs, that would take four-and-a-half days! If you were writing less than a full CD, the time, obviously, would be less—but when pressing a CD, it makes no difference if there is 1 MB or 650 MB of information.

As the numbers increase, it gets even more cost effective—see Table 13.1 for some examples of the costs and time involved. The figures are based on a 12x CD-R drive, writing a full 650 MB. I've also assumed that for the pressed version, the master has already been made, and that it takes ten seconds for each CD, which in turn costs ten cents. These are all conservative estimates—the actual figures for such an exercise are probably much lower.

Table 13.1
Comparing the cost and time of mass production against manually writing CD-Rs

Number of CDs	Duplication Cost ($)	Duplication Time (hours)	CD-R Cost ($)	CD-R Time (hours)
100	70	<1	50	10
1,000	350	3	495	103
10,000	3,500	28	4,950	1,028
25,000	8,750	69	12,375	2,569
100,000	35,000	278	49,500	10,278

Although this appears to be a trivial exercise, it does demonstrate just how quickly you can produce CDs on a production line, compared to the cost and time of doing it manually. You start to break even at 500 CDs and, in fact, once you cost in the time it would take for somebody to sit at a machine and actually write each CD with a CD-R drive, the payback point would be even lower.

Preparing a Master

Aside from the obvious physical differences between a normal mass-produced CD and a CD-R, there are also some differences, however minor, between the production of a CD-R and a CD master. The production and development of the content on the CD shouldn't be any different than producing an ordinary CD-R, except that you should be significantly more diligent about the quality of your CD and your testing regime. There is a lot more to lose by duplicating 10,000 CDs compared to duplicating only ten.

If you are planning to produce a CD that will be used as the master for mass duplication, keep the following in mind:

1. Check the format required by the duplication company. Most will request a data CD written in disc-at-once mode, rather than track-at-once. You'll probably need to make a special request if you want to write a track-at-once, multi-session, or mixed format disc, as these require more care during the development of the master.

2. Follow the advice in Chapter 12, and make sure that you properly test everything on the CD. There's a lot more at stake when you are duplicating 10,000, or even just 1,000, CDs than when you are producing only one.

3. Make absolutely certain that the source CD is virus free. Although you will probably have a software license to support the use of a disk or some other document that limits your liability, distributing a virus on your CDs is not good public relations. You can find examples of software licenses by looking at those supplied with other software. They are usually attached to the CD case or on a separate sheet that came with the manuals.

4. Have some proof that your CD-R original worked fine before it was duplicated so that you have something to compare against. Although it's unlikely, there have been cases where the pressed CD does not work, but the original does—the duplication company should be duplicating the original CD-R and it should work.

5. Get the CD duplication facility to test the CD on its equipment both before and after production. Most duplication companies have a number of different CD-ROM drives and computers in which to test the CDs that are being pressed. Getting them checked here will not only highlight any production problems (which are rare), but also any other problems with the source CD.

Finally, and above all else, remember that this CD will be going to a wide variety of people with different abilities, needs, and equipment. Try to make your CD as easy to use, well documented, and as well laid out as possible. Creating a CD that will go to thousands of people can do more for your publicity department than a year's worth of advertisements, and bad publicity will not be helpful.

Personal CD Duplication

Not everybody wants to create 1,000 or more CDs. Often, what you want is just ten or twenty copies of a CD to distribute to prospective clients, family, or just to make doubly sure that you've got extra copies of important data. There are three ways in which you can create multiple copies of the same CD using a standard CD recorder:

▶ Write the same CD using the same layout and other information a number of times (Write Many).

▶ Write the CD once and then using the duplication feature of the CD software to copy the first CD onto additional CDs (Write Once, Copy Many).

▶ Create an image of the CD you want to write and then write the image to the CD (Write Image).

Each method has its advantages and disadvantages, and we'll look at them here to see the individual benefits.

Write Many

The Write Many method is quite time consuming and can be prone to many different problems. The biggest disadvantage is that because you are writing information to the CD from the same source, you run the risk of making modifications to a file set that you may not want to change. The second problem is that because you are always writing information from the source files, you are prone to the same speed and transfer problems as when writing any other CD. A minor interruption could ruin the CD—you may even have to lower the speed at which you normally write your CDs, which, in turn, will lengthen the time it takes you to duplicate them. The main advantage of the Write Many method is that if you are creating CDs to go to a different number of clients, you could tailor each CD to be mildly customized for each user. Obviously, this is not quite the normal duplication process and probably, in the true sense, isn't duplication at all.

The entire process of Write Many is generally longer than other methods, as you will not only need to write each CD but also check each individual CD to ensure that the writing process has completed successfully. Although you won't need to do a full check on each CD, you will need to ensure that each one is readable before distribution.

Write Once, Copy Many

With the Write Once, Copy Many technique, you write the CD once and then use that CD as the master from which you do a number of CD duplications. Most CD software allows you to copy or duplicate a CD, so all you have to do is set the duplication process in motion. This process is slightly quicker than the Write Many method, because you can always read information from a CD quicker than you can write it and interruptions are less likely to cause any problems during the process.

You also know that each CD will be identical to each other, and you can be sure that any changes to the source will have no effect on the rest of your CDs. When it comes to verification, you can also usually get by with checking only the first CD—and you can do a thorough check of the entire CD, safe in the knowledge that all the other CDs should be perfect.

However, not all CD duplication processes are problem free. Occasionally, the process fails—even if you try a single-speed or direct bit-by-bit copy, usually because of small interruptions to the CD reading process.

Write Image

If you create an image of the CD that you are about to write, either by creating it directly from the source or by writing the CD and then creating an image of that, you get all the benefits of the Write Once, Copy Many technique, but without the pitfalls of the CD duplication process.

Most CD software allows you to create an image from an existing disc—if you create an ISO9660 image, you should be able to recreate just about any disc—including those that use Rock Ridge or Joliet extensions. Under a Mac, creating an image of a CD is much easier. Toast allows you to create an image from within the application that you can use as a direct source, but you can also use Disk Tools to create an image that can be used as the source volume. See Chapter 12 for more information.

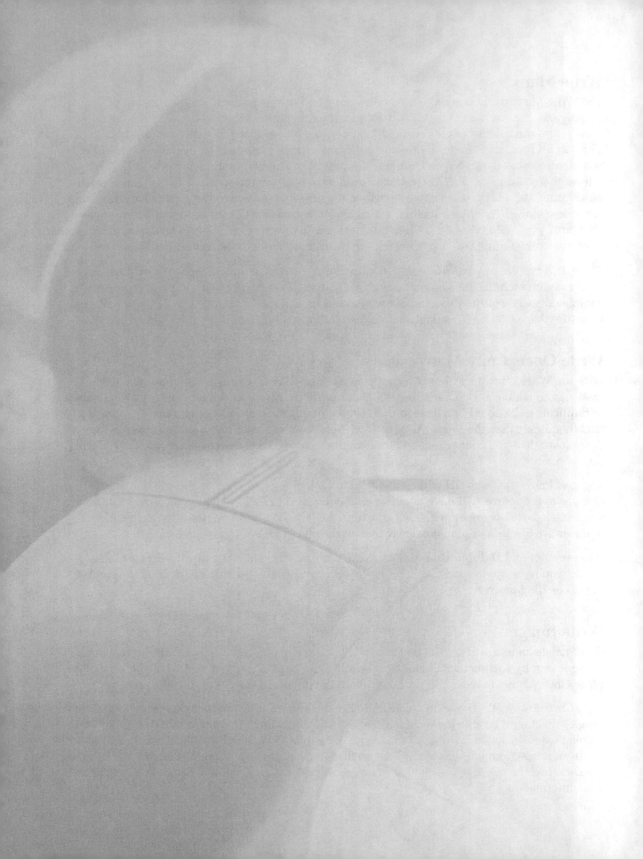

Section IV
CD Writing Software

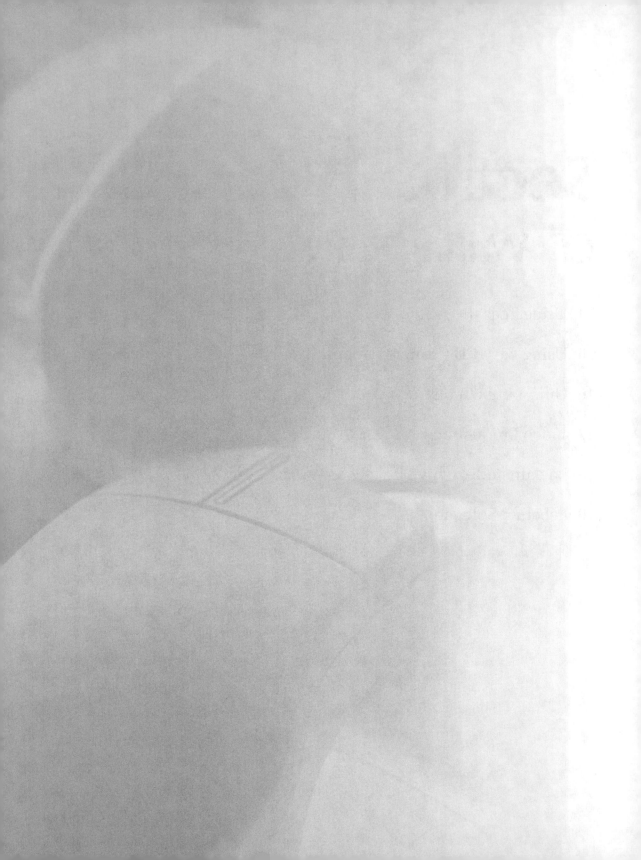

14

Using Toast (Mac OS)

Toast is the best known and used CD recording software available for the Macintosh platform. Although there are other packages, Toast leads the way in terms of features and ease of use. It's also the most likely package to be included with your CD-R drive.

Toast 5.0 is actually made up of a number of different components that allow you to assemble, build, and write a CD. The main component is the Toast application itself, which supports CD writing in a number of different formats, CD copying, and some utility operations such as the creation of temporary partitions and the creation of disk images. Toast also comes with CD Spin Doctor, which allows you to record audio from a tape or record deck; Toast Audio Extractor, which rips tracks from an audio CD; PhotoRelay, a simple image cataloging program; and Magic Mouse Discus, a CD labeling program. You also get some templates for creating labels and AppleScripts for speeding up the process of writing folders and audio tracks to CD.

In this chapter, we're going to concentrate on the Toast application itself. For more information on CD Spin Doctor and Toast Audio Extractor, see Chapter 9, which covers the intricacies of making audio CDs from a number of different sources. For details on how to use the label templates, see Chapter 19.

Installing Toast

Toast typically comes on a CD with your CD-R/RW drive, but you must install the software before you use it:

1. Insert the CD into your existing CD-ROM drive (not your CD-R/RW drive)—the contents of the CD will be displayed in a new window. If it does not launch automatically, click on the Toast 5.0 Titanium icon that appears when the CD is inserted.

2. Double-click the Toast 5.0 Titanium icon.

3. Click through the welcome screens by clicking on the Continue buttons.

4. Click "Agree" if you agree to the software license that is displayed on screen.

5. Check that the installer has chosen the correct drive on which to install the software and then click Install.

Recording a Data CD with Toast

Toast will record files to CD either from files and folders or from an entire volume, including temporary volumes created with Disk Copy (see "Creating a Bootable CD with Toast" later in this chapter for more information). To record any type of data disc with Toast:

1. Run Toast from the disk where you installed it. The main program window is displayed and is shown here in Figure 14.1.

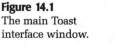
Figure 14.1
The main Toast
interface window.

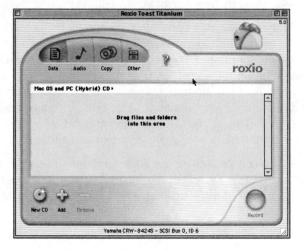

2. Choose the disc type that you want to create from the icons at the top of the CD. Clicking the Data button automatically sets up Toast to create a Data CD that is both Mac and PC compatible. You can select other combinations by clicking the Data button and then choosing the format from the popup at the top of the folder list panel.

3. If you want to create a data disc from an existing disc volume, you can drag and drop the volume into the main window. If you want to record an entire folder or a selection of files and/or folders, you can also drag and drop them into the main window—Toast will automatically change the disc type and set up the disc accordingly.

4. Alternatively, once you've selected the disc type, you can click on the New CD button.

5. If you are copying files, click on the Add button to bring up the Choose Object dialog box (see Figure 14.2). You can select files for your data CD here by clicking on the Choose button. If your source files and folders contain aliases, you can copy original files, rather than aliases, by clicking on the Resolve Aliases checkbox.

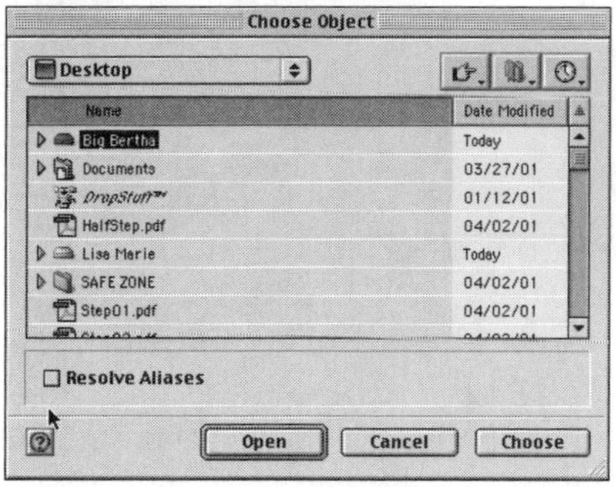

Figure 14.2
Choose files for
your data CD.

6. Put a blank CD into your recorder.

7. Click on the big red Record button—you'll get a new dialog box like the one shown in Figure 14.3.

Figure 14.3
Choosing how to
write your disk.

8. Click Write Disc if you want to write and close the entire disc. If you want to write only to a portion of the disc so that you can add another volume at a later stage, choose Write Session. Once the writing process beings, you'll get the window shown in Figure 14.4.

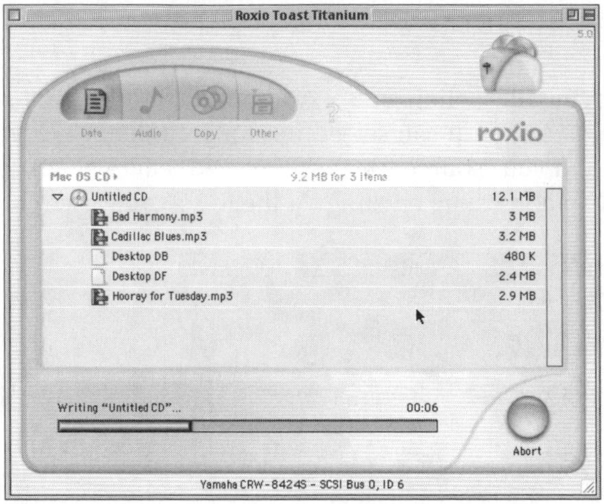

Figure 14.4
Writing a
data CD
with Toast.

Toast will ask you whether you want to verify that the CD was burned correctly, and then it will eject the CD. That's it—all you have to do is let Toast get on with writing the CD.

Recording an Audio CD with Toast

If you want to create an audio CD that you can put into your home or car stereo, you need to record an audio (CDDA) CD. There are two ways to obtain the audio tracks that you want to record onto a CD with Toast:

▶ **Extract the audio tracks with Toast Audio Extractor to your hard disk.** This method allows you to collect and organize tracks from a number of different CDs before you create the new CD—excellent for compilations. See Chapter 9 for more information on using TAE for extracting audio tracks.

▶ **Download MP3s from the Internet or create your own audio tracks from an analog source.** The latter option requires you to connect your audio source to your machine. Again, see Chapter 9 for more information.

Both methods result in a number of files being created on your machine. To write the tracks to CD in the correct format with Toast:

1. Run Toast from the disk where you installed it.

2. Select Audio as the disc type.

3. Add tracks to the CD by clicking on the Add button and selecting previously extracted files, or inserting a music CD into your computer and dragging individual tracks into the main Toast window. Figure 14.5 shows a music CD ready to record.

Figure 14.5
Adding audio tracks
to your CD.

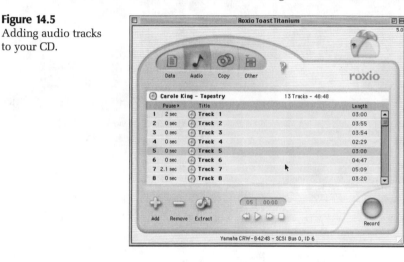

4. Click on the Record button.

5. Click Write Disc if you want to write, and close the entire disc. The Write Session option should be avoided for audio CDs, as most audio CD players are unable to read the audio tracks written in anything but the first session.

Now, let Toast do its stuff.

Copying CDs With Toast

If you want to copy or back up an existing CD in its entirety, insert the original CD in the CD-ROM drive and a blank CD in the CD recorder. Click on the Copy icon (Figure 14.6) and then click Record.

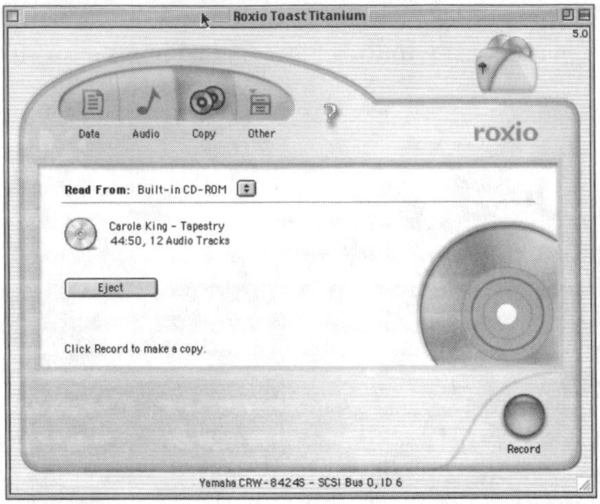

Figure 14.6
Toast is ready to copy
an existing CD.

Recording a Windows/ Unix-Compatible CD with Toast

To create a Windows/Unix-compatible-CD, you need to create an ISO9660 CD. You can create a CD that contains DOS, Macintosh compatible, or Windows compatible filenames. However, a CD written to be DOS/ Windows/Unix-compatible only—even if it uses Mac naming conventions—will write only the data fork of a file to a CD. Because only the data fork is written, you cannot use an ISO9660 CD to hold Mac applications, system folder, or other Mac specific files. If you want to create a CD that can hold both PC and Mac versions of files, use the Hybrid format.

To create a Windows/Unix compatible CD:

1. Run Toast from the disk where you installed it.

2. Click and hold the mouse button on the Other icon and select ISO 9660 as the disc type.

3. Drag and drop files onto the Toast window or use the Select button to open the file layout dialog box (shown in Figure 14.7) and add files and folders.

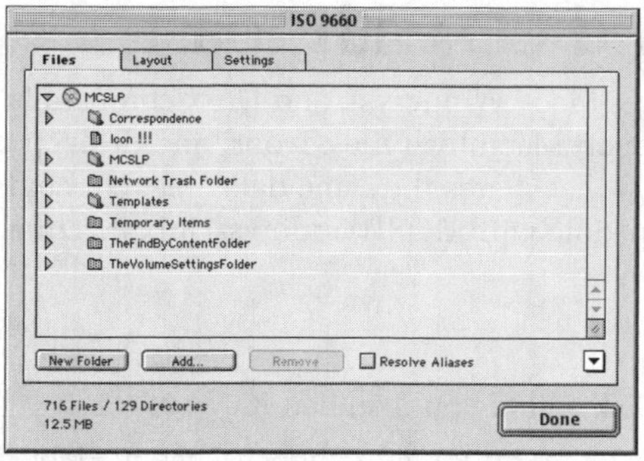

Figure 14.7
Adding files and
changing the layout
on a ISO 9660 disc.

4. Click on the Settings tab in the Data window (Figure 14.8) and configure the settings for the disc you are creating. The most important setting is the Naming system that is being used. Choose ISO 9660 Level 1 if you want to create the most basic ISO CD. Choose Allow MS-DOS Names if you want to create a DOS-compatible CD. Choose Joliet (MS-DOS+Windows) if you want to create a CD that will support long filenames under Windows. You can also opt to support standard Mac OS filename conventions.

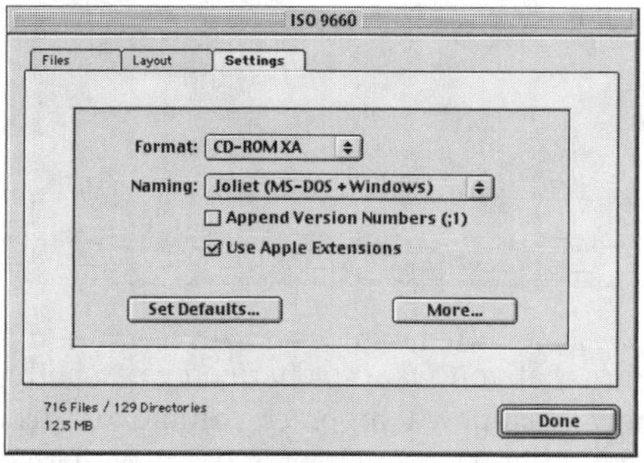

Figure 14.8
Changing the
ISO 9660 settings,
and setting file
naming conventions.

5. Put a blank CD into your recorder.
6. Click on the Record button.
7. Click Write Disc if you want to write and close the entire disc or Write Session if you want to add more data to the CD later.

Once the CD has been created, check the CD in one of your target machine types to verify that the information and filename conventions were written properly.

Recording a Hybrid CD with Toast

You can create a Hybrid CD that is Mac-, Windows-, and Unix-compatible using Toast. Unlike an ISO 9660 CD, hybrid CDs support Macintosh files, icons, and desktop information. What happens is that Toast creates a CD that shares the same data area, but contains two directory areas to allow the CD to be compatible with DOS/Windows/Unix machines and the special file format used by Macs.

To create a hybrid CD:

1. Run Toast from the disk where you installed it.

2. Click and hold on the Other button and choose Custom Hybrid (Figure 14.9).

Figure 14.9
Preparing a hybrid CD.

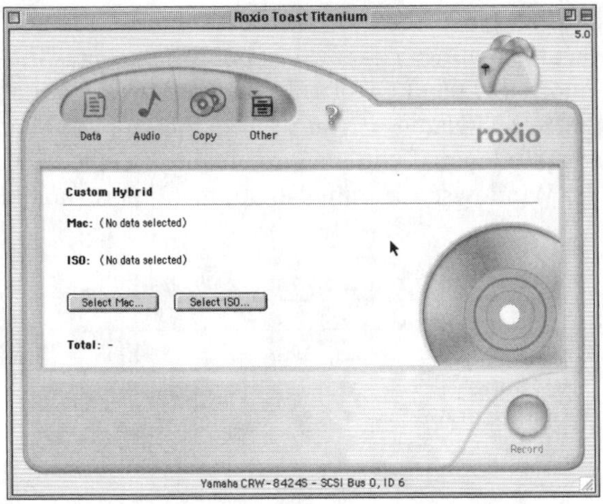

3. You need to put the files that you want to share between both platform types onto a new volume. You can create a new temporary volume for this using Disk Copy. The files on this volume should be Mac versions of the files that you want to share, as Toast will use the volume as the directory for the Mac portion of the CD.

4. Click on the Select Mac button and Choose the volume you just created.

5. Click on the Select ISO button and add the files that you want to be placed on the windows (ISO 9660) portion of the CD.

6. Before clicking the Done button, click on the Settings tab in the Data window and configure the settings for the disc you are creating. The most important setting is the Naming system that is being used. Choose ISO 9660 Level 1 if you want to create the most basic ISO CD. Choose Allow MS-DOS Names if you want to create a DOS-compatible CD. Choose Joliet (MS-DOS+Windows) if you want to create a CD that will support long filenames under Windows. You can also opt to support standard Mac OS filename conventions.

7. Put a blank CD into your recorder.

8. Click on the Record button.

9. Click Write Disc if you want to write and close the entire disc. Write Session is not recommended for writing hybrid CDs.

Once again, make sure you test the CD in PC and Mac machines to ensure that the process has worked properly.

Creating a Bootable CD with Toast

To create a bootable CD with Toast, you should first create a temporary volume using Disk Copy. Then install a system suitable for your machine on to the new image before copying any additional files, applications and installers to the volume. See Chapter 10 for more information on how to create a temporary volume with Disk copy.

Once the volume has been created and you are ready to write the CD, go into Toast, click on the Other button and choose Mac Volume from the list of CD types. Click on the Select button that is presented and choose the mounted Disk Copy volume you created earlier. Make sure you select the Bootable checkbox to ensure that the CD is bootable. Now write the CD as normal.

Once the disc has been created, take the CD you have just written, put it into your CD-ROM drive, reboot your machine, and then hold down the C key to force your machine to boot up from the CD.

If it doesn't work, it may be the fault of the operating system you have installed, rather than the CD itself.

Creating an AutoStart CD with Toast

You can specify any application or file to automatically be opened when a CD is inserted when creating a data disc from an existing disc volume. The file you use for AutoStart has the following limitations:

▶ The file or application must exist at the root of the CD; it cannot be contained within any folder on the CD.

▶ The file or application must be real—aliases to an application or file somewhere else on the disc are not allowed.

▶ The file or application name must have no more than eleven characters.

NOTE

AutoStart on the Mac works only if CD AutoStart has been turned on. You can control this behavior on your machine by using the QuickTime control panel.

To create an AutoStart CD you must use an existing Mac volume. Click and hold the Other button down and select Mac Volume from the drop-down list. See Figure 14.10. Click on the Select button and check the Auto Start box. You'll get a file dialog box where you need to choose the file or application that you want to be started when the CD is inserted. Find the file you want to use, and click Choose. Then continue to add files and folders and write the disc as any other data disc.

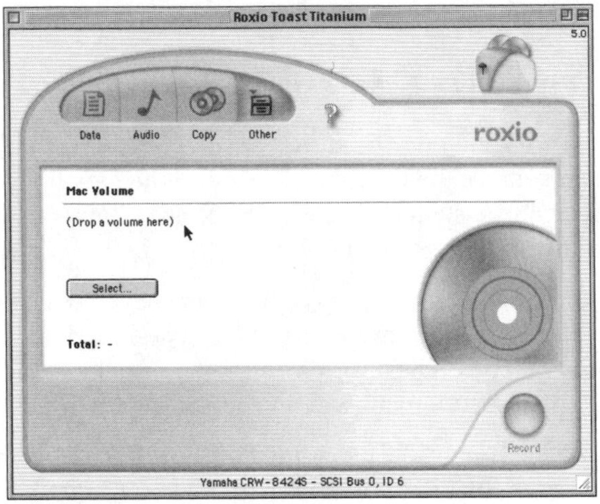

Figure 14.10
Toast is ready to
select a volume.

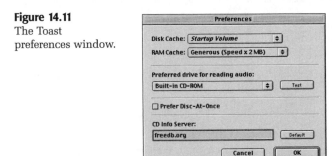

Setting Toast Preferences

Toast is a very powerful package, and part of its power lies in its ability to "do the right thing" in just about every situation. That doesn't mean, though, that you can't configure some of the Toast operations. To change the preferences for Toast, go to Edit > Preferences. When selected, you'll get a window similar to the one shown in Figure 14.11.

Figure 14.11
The Toast
preferences window.

The different options affect Toast as follows:

▶ **Disk Cache**—Toast will use space on one of your hard drives as a disk cache to help assemble items before they are finally written to CD. You can select from the Startup Volume (the Mac OS startup volume), the Application Volume (where Toast resides), or any volume by its name. If you have a Mac with multiple volumes, choose the fastest volume available—that will probably be your startup volume, which is also the default setting.

▶ **RAM Cache**—This controls how much of the available RAM that you have allocated to Toast is actually used for caching information before it is written to disc. The standard amount of RAM that Toast likes to use is equal to 1 MB times the recording speed. So, for an 8x drive, Toast will require 8 MB of RAM to ensure the best results. There is also a generous setting that uses 2 MB instead of 1 MB. Finally, you can define a specific cache size.

▶ **Preferred drive for reading audio**—This is the default drive used when extracting audio before writing the audio to CD. You can use this option if your current CD-ROM drive is not able to extract the audio from a CD digitally, which some older drives can't.

▶ **Prefer Disc-At-Once**—Enable this option if you would prefer Toast to always write discs in Disc-At-Once mode instead of in Track-At-Once mode (see Chapter 5). Not all CD-R/RW drives can record information in Disk-At-Once mode, so make sure you check your manual before enabling this option.

▶ **CD Info Server**—The Internet site where Toast automatically looks for artist and track names to recognize audio CDs.

Once you've configured all of the options, click OK to enable your changes or cancel if you don't want to change any of the preferences.

15

Using Easy CD Creator (Windows)

Easy CD Creator is the best-known software available for writing CDs under Windows. As well as working with traditional CD-R and CD-RW media, Easy CD Creator will also work with the newer DVD-RAM media when using directCD. It combines a core application, Easy CD Creator, that does most of the writing, as well as tools for copying discs, extracting and recording audio files (SoundStream/Spin Doctor), and creating CD labels and jewel case inserts (CD Label Creator), along with a myriad of other tools. It's also often supplied with a further set of sound and image editing/cataloging software and the directCD application for writing CDs in the same way as you copy files to floppy disks.

We'll have a look at Easy CD Creator, CD Copier, and directCD in this chapter. SoundStream and the Spin Doctor extension (for recording analog audio) is covered in Chapter 9, and CD Label Creator is covered in Chapter 19.

Using Easy CD Creator

Easy CD Creator is the tool you use to write data or audio CD projects. You can use Easy CD Creator straight from the Start menu, or use the Project Selector to choose what type of project you want to create.

Installing Easy CD Creator

To install Easy CD Creator:

1. Insert the Easy CD Creator CD into your CD drive.
2. If the product doesn't auto launch, simply double-click on the launch.exe icon within the CD's Explorer window.
3. Follow the on-screen instructions to install the software.

Once the software has been copied over, you will need to reboot your machine.

The Project Selector

Although you can run a lot of the CD writing software directly from the Start menu, most of the software will be accessed though the Project Selector. When you select Start > Roxio Easy CD Creator 5.0 > Project Selector, or right-click on the Easy CD Creator Project Selector icon in the system tray, you'll get a window like the one shown in Figure 15.1. Alternatively, if you have AutoPlay enabled on your system, the Project Selector will be automatically opened when you put a blank CD into your CD-R/RW drive.

Figure 15.1
The Project Selector.

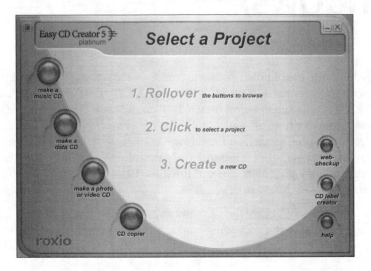

The four buttons on the left allow you to select the primary operation—they are, in order: make a music (audio) CD, make a data CD, make a photo or video CD, or open the CD copier application. The first two are quite obvious in meaning; they take you to software that can help you in the process of creating an audio or data CD. For example, you can see in Figure 15.2 how you can drop into SoundStream or use the main Easy CD Creator application to create a stereo-compatible music CD or an MP3 audio CD for use in your computer or MP3-capable stereo. Figure 15.3 takes you to directCD, Easy CD Creator, or Take Two, which allows you to back up your machine.

Figure 15.2
Music CDs in
Project Selector.

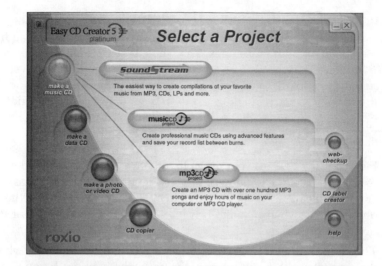

Figure 15.3
Data CDs in
Project Selector.

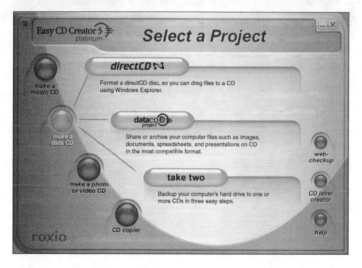

The final three buttons on the main panel allow you to check and, if necessary, update your software over the Internet, start the CD label creator application for printing in CD labels and inserts (detailed in Chapter 19), or get help on using the Project Selector.

Writing a Data CD with Easy CD Creator

The main Easy CD Creator application enables you to write both data and audio CDs, and it uses the same basic layout for both procedures. The whole system is built around a familiar Windows Explorer-like interface, and the process for creating data and audio CDs is very similar. Once you've selected the type of disc you want to record, all you need to do is find the files with the explorer that you want to copy and drag and drop them onto your "CD layout," which is the layout of the files and directories that will eventually appear on the CD.

To create a data CD:

1. Insert a blank CD into your drive. If you have AutoPlay enabled on your CD-R/RW drive, you'll get the window shown in Figure 15.1. Click the make a data CD button, and then the dataCD project button to open Easy CD Creator. If the Project Selector does not start when a blank CD is inserted, open Easy CD Creator Project Selector through the Start menu.

2. The main Easy CD Creator window looks like Figure 15.4. The window is split into three panels, with a button bar at the top of the window. If you click the expand icon, another panel appears. The top two panels operate just like any other Windows Explorer-like browser—the left-hand panel lists the disk and directory structure and the right-hand panel shows the files and directories within the currently selected directory. You use these panels to find the files that you want to add to the CD.

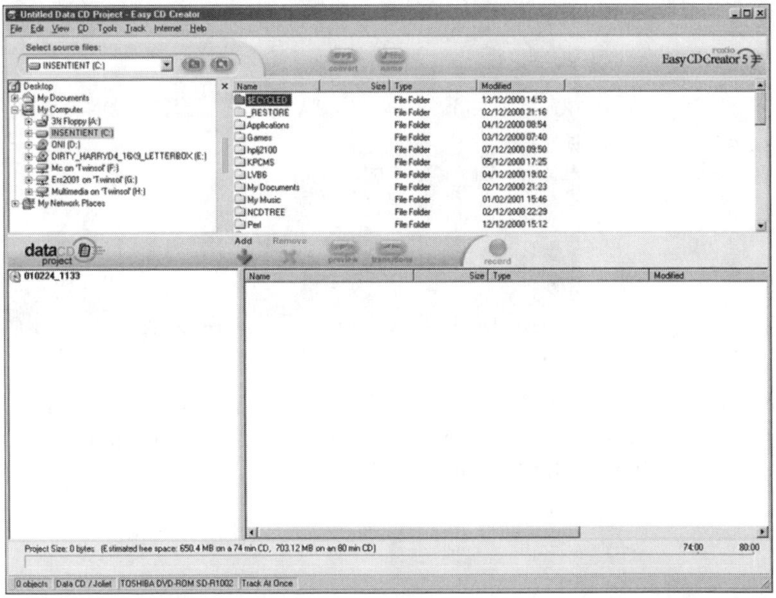

Figure 15.4

A blank Easy CD Creator window with the Windows Explorer-like browser at the top.

3. At the bottom of the window is a scaled bar that shows how much space the files and directories that you have already selected will take up on the final CD. Use this to gauge how much information you have added to the CD layout—figures are shown both for 74- and 80-minute blank media.

4. Use the top panel to find the files and folders that you want to copy to the CD and drag and drop the folders into the lower panel, or select them and click the Add button in the toolbar. You should see the files and folders that you've just added in the bottom panels. Repeat the process until you've added all the files you want to the CD. You can see in Figure 15.5 that I've collected together a set of files and directories relating to a series of projects.

Figure 15.5
The final layout of a CD in Easy CD Creator.

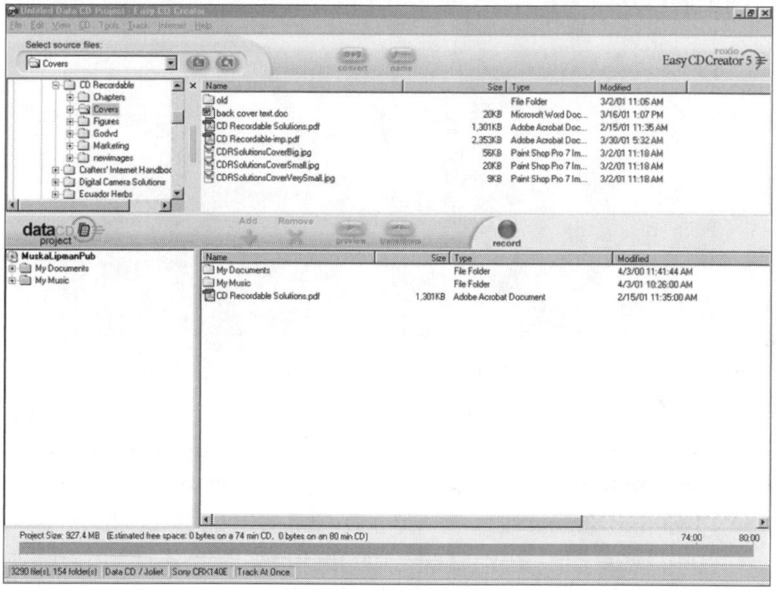

5. Before proceeding, you may want to adjust the properties of the CD you are about to write. See "Setting CD Properties" later in this chapter for more information on these parameters, as they are shared among all CD types.

6. Once you're happy with the layout, you are ready to write your CD. Click on the big red Record button. You'll be prompted with the dialog box shown in Figure 15.6. From this window, you can control the write speed, the number of copies, and the CD-R device that you want to use. If you want to simply go ahead and write your CD, just press the Start Recording button.

Figure 15.6
The basic CD creation window.

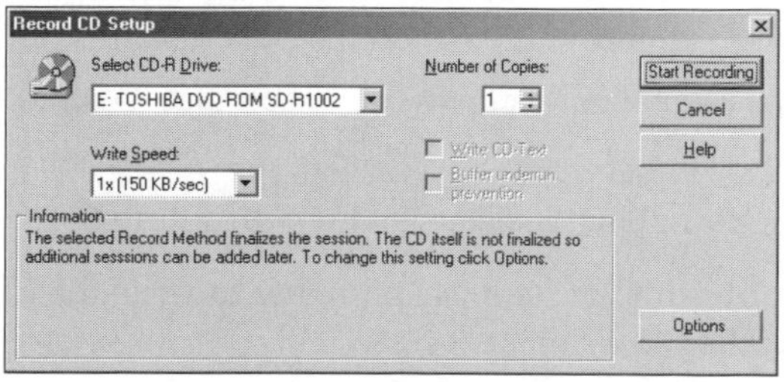

7.   However, if you want to change the way the CD is written, click on the Options
button to get the dialog box shown in Figure 15.7. From here, you can control the
specifics of the CD writing process.

Figure 15.7
Configuring the
advanced properties
for creating a new CD.

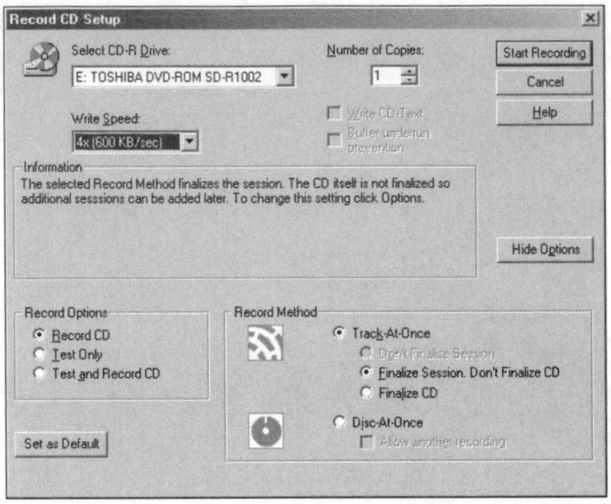

The different options available to you are listed and described below:

▶ **Test Only**—Easy CD Creator will use the "dummy burn" facility, reading the
information from the source discs and determining whether the information can be
written to the CD at the speed you have selected.

▶ **Test and Create CD**—Easy CD Creator will go through the test procedure and then,
providing the test worked, proceed to write the CD.

▶ **Create CD**—Go ahead and write the CD.

When working in track-at-once mode, you can also adjust how the disc is written:

▶ **Don't Finalize Session**—This does not "close" the session, so you can add more
information to the disc at a later stage. But, you won't be able to read the CD in a
standard CD-ROM drive. However, you may be able to read a CD that has open
sessions on the CD-RW in read mode or on another CD-R/RW drive in a different
machine.

▶ **Finalize Session. Don't Finalize CD**—This creates a disc that can be read in any
machine and have further information added to the disc as new sessions at a later
stage. Not all drives support multisession discs, so use this option with care.

▶ **Finalize CD**—This permanently closes the CD so that it cannot be written to in the
future.

If you want to save the options you have selected for all your future CDs, click Set as Default.

8.   Once you are happy with the settings and ready to write the CD, click on Start
Recording to start the CD writing process.

9. The last window (Figure 15.8) shows the progress of the writing process. Easy CD Creator will first attempt to find a suitable drive to use as a source for the files that will be written to the CD. This allows you to write information to a CD from a slower source, such as Zip, Jaz, or even network drive. If necessary, Easy CD Creator then copies the files to a suitable drive (probably your hard disk) before actually writing the track to the CD.

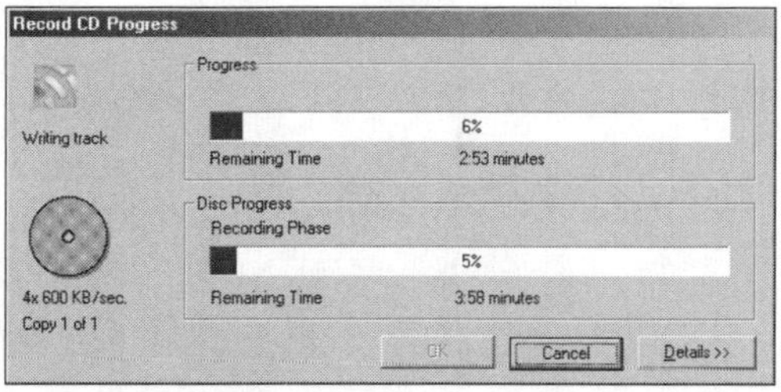

Figure 15.8
Writing a CD with
Easy CD Creator.

Writing an Audio CD with Easy CD Creator

To write an audio CD, click make a music CD from the Roxio Project Selector and then musicCD project to open Easy CD Creator in music CD mode. Once in Easy CD Creator, you follow the same basic instructions as before, only you find and select audio files instead of data files to add to the CD. The exact sequence is:

1. Insert a blank CD into your drive. If you have AutoPlay enabled on your CD-R/RW drive, you'll get the window shown in Figure 15.1. Click make a music CD, and then musicCD project to open Easy CD Creator in music CD mode. If the Project Selector does not start when a blank CD is inserted, open Project Selector through the Start menu.

2. You'll be given a slightly different layout to the data CD layout shown earlier. Instead of a split bottom panel, you have only a single panel showing the audio CD information (artist, title) and the list of tracks to be written to the CD. See Figure 15.9 for a sample.

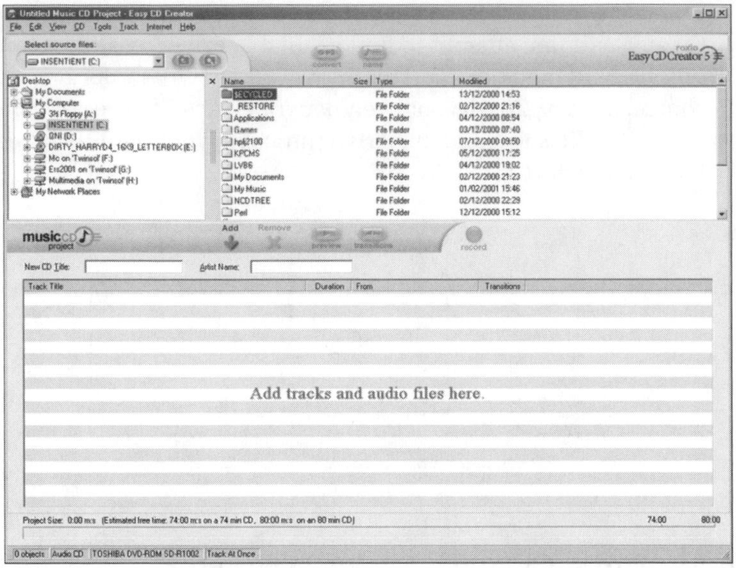

Figure 15.9

The Easy CD Creator window for audio CDs.

3. Using the explorer panel, find the files you want to use. Easy CD Creator will tape WAV and MP3 files from your hard disk and will also rip audio CD tracks from an existing CD inserted into another drive. Once you've found the files or tracks you want, drag them over to the lower panel—you can use the Control key to copy more than one file into the list. Remember to monitor the space you have used up on the CD—a standard audio CD holds seventy-four minutes of music, and the bar at the bottom of the window will let you know how much space you have left.

4. Once you are happy with all the tracks on the CD, you can change their layout and the transition parameters when changing between tracks during playback. To change the order, simply drag and drop the tracks into their new location. The audio effects you can control are accessible by right-clicking on the track and selecting Transition Effects from the menu. You'll get a dialog box similar to the one in Figure 15.10.

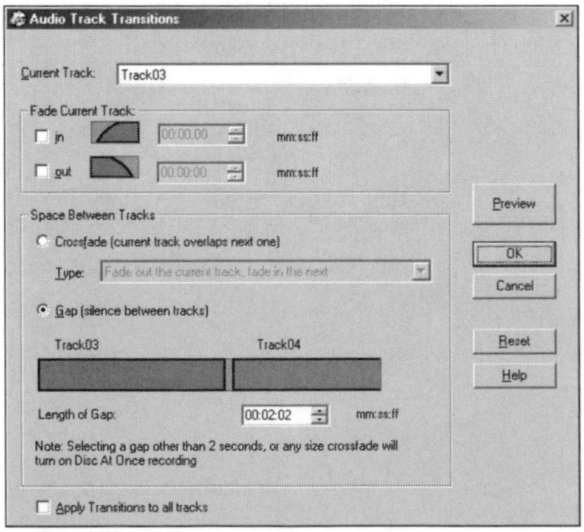

Figure 15.10

Setting the audio effects for a track.

There are four basic parameters you can adjust—the fade in (and out) of the track while it is being played, and the space between tracks. There is also a combined option, crossfading, which is essentially a combination of all three systems—more specific information on each parameter is given below:

— **Gap (silence between tracks)**—The "gap" between tracks. When using an existing audio CD source, you cannot change this value. However, if you have previously ripped the audio tracks from a CD into WAV, AIFF, or MP3 format or downloaded the track from the Internet, you can modify this gap value. The default is two seconds (the same as that used on prerecorded audio CDs). You may want to shorten the time if the tracks you are recording are spoken word tracks—a delay would cause a break in the story telling. Alternatively, you can click on the convert button when you've selected an audio track to have it converted to an MP3 or WAV file, which you can then select within Easy CD Creator as part of your audio project.

— **Fade In**—The amount of time to fade in the audio at the beginning of a track. The volume level will start from zero and gradually rise to the normal level for the duration you specify.

— **Fade Out**—The amount of time to fade out the audio at the end of the track. The volume level will fade from the normal level to zero for the duration you specify.

— **Crossfade**—The amount of time to blend two tracks. This uses a combination of fade out of the previous track and fade in of the current track. This is useful for merging music tracks together to create continuous music for parties and background tracks at businesses and restaurants. If you want to use this, make sure you set the pause value to zero.

5. You can also set the CD title and artist information; this information will be recorded so that the CD will be recognized next time you play it. You can also name any tracks on the CD that haven't already been recognized using the CDDB system. Note that this information will not actually be stored on the CD, just on your computer.

6. Click on the Record button.

7. You'll be prompted with the dialog box shown in Figure 15.6. Click on the Advanced button if the advanced dialog window is not already visible, then click on the Disc-at-once checkbox—providing your drive supports it—this will help to prevent any annoying clicks from appearing on the audio CD when played on some audio CD players.

8. Click Start Recording to start the process.

Creating a Bootable CD with Easy CD Creator

Many years ago, when hard disks were expensive, many computers had two floppy drives—one to hold the operating system, and the other to hold the application or data files that you were using. Machines booted up from a floppy disk all the time. Even when hard disks were introduced and started to become affordable, the humble floppy disk remained as the "backup" bootable device—if you had a problem, you booted from floppy and used the tools on the disk to try to rescue and repair the machine.

Bootable CDs for PCs, running everything from DOS to Windows and even Unix and Linux, use the El Torito! format. Because of the way in which a bootable CD is produced, we are somewhat limited as to what we can put on a bootable CD. We cannot, for example, install Windows onto the CD—there are a number of reasons for this, starting with the way in which Windows works, especially with respect to virtual memory (if the CD is not writable, Windows has nowhere to store the virtual memory file, and disabling VM is difficult without running Windows!). We can, however, put DOS onto the CD and enough other tools such as scandisk (or chkdsk), fdisk (for disk formatting), and installers and other information.

To record a bootable CD, you must first make a bootable floppy. There are two ways of doing this, and they each create a different set of functionality:

▶ **Using format**—The first method is to format a floppy disk, and ask Windows to copy the system files to the disk. You'll need to add suitable config.sys and autoexec.bat files to make the disk properly bootable. This option is supported only on Windows 95, 98, and NT, and it installs only a very basic version of DOS.

▶ **Using Add/Remove Programs**—The second is a more complete solution. Insert a blank floppy disk into your drive and then open the Add/Remove Programs control panel, shown in Figure 15.11. Click the Startup Disk tab and create a new disk. The disk that is created with this method also includes the drivers, autoexec.bat, and config.sys files required to not only boot the machine but also the other diagnostic tools and CD drivers.

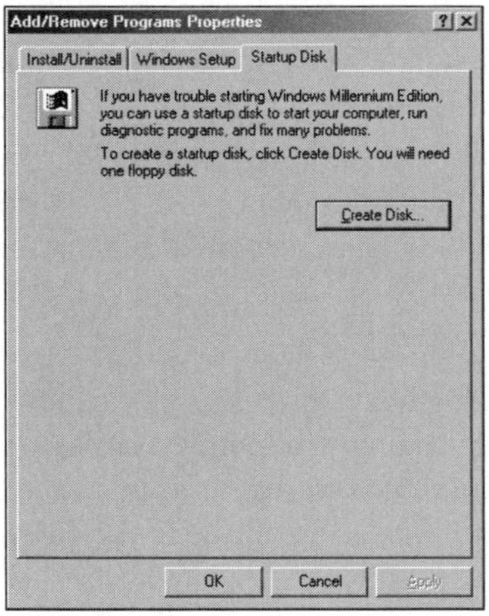

Figure 15.11
Creating a bootable
floppy using Windows.

Once you've created the disk, check it by booting your machine using the floppy. If it doesn't work, you'll get a message saying "Non-system disk." Eject the disk, reboot from the hard drive, and try recreating the disk again.

Now that you've got a bootable floppy, you need to create the CD itself:

1. Open Roxio Easy CD Creator.

2. Insert a blank CD into your CD-R/RW drive.

3. Click File and select the New CD Project menu item, followed by the Bootable CD from the submenu.

4. You'll be prompted with the dialog box shown in Figure 15.12. Select the type of bootable CD that you want to create.

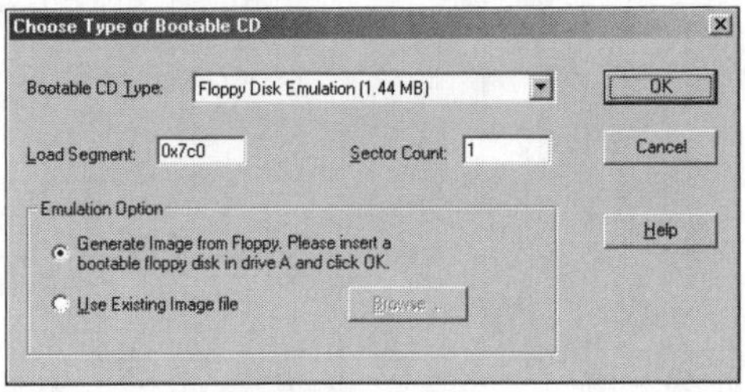

Figure 15.12
Adding the contents
of a bootable floppy
to the CD layout.

There are four different types to choose from:

— **Floppy Disk emulation (1.44MB)**—forces the bootable CD to emulate a 1.44MB bootable floppy.

— **Floppy Disk emulation (2.88MB)**—forces the bootable CD to emulate a 2.88MB bootable floppy.

— **Hard Disk emulation**—allows you to create a 'full size' CD with as many installers and additional data as you need. You'll need to have a suitable bootable image file available to write to the CD; you can use a floppy image if you wish.

— **No Emulation**—Don't emulate a floppy or hard drive.

If you want to use an existing image, click on the Browse button to find the bootable image file. Don't adjust any of the other parameters—you shouldn't need to change these figures.

5. If you've opted to emulate a floppy disk, you'll be prompted (see Figure 15.13) to insert the bootable floppy disk that you just created into the floppy drive. Insert the disk and click OK. Roxio Easy CD Creator will copy the bootable information from the floppy disk and store it within two files, BOOTCAT.BIN and BOOTIMG.BIN within your final layout.

6. All you need to do now is add any further information, installers, applications, etc., that you may want to use on the bootable CD to the CD layout, just as you would for an ordinary data CD.

7. Once you are finished, click on the Record button to write the information to CD.

8. Once the CD has been written, you will need to configure your machine so that it can boot up from the CD in preference to the floppy drive or the hard drive. To do this, you will need to configure your BIOS, which you usually do by pressing a key (F2 or delete) during the startup process when you first turn the machine on. See Figure 15.13 for an example—in this case, we need to press F2.

Figure 15.13
Dropping into the
BIOS from the main
BIOS boot screen.

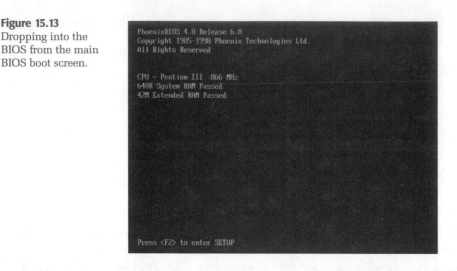

Once there, change to the boot options page or the BIOS Features page using the on-screen menus. You'll need to change the priority with which the BIOS searches for a bootable disc and operating system. The default is normally to boot from the hard disk or from the floppy if one has been inserted into the drive. Change the priority so that the CD-ROM is either first, or immediately after, the floppy drive. You can see in Figure 15.14 that I've configured the CD-ROM drive to priority over floppy and hard disk devices.

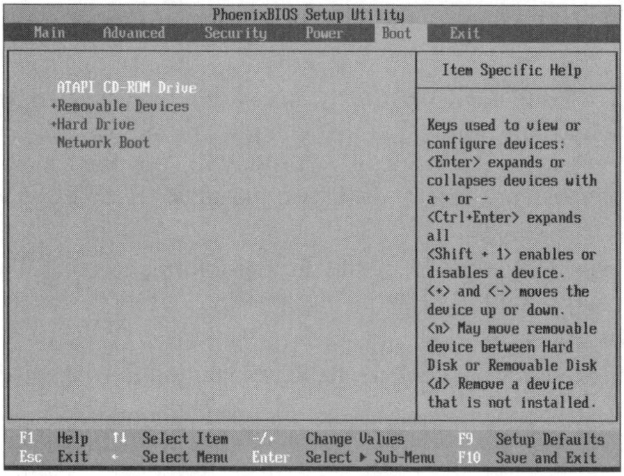

Figure 15.14
Setting the BIOS for
booting from CD.

To boot from the CD, insert the CD before a restart or during the BIOS startup and then wait while the system searches for a bootable device. If it doesn't boot up from your CD, something went wrong and you'll need to check the CD.

Solving Problems with Disc Images

Disc images can solve a few problems that you may experience when writing CDs. When you create a disc image, what you produce is a single file that consists of the files you want to copy to CD, all in one big file. The file is therefore just a copy of the CD, but because it's all in one file, you don't suffer the same fragmentation or file-reading problems normally experienced on slower machines or machines with very fast CD-R drives.

You can also create an image to be used for duplication, or you can create an image on a machine that does not have a CD-R/RW drive attached—you can then copy it over a network, or with a Jaz drive, to a machine that does have a drive or connect a FireWire, USB, or parallel drive to the machine when you want to write the CD.

To create a disc image:

1. Build your CD as normal using the instructions earlier in this chapter.
2. Choose File > Create CD Hard Disk Image. You'll be prompted with a normal file dialog box, as shown in Figure 15.15.

Figure 15.15
Choosing the location where you want to save a disc image.

3. Find the directory in which you want to save the image—you'll need about 700 MB to store an entire disc—and give the file a name.
4. Click Save. Easy CD Creator will go through the normal recording process, but it will write the information into the image file.

To write a CD from an existing disc image:

1. Open Easy CD Creator.
2. Choose File > Record CD from CD Image.
3. You'll be prompted with a standard Open file dialog box; find the file you want to choose and click Open.
4. Once the image has been identified and the information read from the image, you'll be prompted with the normal CD Creation Setup dialog box, shown in Figure 15.16. Note that you cannot leave a CD open when writing an image.

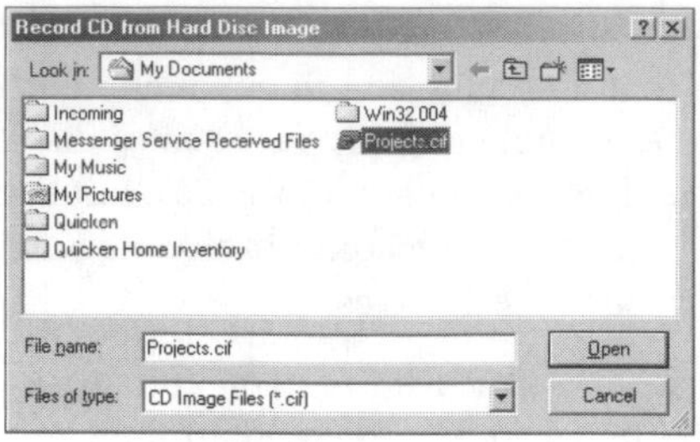

Figure 15.16
Selecting an existing
Easy CD Creator Image
for writing to CD.

5.   Insert a blank disc and click OK.

Setting CD Properties

You can control the format and properties of each CD you create by right-clicking on the main
CD icon and choosing Properties. The CD Project Properties window can be seen in Figure
15.17, showing the General panel.

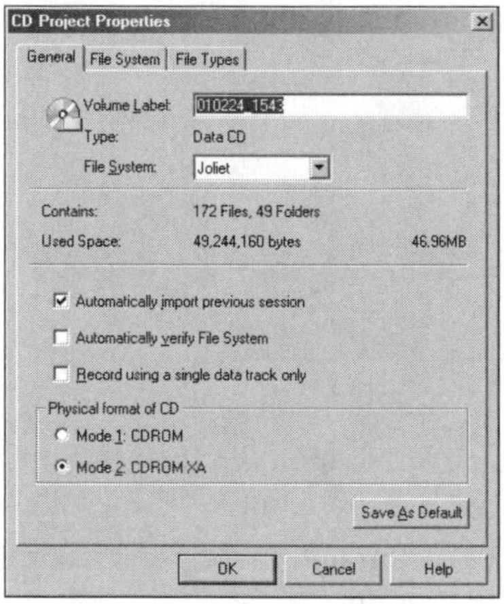

Figure 15.17
Changing the
general options.

On this page, you can control:

▶   **Volume Label**—The name of the CD once it has been created; the default is the date
and time the CD project was created.

▶   **File System**—Either Joliet, for a standard Windows CD, or ISO9660 for an ISO-
compatible CD. This option is disabled for audio CDs.

▶   **Automatically import previous session**—Automatically loads the information about
the previous session if you are creating a multisession disc.

▶   **Automatically verify File System**—By checking this option, the CD will be compared
against the original files to make sure that the information was written properly.

▶   **Record using a single data track only**—This guarantees that the CD will be written
using one continuous track, important if you are creating a CD that will be used as
the master for duplication.

Section IV CD Writing Software

▶ **Mode 1/Mode 2**—Choose Mode 1 for a more compatible CD, but Mode 2 if you want to create a multisession CD or CD Extra CD-ROM.

The File System tab (shown in Figure 15.18) controls the catalog information added to the disc and how the dates on the CD are set.

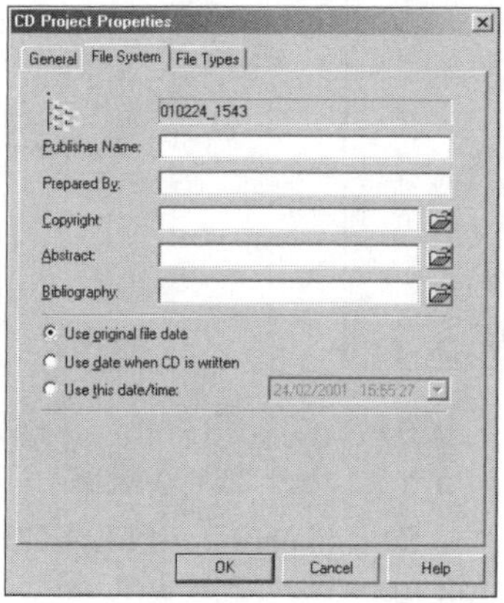

Figure 15.18
Changing the file
system options.

The options you can configure are:

▶ **Publisher Name**—Enter your name or your organization's name, up to 128 characters (optional).

▶ **Prepared By**—Enter the name of the disc creator—usually your name (optional).

▶ **Copyright**—Enter the copyright text for the material on the disc or select the name of the file that contains your copyright statement (optional).

▶ **Abstract**—Enter the content description for the disc or select the name of the file that contains the information (optional).

▶ **Bibliography**—Enter the bibliographical reference or select the name of the file that contains that information (optional).

▶ **Date/Time Stamp**—Select the date and time that you want to apply to each file. Using the original file date is probably the best option, but you can also set the date of each file to the date the CD was written or to a specific date.

Finally, you can also filter the types of files written to the disc. You can use this to ensure that all the space on the disc is taken up with files you need and not with backup files, temporary files, and, in some cases, application and system files. To control the operation of which file types are added:

▶ **Add all files/Excluding file types**—These two radio buttons allow you to select which files to add by their file extension. Selecting Add all Files will obviously disable any filtering system. If you select Do not add files of the following Types, then you need to type the file extensions you want to exclude from the CD in the box below the option. You can see in Figure 15.19 that I've filtered files with the extensions BAK, TMP, EXE, DLL, and COM, which excludes most application files and temporary or backup files.

Figure 15.19
Excluding file types
from a CD.

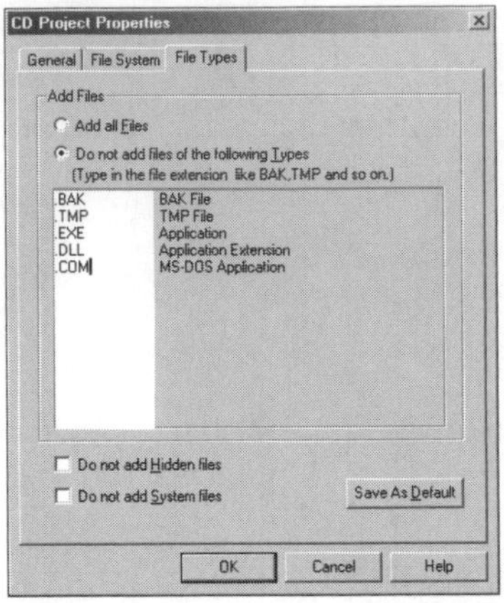

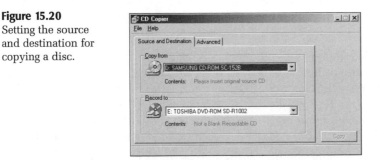

> ► **Do not add Hidden files**—Check this field if you want Easy CD Creator to ignore hidden files of any type or extension from the CD it writes.

> ► **Do not add System files**—Check this field if you want Easy CD Creator to ignore any system files of any type or extension from the CD it writes.

Once you've configured all the options, click OK to save the changes.

Copying a Disc with CD Copier

If you want to create a duplicate of an existing CD, perhaps for backup purposes or because you need to duplicate a number of CDs for further duplication (see Chapter 13), you should use CD Copier. You could use Easy CD Creator, but you cannot rely on the speed of the source CD to ensure a good writing process, and you may end up creating a large number of coasters!

To use CD Copier:

1. Insert the CD that you want to copy into your CD-ROM drive.

2. Open the Easy CD Creator Project Selector and then click on the CD Copier button to open CD Copier.

3. You'll be prompted with a window like the one shown in Figure 15.20. Choose the source CD-ROM drive that will contain your original and the CD-R/RW drive that you want to use.

Figure 15.20
Setting the source
and destination for
copying a disc.

4. Insert a blank CD.

5. Click on the Advanced tab (shown in Figure 15.21) and select or set any of the available options. From here, you can control the record speed, the number of copies, whether to test the speed, test and then copy or simply copy the CD, and whether to use disc-at-once mode (recommended). You can also opt to copy the disc to your hard drive first. This may be a more reliable method of writing a CD if you have a slow CD-ROM drive or if your CD-R/RW drive is the only CD drive you have in your machine. If your drive supports it, you can also enable the Buffer Underrun Prevention to avoid creating too many coasters!

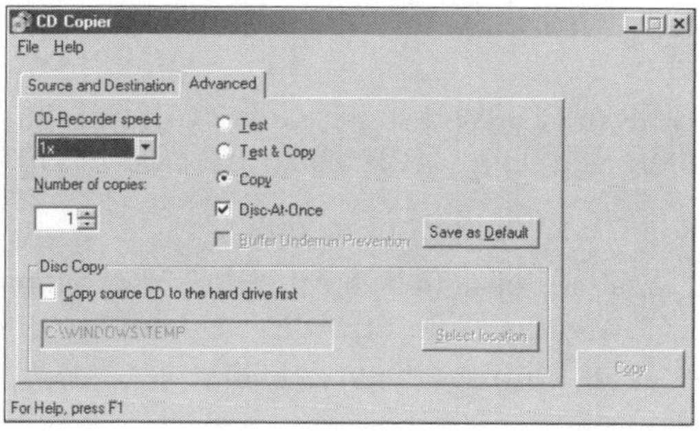

Figure 15.21
Setting the advanced options when copying a CD.

6. Click back to the Source and Destination tab and click the Copy button. CD Copier will now copy across the files, using your hard disk if you asked it to, from the source CD to the CD-R/RW drive.

Using directCD

The traditional method of writing CDs—collecting together the files and then writing them all to the CD in one go—is a time-consuming and, to many people, counter-intuitive task. Most people expect to put a CD into their drive and start copying files straight over to the CD just as they would with any other type of removable media. Until recently, this wasn't possible, but modern CD-R/RW drives support packet writing and UDF (universal disc format), which with suitable software enables you to do exactly what I've just described.

directCD, which comes as part of the Easy CD Creator package, supports packet-writing CDs and allows you to copy files as easily as dragging and dropping them. Better still, when combined with a CD-RW drive and media, you have access to a real 650 MB removable disc on which you can continually change the contents, while always having a reliable copy of the information.

The advantages of directCD are:

▶ **Easy to use**—You just copy the files you want to CD as with any other file.

▶ **Quick**—There is no special preparation involved, so using directCD is usually quicker than Easy CD Creator.

▶ **Fool-proof**—If you are using CD-R, then using directCD is a great way of keeping a permanent, unmodifiable version of a file or project. An automatic archive!

▶ **Makes CD-RW a proper removable storage solution.**

There are some disadvantages, however:

▶ **Format**—You are limited to creating Windows CDs. directCD does not allow you to easily choose the format. Although ISO9660 mode is possible, you cannot use directCD for recording audio CDs.

▶ **You can't change your mind**—With CD-R, once you've copied the files over, they are on the CD. Although you can delete them, it only removes their catalog entries on the final disc; you can't reclaim the space.

We'll have a look at the different ways of using directCD in this section.

Formatting the Disc

Before you start to write to a CD-R or CD-RW disc with directCD, you must format it, in much the same way that you would format a floppy disk. To format a new CD:

1. Load a blank CD-R or CD-RW into your recorder.

2. Open the Easy CD Creator Project Selector if it does not automatically open for you. Select make a data CD and then select the directCD button. directCD should display format utility window, as shown in Figure 15.22.

Figure 15.22
Formatting a new disc with directCD.

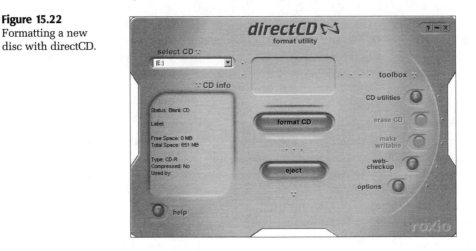

3. Click on the Format button to start the formatting process. You'll be prompted with another window shown in Figure 15.23. Here you can name the disc and enable compression. The name can be up to eleven characters and display in windows and file selection dialogs, just like any other disc. Use compression only if you are willing to sacrifice some level of compatibility—discs that are formatted with compression enabled can be read only on machines that have Roxio Easy CD Creator installed or those that have the UDF Reader application installed. The formatting operation of directCD will automatically copy the USD Reader application to the disc in uncompressed form so that it can be installed on other machines to allow them to read the compressed portion.

Figure 15.23
Naming your new
directCD CD.

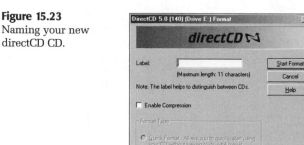

4.   Once you've named the CD and decided whether you want to enable compression, click Start Format and directCD will format the disc. The process takes less than a minute.

5.   Once the CD has been formatted, you'll get a CD Ready window like the one shown in Figure 15.24.

Figure 15.24
directCD, showing
the CD Ready
dialog box.

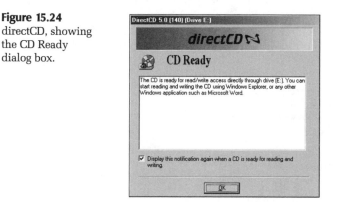

Your disc is now ready to use.

Note that you cannot eject the disc as you would any other CD-ROM—you *must* eject the CD using directCD. You can check the status of the disc by moving the mouse over the directCD icon in the system tray—you'll get a message stating that the CD has been locked. While a directCD CD-R/RW is loaded in the drive and ready to be written to, a small red lock appears over the directCD icon.

Copying Files to the Disc

Although the disc appears in My Computer just the same as any other disc (see Figure 15.25), the disc you have just inserted is not read-only. You can copy files to the disc just as if it were a floppy.

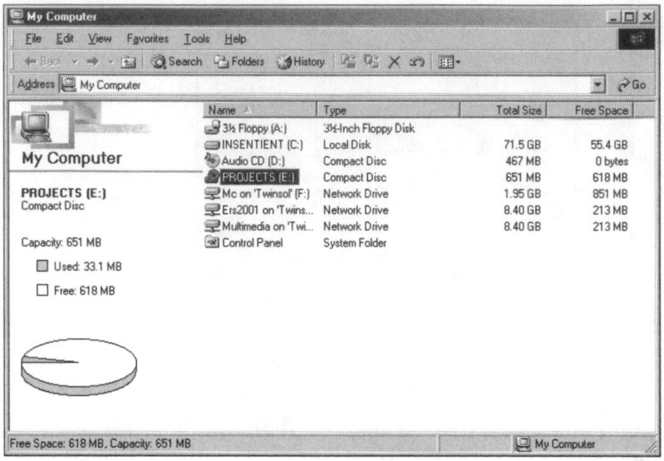

Figure 15.25
The new CD as it
appears in My
Computer.

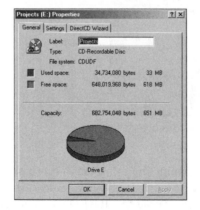

Before you start copying information to the disc, it's a good idea to first check the free space on
the disc. There are a number of ways you can do this, but the best way is to select the CD in
the My Computer window. If you are in icon view, a quick overview of the capacity and
amount of disc used and free is shown in the window in the left-hand panel, shown in Figure
15.25. For a more detailed breakdown, right-click on the disc's icon and select Properties from
the popup menu or press Alt-Return. You'll get a properties window like the one shown in
Figure 15.26.

Figure 15.26
Getting more
information on
the capacity of a
directCD disc.

Finally, for a more detailed view, especially on discs that have compression enabled, you'll need
to open directCD. When a formatted disc is inserted into the drive, directCD gives extended
information about the space on the disc. You can see an example here in Figure 15.27.

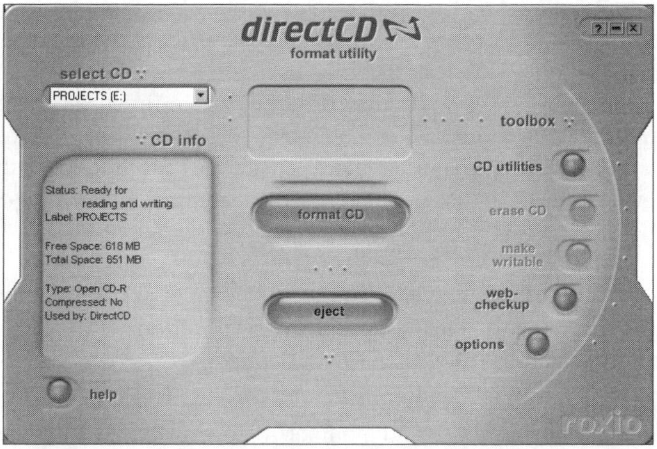

Figure 15.27
Using directCD
to get further CD
information.

NOTE

If you check the spare space on the disc, you'll notice that a significant amount of space has already been used on your CD—typically 40 MB. The information is not a mistake—the 40 MB is reserved for recording information about the file system and the files you copy to the disc. Depending on how many files are copied to the disc, you may be able to reclaim some of the space on the disk, but not all.

Once you have verified that there is space on the disc for you to use, you can just start adding files to it. You can drag and drop files to the disc and you can even save files direct to the CD from within an application. directCD will handle all of the communication with the drive and how to update the table of contents and other information.

Ejecting the Disc

As I said earlier, you cannot simply eject the CD, put the disc into another machine, and start using it. The reason for this is that the disc has not been properly closed. To eject and close the disc so that it can be used in other machines, you must eject the disc through directCD. However, there are three modes in which you can leave the disc once it has been ejected:

▶ **Leave As Is**—This will allow you to eject the disc so that it can be added to and re-used later, but you will be unable to use the disc in another machine. Use this method if you are using directCD as a way to incrementally append information to the disc, without needing to read the information until the disc has been written.

▶ **Close to UDF v1.5**—This closes the disc so that it can be used on machines which have had the UDF v1.5 Reader driver installed on them. If the drivers have not been installed, then the CD will be unreadable.

Close to Read on Any Computer—This mode closes the current session so that the disc can be read in most other machines and drives. Use this method if you want to read the information on another machine or if you have completed writing information to CD. The process takes a while, as directCD has to finish setting up the CD. Although this method makes the disc readable by another machine, it does not "close" the disc so that it cannot be appended later. You get the option to force the "close" operation, however, so that the disc cannot be used again (unless it's a CD-RW).

To eject the disc with directCD:

1. Right-click on the directCD icon in the system tray and select Eject from the pop-up menu. Alternatively, you can press the eject button on the CD drive, or click on the eject button within the directCD application.

2. You'll get a window like the one shown in Figure 15.28. Select the type of eject operation you want to use, remembering to check the Protect box if you want the CD to be closed so that other files cannot be added to the disc later.

Figure 15.28
directCD asking
you to confirm your
ejection request.

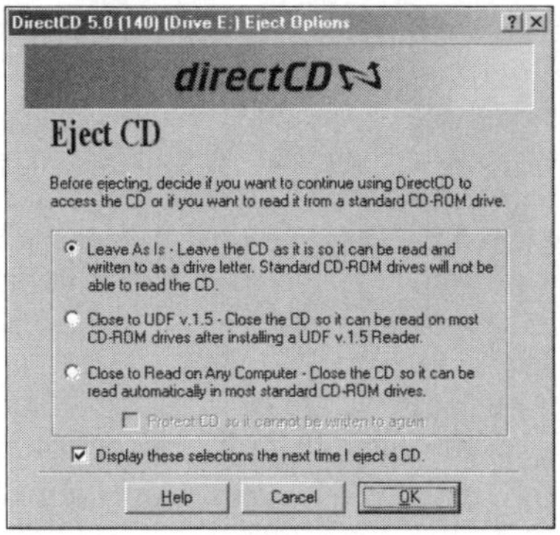

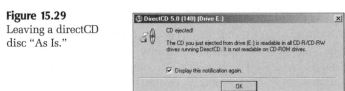

3. Click Finish to complete the operation and eject the disc. If you decided to leave the disc as is so that you can add more information to it later, you'll be prompted with the dialog shown in Figure 15.29. If you decided that you wanted to add more information to the disc later, then the fixing process will take place, with a progress bar to indicate how long it will take. Once completed, you'll get a message like the one shown in Figure 15.30.

Figure 15.29
Leaving a directCD
disc "As Is."

Figure 15.30
Fixing the CD with
directCD.

Adding More Files

To add more files to a CD that you have ejected, all you need to do is put the CD back in.
Providing you ejected the CD in "Leave As Is" mode, you can start to use the disc again, copying
files and saving documents just as you did the first time you inserted the CD.

If you chose "Organize" and left the disc open, directCD will update the table of contents and
allow you to add new files. This process will take slightly longer than the normal copying
process, as it has to update the contents each time, instead of just picking up where you left off.

Deleting Files

To delete files from a CD-R or CD-RW, all you need to do is select the files in Windows Explorer
and press the Delete key. You'll be asked to confirm that you want to delete the files you have
selected.

Depending on which type of disc you are using, the effects of the process will change:

▶ **CD-R**—If you delete files from a CD-R with directCD, what happens is that the
   directory entries for the files are removed, but the actual files and the blocks they use
   up on the disc remain. Unfortunately, although the files will disappear, they will still
   use up space on the disc—there is no way to reclaim the lost space. Be aware that
   this method also allows experienced users to read the information from the disc, even
   though the directory entries no longer exist, which makes this option very dangerous
   from a security point of view if you are worried about the content of your CDs.

▶ **CD-RW**—Because a CD-RW disc is rewritable, directCD takes full advantage of the
   fact and deletes the files and the blocks they are using. Unlike CD-R, this means that
   you reclaim the space that was being used by the files, and there is no penalty for
   copying files to the CD with directCD.

Setting directCD Options

The options button in the main directCD panel allows you to control certain properties of the
directCD process and operation. You can see an example of the panel in Figure 15.31, and an
explanation of each of these items is given below.

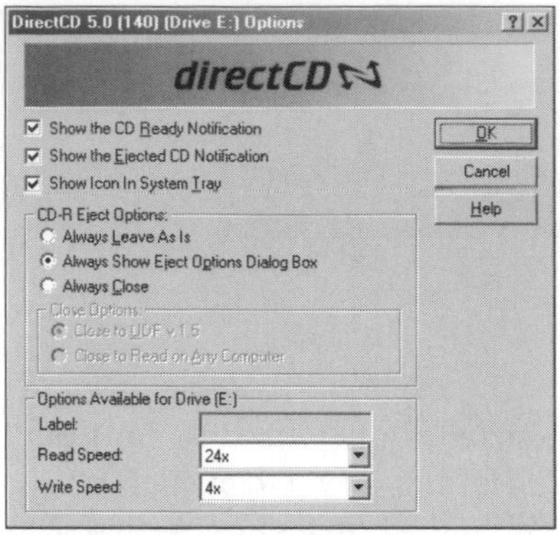

Figure 15.31
Configuring the
directCD Wizard.

▶ **Show the CD Ready Notification**—Forces directCD to show the Disc Ready window
when a disc is ready to be used, either after formatting or when inserting a
previously opened disc.

▶ **Show the Ejected CD Notification**—You always want to have an information window
shown after a CD has been ejected.

▶ **Show Icon in System Tray**—Displays a quick-link icon in the system tray to allow
you to open directCD and set options.

▶ **CD-R Eject Options**—Here you can control what happens when you choose to eject a
CD. You can choose that the CD is automatically left "as is"—you would have to use
the directCD application to close the CD. Alternatively, you can force the CD to
automatically be closed, either for reading on a computer with the UDF Reader
installed or suitable for any machine. This is useful if you want to use directCD as an
alternative to the Easy CD Creator application. Alternatively, you can be prompted to
choose the method to use when you decide to eject the CD.

▶ **Options Available for Drive**—You can use this section of the window to choose the
speeds at which to read and write information to and from the CD.

16

Unix/Linux Tools

Under Unix and Linux, we have a slightly different set of issues surrounding CD writing compared to Macs and Windows. The primary consideration is the interface. Unix is not an operating system that was designed with a GUI in mind. In fact, the best CD-recording tool on the market—**cdrecord**—is a command-line tool. The **cdrecord** tool is a professionally written piece of software and it can do everything that either Toast or Easy CD Creator can manage. It's also compatible with different versions of Unix. I have **cdrecord** running on my Intel-based Linux box and an Intel-based Solaris box, and it should work fine on BSD and other OEM Unix flavors without a problem. Although **cdrecord** is command-line based, there are a number of GUI interfaces that sit on top of **cdrecord** and allow you to select and produce CDs using a similar interface to that offered under Mac OS and Windows. What's really good, though, is that because there are so many interfaces, if you don't like one, you can change to another without losing any of the functionality of the core tool. Furthermore, the accessibility of these front-end tools is far more flexible than either Mac OS or Windows—you can even write a CD on a remote machine by controlling the drive through a Web interface!

In this chapter, we're going to look at **cdrecord** and some of the interfaces available for it, including details of how to build and compile the tools before using them to write your CDs.

Obtaining and Compiling Unix/Linux Tools

Your best resource for obtaining just about any Unix tool is to visit **www.freshmeat.net**. The site contains links to nearly all of the Linux software that is out there, from freeware and shareware to demo and even commercial products. All the links and information you should need are there. You can see the main freshmeat.net page in Figure 16.1.

Figure 16.1
The Freshmeat
Web site.

Most tools on freshmeat.net are supplied in their source form, which means you'll need a compiler, the **make** utility and probably **gzip** or **bzip2** to decompress the package to your machine. The best option for a compiler is **gcc**—the GNU C compiler—which comes as standard with Linux. Alternatively, if you are on a commercial system, then the standard **cc** compiler that comes with your OS should be fine.

TIP

Most Solaris installations come with Forte, but if your Solaris installation doesn't come with a C compiler, visit **www.sunfreeware.com**, which supplies the GNU compiler in Solaris package format. Most other Unix variants, including Linux, will come with GNU C.

Once you've found the piece of software that you're looking for, it needs to be compiled and then installed—but the process is not quite as manual as it sounds. In fact, the process for extracting, compiling, and installing the tool is usually just a case of a few steps:

1. Extract the sources—the following should work:

    $ gunzip -c package.tar.gz | tar xf -

    Just remember to change **package.tar.gz** for the files that you've downloaded. If the package ends in **.bz2,** then it's a **bzip2** file and you need to use:

    $ bunzip2 -c package.tar.bz2 | tar xf -

2. Change to the newly created directory:

    $ cd package

    The package will probably be a combination of the package name and its version number—use **ls** to determine the final directory name if you're not sure.

3. Run **configure**—This goes through and checks your system to determine whether you have everything required to build the software in question. The process can be quite time-consuming and could take anywhere from thirty seconds to ten minutes to complete. You can usually simply get away with:

    $ ./configure

    But check the **INSTALL** or **README** files to determine if there are any command-line options you might need to add. Note that if any errors are reported during this process, you will need to check why they occurred—it might be a library that's missing, in which case you'll need to install that first, or it might simply be a warning that something is missing and can usually be ignored.

4. Run **make**—This actually compiles and builds the application for you. Again, you can normally get away with:

    $ make

    You should watch your screen during this process, as **make** may report problems. These should have been picked up by the **configure** script, but it won't always be the case.

5. Run **make test**—Assuming that the compilation process has completed successfully, this will test that the application works and does what it should:

    $ make test

    Don't worry if you get an error such as "no such target" or "no rule to make target test"—this just means that the package doesn't include its own testing routine, not that the build process has failed.

6. Run **make install**—This installs the application into its final location, ready for you to use it:

    $ make install

Once this final stage has been completed, the package has been installed and is ready for you to use. The default installation location is usually /usr/local/bin—make sure that the path into which the package was installed is added to the **PATH** environment variable in your **.profile**.

Installing cdrecord

The main tool you will need for recording CDs under Unix is, as we already know, **cdrecord**. The main application includes a special driver that enables **cdrecord** to talk to most CD-R drives, whether they use IDE/ATAPI, parallel port, or SCSI as their connection method. You should be able to follow the instructions above for building and installing **cdrecord**; it doesn't really have any surprises. But be warned that it will take a long time to compile—even on a fairly fast system, it will take ten minutes to compile all the files necessary for the core application.

The latest stable version available at the time of writing is version 1.9, although a new version is under development, with the latest developmental release being 1.10a07, released in November 2000. New updates and fixes were being released almost weekly. Support in all versions above 1.8 includes Linux, SunOS (4.x), Solaris, AIX, HP-UX, SGI IRIX, Net/Free/OpenBSD, OSF-1, NeXTstep, Mac OS X, BeOS, VMS, and also Windows 95/98/Me/2000 and NT 3.5 and 4.0.

I've personally tried the software under Solaris, Linux, and Windows 98 and not had any problems with the results. For more information on **cdrecord**, visit **www.fokus.gmd.de/research/cc/glone/ employees/joerg.schilling/private/cdrecord.html**.

TIP

If you are using Solaris 8, check the Software Companion CD—**cdrecord** is one of the applications that can be installed in its precompiled form without you having to manually build the software. Although it may not be the most recent version, it will be enough to get you started.

Installing a cdrecord Front End

Remember, **cdrecord** is classed as a CD-R burn engine—its sole purpose is to provide the core methods required for writing CDs, and although it can be used directly for creating a CD, you'll probably want a front end to help you control all of the features.

Most of the front ends available rely either on the **Tk** or **gtk** interface toolkits. You can download **Tk** from **www.scriptics.com**—the latest version at the time of writing was 8.3.2, but most packages will be fine with the 8.0.5 version. You will need to install both **Tcl** and **Tk** and also build and compile them in that order. For **gtk,** you'll need to install the **glib** and **gtk** libraries, again in that order. The latest official version at the time of writing was 1.2.8, although a new 1.3 release was already in development. You can download **gtk** from **www.gtk.org**.

Whichever front end you choose, you will need to check the **INSTALL** and/or **README** file to get precise installation instructions. The CDR Toaster application, for example, uses the **wish** shell installed with **Tk;** others may need to be compiled and built just like **cdrecord** itself.

Using cdrecord

Because **cdrecord** is a command-line tool, its configuration and use is done through a set of command-line switches when you invoke the program. You can get a list of all the options to **cdrecord** if you just execute the command without any command line options:

```
$ cdrecord
cdrecord: No CD/DVD-Recorder device specified.
cdrecord: Usage: cdrecord [options] track1...trackn
Options:
-version        print version information and exit
-v              increment general verbose level by one
-V              increment SCSI command transport verbose level by one
-debug          print additional debug messages
dev=target      SCSI target to use as CD/DVD-Recorder
timeout=#       set the default SCSI command timeout to #.
driver=name     user supplied driver name, use with extreme care
driveropts=opt  a comma separated list of driver specific options
-checkdrive     check if a driver for the drive is present
-prcap          print drive capabilities for MMC compliant drives
-inq            do an inquiry for the drive end exit
-scanbus        scan the SCSI bus end exit
```

-reset	reset the SCSI bus with the cdrecorder (if possible)
-ignsize	ignore the known size of a medium (may cause problems)
-useinfo	use *.inf files to overwrite audio options.
speed=#	set speed of drive
blank=type	blank a CD-RW disc (see blank=help)
fs=#	Set fifo size to # (0 to disable, default is 4 MB)
-load	load the disk and exit (works only with tray loader)
-eject	eject the disk after doing the work
-dummy	do everything with laser turned off
-msinfo	retrieve multi-session info for mkisofs >= 1.10
-toc	retrieve and print TOC/PMA data
-atip	retrieve and print ATIP data
-multi	generate a TOC that allows multi sessions
	In this case, default track type is CD-ROM XA2
-fix	fixate a corrupt or unfixated disk (generate a TOC)
-nofix	do not fixate disk after writing tracks
-waiti	wait until input is available before opening SCSI
-force	force to continue on some errors to allow blanking bad disks
-dao	Write disk in DAO mode. Option will be replaced in the future.
tsize=#	Length of valid data in next track
padsize=#	Amount of padding for next track
pregap=#	Amount of pre-gap sectors before next track
defpregap=#	Amount of pre-gap sectors for all but track #1
mcn=text	Set the media catalog number for this CD to "text"
isrc=text	Set the ISRC number for the next track to "text"
index=list	Set the index list for the next track to "list"
-audio	Subsequent tracks are CD-DA audio tracks
-data	Subsequent tracks are CD-ROM data mode 1 (default)
-mode2	Subsequent tracks are CD-ROM data mode 2
-xa1	Subsequent tracks are CD-ROM XA mode 1
-xa2	Subsequent tracks are CD-ROM XA mode 2
-cdi	Subsequent tracks are CDI tracks
-isosize	Use ISO9660 file system size for next data track
-preemp	Audio tracks are mastered with 50/15 µs pre-emphasis
-nopreemp	Audio tracks are mastered with no pre-emphasis (default)
-pad	Pad data tracks with 15 zeroed sectors
	Pad audio tracks to a multiple of 2,352 bytes
-nopad	Do not pad data tracks (default)
-shorttrack	Subsequent tracks may be nonRed Book < 4 seconds if in DAO mode
-noshorttrack	Subsequent tracks must be >= 4 seconds
-swab	Audio data source is byte-swapped (little-endian/Intel)

The type of the first track is used for the TOC type.
Currently, only form 1 tracks are supported.

You can see from this quite voluminous list that the configuration options available to you are quite complex, and this is just one reason why most people use a front end, such as CDR Toaster, to control the operation of cdrecord. The front ends take the complexity out of using cdrecord directly and avoid the need to write commands that could easily be two or three lines long if typed manually.

That's not to say that **cdrecord** cannot be used from the command line in some situations. Because of the complexity, we won't be covering the process in detail in this book—instead we'll use one of the many interfaces available.

Selecting the Right Drive

Before you start to use **cdrecord**, you must determine the address to use for your CD-R drive. Although there are many different systems for determining your drive, many of which differ from machine to machine and OS to OS, **cdrecord** supports its own very simple system. First, run **cdrecord** with the **-scanbus** command line option. This will list the compatible devices installed in your system and whatever device chain (SCSI or IDE) they are connected to. You can use this information to identify your CD-R device:

```
$ cdrecord -scanbus
Cdrecord 1.10a05 (i686-pc-linux-gnu) Copyright © 1995-2000 Jörg Schilling
Linux sg driver version: 2.1.36
Using libscg version 'schily-0.4'
scsibus0:
        0,0,0    0) 'IBM     ' 'DNES-309170    ' 'SA30' Disk
        0,1,0    1) 'IBM     ' 'DNES-309170    ' 'SA30' Disk
        0,2,0    2) *
        0,3,0    3) *
        0,4,0    4) *
        0,5,0    5) 'PLEXTOR ' 'CD-R   PX-R820T ' '1.03' Removable CD-ROM
        0,6,0    6) 'OnStream' 'SC-30          ' '1.06' Removable Tape
        0,7,0    7) *
```

The appropriate device in this case is the PLEXTOR CD-R drive. The leading three digits to each line give the reference number that we can use to tell **cdrecord** which drive to employ. This saves us from determining the device information manually. In this case, our Plextor drive is device 0,5,0, which we can use both with **cdrecord** and in applications like CDR Toaster that use **cdrecord** to do the recording for them.

Writing a CD with cdrecord

Despite the fact that it's possible, I don't remotely suggest using **cdrecord** as the method for creating a CD. Most people use **cdrecord** in combination with the **mkisofs** utility, which generates a data disc on the fly. For example, the following command-line would create a Joliet-compatible disc:

```
$ mkisofs -joliet /usr/local/cd | cdrecord -v -eject dev=0,5,0 speed=8 -data -
```

This generates the output shown below, charting the progress of the writing process:

```
Disk type: Long strategy type (Cyanine, AZO or similar)
Manuf. index: 25
Manufacturer: Taiyo Yuden Company Limited
cdrecord: WARNING: Track size unknown. Data may not fit on disk.
Starting to write CD/DVD at speed 8 in write mode for single session.
Last chance to quit, starting real write in 1 seconds.
Waiting for reader process to fill input buffer ... input buffer ready.
Performing OPC...
Starting new track at sector: 0
Track 01:   5 MB written (fifo 100%).  1.58% done, estimate finish Mon Nov 20 19:18:02 2000
Track 01:  15 MB written (fifo 100%).  3.15% done, estimate finish Mon Nov 20 19:11:41 2000
Track 01:  25 MB written (fifo  98%).  4.72% done, estimate finish Mon Nov 20 19:09:13 2000
...
Track 01: 591 MB written (fifo 100%). 95.97% done, estimate finish Mon Nov 20 19
```

```
:04:52 2000
Track 01: 601 MB written (fifo 100%). 97.54% done, estimate finish Mon Nov 20 19
:04:52 2000
Track 01: 611 MB written (fifo 100%). 99.11% done, estimate finish Mon Nov 20 19
:04:51 2000
Track 01: 616 MB written (fifo  98%).Total translation table size: 0
Total rockridge attributes bytes: 0
Total directory bytes: 0
Path table size(bytes): 10
Max brk space used 67e4
317824 extents written (620 Mb)
Track 01: 620 MB written (fifo 100%).
Track 01: Total bytes read/written: 650903552/650903552 (317824 sectors).
Writing  time:  541.742s
Fixating...
Fixating time:   34.256s
cdrecord: fifo had 10254 puts and 10254 gets.
cdrecord: fifo was 0 times empty and 6548 times full, min fill was 87%.
```

Instead of using **cdrecord** directly, use a front end—we use CDR Toaster throughout the rest of this chapter.

Using CDR Toaster

CDR Toaster is probably my favorite interface to the **cdrecord** utility, mostly because of its very clean interface and design. It's as easy and straightforward to use as either Easy CD Creator or Toast and, in some cases, actually easier to use than either tool. CDR Toaster is built around a single window that provides all of the information, direction, and structure required to build a CD. You can see the window in Figure 16.2.

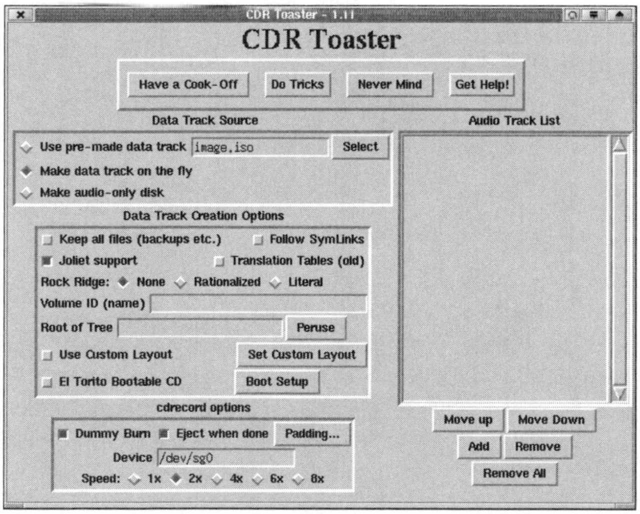

Figure 16.2
The CDR Toaster
interface to cdrecord.

The window is split into five sections. The top panel (shown in Figure 16.2) contains the buttons and popups that control the operation of the **cdrecord** tool. For example, **Have a Cook-Off** actually writes the CD, while **Do Tricks** is a popup button set that allows you to read existing CDs and CD-ROMs for copying and audio production, as well as blanking a CD-RW disc.

The Data Track Source panel (Figure 16.3) controls the source and destination format, allowing you to use an image, a data disc, or an audio disc. The Data Track Creation Options panel (Figure 16.4) controls the specifics of the writing process, including picking the location of the directories and files and whether to follow symbolic links. It even supports the ability to create a bootable CD.

Figure 16.3 (left)
The Data Track Source panel in CDR Toaster.

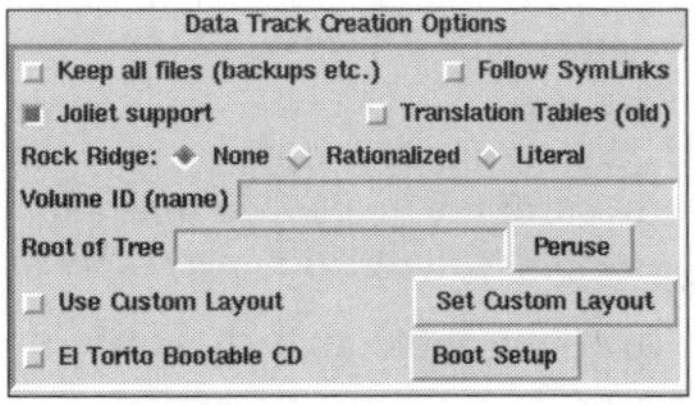

Figure 16.4 (right)
The Data Track Creation Options panel in CDR Toaster.

The cdrecord options panel (Figure 16.5) controls the process of actually writing the CD—selecting the correct device, specifying the writing speed, and whether padding should be used. Audio Track List (Figure 16.6), allows you to add and control the order of the audio tracks that you want to write to the CD.

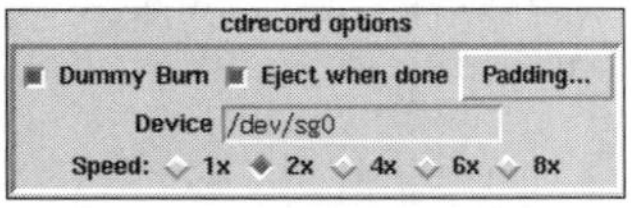

Figure 16.5
The cdrecord options panel in CDR Toaster.

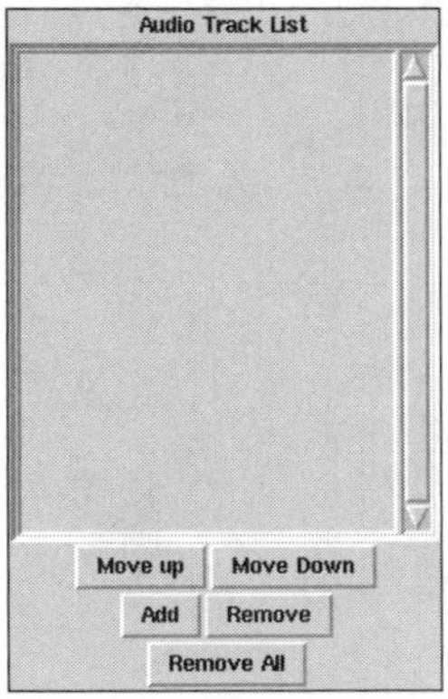

Figure 16.6
The Audio Track List panel in CDR Toaster.

Writing a Data CD with CDR Toaster

Writing a data CD with CDR Toaster could be easier:

1. Copy all the files and folders that you want to appear on the CD into a new directory. You can play with the layout and naming in this new directory—exactly what appears here will be written to CD.

> **TIP**
>
> If you are running short of space, create symbolic links to the directories and files you want on the CD and check the **Follow Symlinks** option.

2. Start CDR Toaster by typing **cdrtoaster** at a shell prompt while running X Windows.

3. Make sure **Make data track on the fly** is checked.

4. Click what type of file system support you want—Joliet support creates a Unix- and Windows-compatible CD; you can also add Rock Ridge extensions if you wish for better Unix support.

5. Click on the Peruse button and then use the dialog box seen in Figure 16.7 to find and select the directory into which you copied the files. Click on the Accept button when you have found and selected the directory.

Figure 16.7
Selecting the directory to use as the root source for data CDs n CDR Toaster.

6. Set the device address, the speed you want to write the CD, and whether you want to perform a dummy operation, which doesn't create the CD but just checks the speed.

7. Insert a blank CD into your drive.

8. Click **Have a Cook-off** to start the writing process.

CDR Toaster will now open a new **xterm** window, in which it will start **cdrecord** to begin the writing process. You can follow the output and progress using that **xterm** window.

Writing an Audio CD with CDR Toaster

You can write AIFF, WAV, and MP3 files to CD using CDR Toaster. Writing MP3s requires the **sox** toolkit, which you can download from Freshmeat and install according to the generic instructions above. Because the MP3 files need to be uncompressed, you need a disk with about 800 MB to hold the audio files for an entire 650 MB CD.

To record an audio CD with CDR Toaster:

1. Start CDR Toaster by typing **cdrtoaster** at a shell prompt while running X Windows.

2. Check the **Make audio-only disk** option.

3. Click the Add button underneath the Audio Track List—you'll be prompted to specify the location of an audio file explicitly—it's not a browsing window. Enter the path and then click OK.

4. Set the device name again in the Device box and set the speed at which you want to write the CD.

5. Click the **Have a Cook-off** button.

6. If you've selected MP3 files, you will be warned about the quality issue. If you've selected any type of audio file except a raw extracted audio file, you will be asked to select a directory in which the audio conversion can take place before it is written to CD. Select the directory to use, and click Accept.

Depending on the number of tracks, source format, and the speed of your machine, it will take some time to assemble the files before they are finally ready to be written to CD. It may take two or more times the normal period required to write a CD at the speed you have selected. You can monitor the progress using the **xterm** that is started by CDR Toaster during the writing process.

Copying a Disc with CDR Toaster

Copying an existing disc is a case of first making an image of the disc. Because the image that we create is a direct copy of the raw data on the disc, you can copy any type of disc, including audio and data discs. To create the image:

1. Start CDR Toaster by typing **cdrtoaster** at a shell prompt while running X Windows.

2. Choose Do Tricks > Read CDROM to create ISO image—you'll be prompted with a dialog box, shown here in Figure 16.8.

Figure 16.8
Saving a CD-ROM to
a disk image.

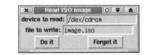

3. Enter the name of the device to use as the source—this will be /dev/cdrom for the first CD-ROM drive in your machine, and /dev/cdrom#, with # being the number of the next CD-ROM drive.

4. Enter a name to use to store the image that will be created.

Once the image has been read and saved to a file, you'll want to write the image back:

1. Start CDR Toaster by typing **cdrtoaster** at a shell prompt while running X Windows.

2. Click on the **Use pre-mode data track** button and then enter the name of the file you want to use. You can supply a full path, but it defaults to files in the current directory.

3. Check the device address, and the writing speed.

4. Click on the **Have a Cook-off** button and let **cdrecord** write the CD.

That's it—you should have copied the CD!

17

Video Production

One of the rapidly growing uses for computers in the home is video editing and production. Once the preserve of TV studios and expensive video editing companies, such editing can now be done easily and cheaply at home. As machines get faster and it becomes easier to connect and import video into your machine, it's a trend that's likely to continue.

The process behind editing a video on your computer is very straightforward:

- ▶ Import and convert the video into digital format
- ▶ Edit one or more digital video streams, adding voiceovers, music, and digital effects such as titling and transition between video segments
- ▶ Export the completed project into the desired format

The feature that makes video editing on your PC or Mac possible is the conversion (or transfer) of the video into its digital form. Just like the audio tricks you learned in Chapter 9, once you have information in digital format, you can do whatever you like with it. In the case of audio, it means cleaning it up, cropping the individual tracks, and, of course, converting it into different formats and using it to create new compilations. There are more things that you can do with digital audio, but none of them are relevant to CD recording.

With video, the options are more extensive. Once you have the video, you can make selections on specific frames and even alter the original sequence. You can also add audio background tracks for voiceovers or background music and digital effects such as fading shots between each other or "spinning" a shot into display, just as you would see on TV. For that final professional touch, you can also add titles to the video that are either static or that move across the screen like the credits at the end of a TV show.

Editing video on your machine requires a fairly fast computer (Pentium III or G3/G4 Mac) and some suitable software. In addition, you need to be able to import and export video information. Importing video relies either on a FireWire interface and a camera or media converter or an analog digitizer.

Exporting the final video is far more flexible. Most people output back to their camcorder or to a traditional videotape recorder. However, there's nothing to stop you from exporting the video either to CD, in the form of a video CD, or—by using the new DVD-R drives due on the market this spring—to DVD.

In this chapter, we're going to look quickly at two products that can be used to create videos that can be placed onto CD or DVD. The first is Apple's iMovie 2.0, a video-editing package that comes free with most Apple iMac, G3, G4, and PowerBook machines. The second is Ulead VideoStudio 5.0, which is a general-purpose video editing package that allows you to export the video into a number of formats, including that suitable for Video CD, Web publishing, and even DVD.

Video Sources

Both the packages that you will learn about in this chapter take input and import media from a number of different sources. There are two main video formats that you can use: DV camcorders and, of course, traditional analog video. However, there are times when you want to introduce other formats, and both programs allow you to insert digital stills (in the usual formats) and audio for voiceovers and background music.

DV Camcorders

The MiniDV video camera is a relatively recent invention, with most companies moving to the DV format by the start of 2000. Because the DV format is entirely digital, we can take raw DV video footage into VideoStudio, iMovie, or similar software without any need for conversion. All MiniDV camcorders come with a FireWire (or i.Link or IEEE1394) port to allow you to transfer the video signal from the tape within the camera to your machine. The iMac DV range and all other modern Apple Mac computers come with a FireWire port. On the PC, you will need to buy a FireWire card—you could purchase one for as little as $50 at the beginning of 2001.

FireWire is rapidly becoming the interconnect standard for both video and audio systems in the consumer world. It uses a very simple 3-pin cable, allows for transfer rates of 400 Mbps and can be used and connected to a wide range of devices. FireWire ports are now standard in many consumer products, allowing you to connect your DVD player, television and stereo system.

It may not be too long before you will be able to connect your DV camera to your FireWire-enabled DVD recorder and transfer your home videos straight to DVD. Until then, we have to use a computer—which also provides us with a solution for editing the video before it is written!

Traditional Video

Older camcorders (supporting the 8 millimeter, Hi-8, and VHS/VHS-C formats) and your household video recorder can also be used, but you will need either a media converter or an analog digitizer to get the video into a suitable format for editing on your PC or Mac.

Media converters translate the video signal from traditional video devices (via the S-VHS or composite connectors) and stereo audio into the DV format. Sony makes a suitable product called DVMC-A2 (priced at about $500), currently available only in the United States and supporting only the NTSC format. There are other products on the market, many of which share the same ability as the Sony product and its two-way conversion, allowing you to both take in and output the information in DV format for recording back to a standard video. Alternatively, many MiniDV camcorders come with the ability to record and, in some cases, convert information from an external composite or S-VHS source.

Analog digitizers used to be the only way of getting the older analog video format into your computer. The digitizer offers the video equivalent of the ADC built into most PC sound cards, basically digitizing each frame of the video signal into digital format and creating either a raw (uncompressed) video stream or, in the more expensive systems, by converting it into an MPEG-1 or -2 video stream. The problem with digitizers is that they can sometimes produce substandard results. This is not the fault of the manufacturers but has more to do with the high development and production cost of the equipment required compared to how much the average person is willing to pay. There are numerous products available, including the Belkin USB VideoBus II, which allows you to import digital information through your USB port. You can also find solutions that utilize both PCI cards and FireWire ports.

Video Formats

There are numerous video formats that you can distribute movies in once you have edited your video. Some of the different formats are listed below. One of the problems with home editing, aside from getting the video into your machine, has been dealing with the sheer volume of information in the first place. Uncompressed raw video runs at 15 MB per second—the average 20 GB hard disk could store only twenty-three minutes of video!

Such a high data rate would obviously be impossible to use in terms of Video CD, DVD, or over the Internet—in fact, your average DVD holds only six minutes of video at that rate. The solution is to compress the video information in some way to reduce its data rate and, therefore, the overall video stream size. There are many different video compression and raw video source formats, some of which are listed below.

MPEG

MPEG was developed by the Moving Picture Experts Group, a group of engineers that was given the task of creating a standard for delivering moving pictures in digital format. MPEG uses a number of different techniques, from recording only the changes between frames, to using a similar style of compression to that used on JPEG images. MPEG comes in a number of standards: MPEG-1 is used on Video CD and MPEG-2 is used on DVD (see below for more details on both formats). The MPEG format is generic and can be read both by home consumer equipment and by most OS platforms.

Until recently, generating an MPEG stream was a problem. Computers simply weren't fast enough to produce the MPEG video stream on their own and normally required special hardware. Modern computers can output MPEG at a more reasonable rate, but most machines are still limited to producing MPEG at less than real time. On my PIII 800 MHz PC, it took seventy-five seconds to create a thirty-one second video at DVD (PAL) quality. Scaling that up, a full hour of video would take about two-and-a-half hours to generate the required 2 GB file!

QuickTime

QuickTime was developed by Apple as a generic media API and framework for video and audio. It has gone through a number of revisions over the years, and currently supports both static formats—where you must download the file before playing it—and streaming formats, as used when you want to view a movie or broadcast "live" over the Internet. QuickTime does not rely on a single format; instead, it encapsulates an MPEG or other media format within the file, which is then decoded by the QuickTime system during playback. QuickTime is supported on Macs and Windows machines only.

RealAudio/RealVideo/RealMedia

The Real audio and video formats are completely proprietary and were specially designed for streaming audio and video over the Internet and other low-bandwidth connections. The format supports a number of resolutions and compression methods to lower the overall size and data rate required to transfer the information. However, because RealAudio and RealVideo are proprietary, you need to use the RealAudio player to listen to them; converting from RealAudio or RealVideo to another format is impossible without special software, which can be expensive. Creating RealVideo is easier (VideoStudio does it natively), but be aware of the compatibility issue and limitations of using such a closed format.

AVI

The AVI format was developed by Microsoft as a video solution for Windows 95. The AVI format is proprietary and, like many other generic formats (such as QuickTime), it can use a number of different codecs to compress the video and/or audio to different standards. AVI is supported under Windows and Mac OS (when using QuickTime), but because of the variety of codecs available, reading certain AVI files using unsupported encoders on the Mac is impossible.

Video CD

The Video CD format was an early form of what we now know as DVD. Video CD uses the 650 MB on a CD-ROM in combination with the MPEG-1 standard, providing an image that is roughly the same quality as home-recorded videotape (actually 352x240 pixels/30 fps for NTSC and 352x288 pixels/25 fps for PAL). The quality is not quite as good as a pre-recorded video, but the advantage of CD-ROM makes it an attractive alternative. The only problem is the size of a CD-ROM, which becomes limiting. A Video CD can hold between forty-five and ninety minutes of video at the above quality, including a stereo audio track.

Video CDs can be played on most computers, and many DVD players—which must have the MPEG decoder built in for playing DVDs—will also play Video CDs. However, many DVD players are unable to read CD-R and CD-RW media, even when working with normal audio CDs. After trying a number of different DVD players when working with a Video CD, only one—a Philips—would actually play the Video CD at all.

DV

Digital Video is the format used by digital camcorders. The DV standard has the same resolution as DVD (720x480 pixels/30 fps for NTSC and 720x576 pixels/25 fps for PAL), making it an ideal source both for creating normal videos (where the quality is reduced) and for writing to DVD using suitable software or hardware. The DV format also includes a stereo soundtrack working at normal CD quality (44 kHz/16-bit).

DVD

The DVD standard uses the MPEG-2 video format and an identical resolution to the camcorder DV standard. Aside from its basic format and video stream details, the rest of the DVD standard relates to how the information is laid down onto the DVD disc, while also providing the menu and multitrack video/audio standards. We looked in more detail at the DVD standard in Chapter 2.

iMovie

Apple's iMovie was introduced with the iMac DV as a consumer-oriented solution for video editing. The unique ability of the iMac DV at the time was its inclusion of a FireWire port as standard, making it possible to easily import digital video from an external MiniDV camcorder. You could import the information straight from a camera (the iMac DV even included a suitable cable), edit it on your iMac in almost real time, and then export the video back to your DV camcorder for transfer to your standard video player.

At the beginning of this year, Apple also released the iDVD product, which comes as standard on the new top-of-the-line G4 desktop machine. This uses the new Pioneer-developed DVD-R drive, also fitted to the machine, to allow you to write DVD discs. You can import a movie into iMovie and then export the iMovie project to iDVD. Here, you add the necessary menus and catalog information to create a properly formatted DVD before writing the whole iDVD project out to a DVD-R disc. The resulting disc can be played in any DVD player from consumer set-top boxes to those built into computers.

Unfortunately, iDVD is too new to be covered in this book; at the time of this writing, most people hadn't even received the machines they had ordered on the day of the announcement! Look for an update on using iDVD on the book's Web site (**www.mcwords.com/projects/books/cdr/**).

Beyond the ability to export the movie back to a DV camcorder, or to pass it on to iDVD, the only other format supported for export by iMovie is as a QuickTime file. You can write a QuickTime file just like any other to a normal data CD without requiring special treatment.

We'll have a quick look at iMovie and some of the special treatments available to you when editing movies, as well as how to export the movie in QuickTime format. Throughout the example below, I've used the sample tracks and effects that come with iMovie when it's supplied on CD so that you can try out the sequences for yourself using the same clips.

Importing Video from a DV Device

Your first job should be to import some video from your video camera. The process is very straightforward—just follow these steps to get the video onto your machine:

1. Open iMovie and choose to start a new project, or open an existing project if you are adding new material to an existing movie. You'll be presented the window shown in Figure 17.1. The window is split into three sections: The panel on the top left allows you to play your movie and record from a DV source; the panel on the top right is your "shelf" and gives you access to all of your video clips, transitions, effects and titles, and

the interface for adding an existing audio track or actively recording a new one; and the bottom panel shows either the clip viewer (the top tab) or the timeline viewer (the bottom tab). We'll look at the difference between the two in the next section.

Figure 17.1
The main iMovie window.

2. Change the movie panel to Camera mode by clicking the blue button at the bottom left of the panel to the DV camera icon (see Figure 17.2).

Figure 17.2
Switching to Camera mode.

3. Switch on your camera and rewind the tape to a point just a few seconds before where you want to record.

4. Click on the Play button within the movie panel—this tells your video camera to start playing the tape. When you get to the point that you want to start recording from, click the Import button.

5. When you have finished recording, click the Import button again.

Your video clip should appear in your shelf and can now be inserted into an active storyboard or timeline.

Laying Out Your Story

Once you've got all of the material from your camera, you can start to lay out the individual clips and portions of larger clips into the layout and sequence of the final movie. The entire process is controlled through the bottom panel, which displays your movie in the clip or timeline viewer:

▶ **Clip viewer** (also called storyboard mode) is used to lay out the sequence of clips within your final movie. For example, with a wedding, you'd probably lay out a storyboard that started with the pre-wedding sequence, followed by the wedding itself, and then the wedding breakfast and party afterward. Storyboard mode gives you a quick view of the sequence of shots within the movie, but it doesn't allow you to control the precise timing of these shots—they are simply sequenced one after another. You can see a sample of the mode in Figure 17.3.

Figure 17.3
The Clip viewer
in iMovie.

▶ **Timeline viewer** (also called timeline mode) is used to control the timing of individual tracks within the final module and also to control the timing between tracks. There are three tracks to every iMovie project—one video track and two audio tracks. By using the timeline, you can control precisely when fading between movie clips will occur, as well as when different audio clips are overplayed on the video track. Without timeline view, it would be impossible to sequence multiple tracks. You can see a sample of a timeline view in Figure 17.4, showing a sequence of video tracks, transitions, and audio clips across all three tracks.

Figure 17.4
The Timeline viewer
in iMovie.

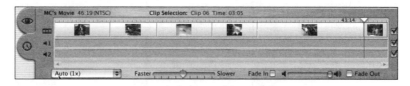

To add video and audio clips to your movie project, use the clip shelf to select the clip you want and then drag the clip to the viewer panel. If you are using the clip viewer, you can control the sequence of the individual clips. If you are using timeline viewer, you can set audio clips to run in tandem with existing video clips and adjust the starting time of each clip.

To edit the tracks so that you can remove unwanted frames, use the video panel to find the section you want and then hold down the Shift key while selecting the frames you want to delete. When you have selected the section you don't want, press the Delete key to kill it.

Adding Transitions

Transitions control how the movie progresses from one clip to another. Simply moving from one sequence of video to another can be confusing for the viewer, which is why most editors and movie directors like to use wipes (where the new clip wipes across the screen) or dissolving (where the old clip fades out and the new one fades in). These transitions indicate to the viewer that the scene is changing, either because it's being shown from a different angle or because we're changing to a completely different location.

iMovie supports a wide range of different transitions, none of which can be easily demonstrated on paper. However, some of the transitions and a description of their effects are listed below:

▶ **Circle Closing/Opening**—The old frame is overloaded with a circle that increases or decreases in size, replacing the old clip with the new clip.

▶ **Cross Dissolve**—The two clips are faded, the old being faded out and the new faded in.

▶ **Fade in/out**—These are useful for opening sequences or when moving from a solid screen to a new scene and vice versa.

▶ **Overlap**—Like Cross Dissolve, except that the new clip is first overlaid on the existing clip.

▶ **Push**—The new clip pushes the old clip out of frame from any of the four sides.

▶ **Radial**—The new clip is "wiped" in like the hand of a clock.

▶ **Scale Down**—The old clip frame is slowly reduced to nothing, while revealing the new clip.

▶ **Warp In/Out**—The new (or old) clip is expanded from a star in the middle of the screen until it fills the screen (or reduces to nothing).

The best way to get an idea of these effects is to try them. Luckily, iMovie provides an easy way of doing this by simply selecting the transition from the list (shown in Figure 17.5). iMovie will show you a quick preview of the process.

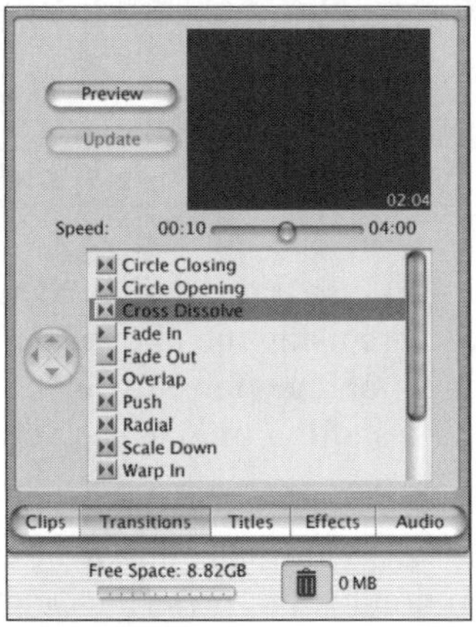

Figure 17.5
The Transitions shelf
in iMovie.

To add a transition, change the shelf to show the transition panel, select the transition you want from the list, and, if relevant, choose the direction of the transition. You can also control the period of the transition using the Speed slider from 1/10 of a second up to 4 seconds. Once you've selected and configured the transition, drag and drop the transition between two of your clips in the timeline.

The transition will need to be "rendered"; this is the process by which the appearance of each frame in the transition is calculated. Transitions must be rendered before they can be played properly. You can monitor the rendering process by looking at the red bar underneath the transition icon within the clip or timeline viewer.

Adding Titles

Watching a film without titles does not necessarily mean you are missing out on anything, but it can make the plot difficult to follow on everything from the latest big-budget blockbuster to your daughter's tenth birthday party. Titles are simply pieces of text that are overlaid onto frames within your video.

To add titles, change the shelf to show the Titles panel (shown in Figure 17.6). From here, you can control the size of the titles, what sort of titles appear (i.e. a multi-line list or separate blocks), and the font and color used to display the titles on screen. Once you've selected your title style and text, drag and drop the title style onto the movie clip to which you want to add the text.

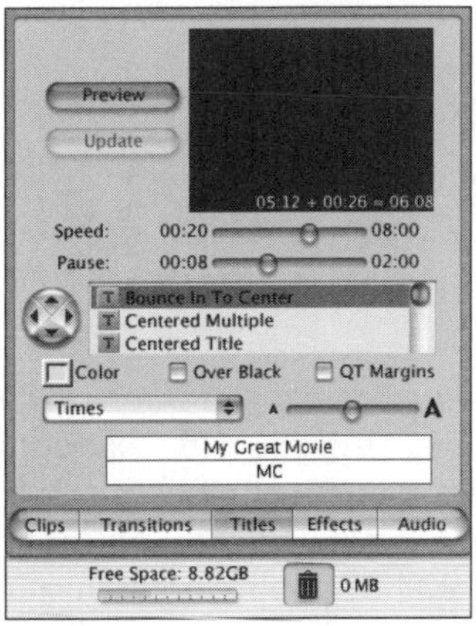

Figure 17.6
The Titles shelf
in iMovie.

Adding Effects

Watching ordinary movies can be pretty boring, so it's fun to sometimes modify the movie a little to give it a bit more life. Under iMovie, this is called adding effects. Effects change a proportion of a clip and allow you to adjust the colors, contrast, and other basic features, along with adding more complex effects such as water ripples and soft focus. Soft focus is great if you want to make a film seem romantic (or "dream-like"), while the Sepia Tone effect changes the movie to be in the brown and white tones characteristic of very old photos.

To apply an effect, use the movie viewer to select an area of the film to which you want to apply the effect. Change to the Effects panel in the shelf (see Figure 17.7), then select the effect you want and any options for the effect. You can preview the changes or just click on the Apply button to make the changes to the live movie track. As with transitions, it will take a while for the effects to be rendered. To undo an effect, click Restore Clip; to make an effect permanent, click the Commit button.

Figure 17.7
The Effects shelf
in iMovie.

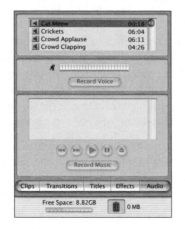

Adding Music/Voiceovers

With the timeline viewer active, you can drag and drop onto one of the audio tracks any sounds that you already have on your audio shelf. Audio clips can overlap each other and you can have as many clips as you like within a project.

In addition to the little music clips that come with iMovie, you can record music from a CD so that it can be added as a music track to the movie. Also, you can record direct from a microphone or external audio source and add that to the movie. In either case, change to the Audio shelf (see Figure 17.8), then use the controls to either record from a microphone or to select an audio track from the CD currently in the drive. In the case of Microphone input, the audio you record will automatically be placed into Audio Track 1, while music will be added to Audio Track 2.

Figure 17.8
The Audio shelf
in iMovie.

Exporting a QuickTime Movie

You've played, you've fiddled, and you've added titles, effects, and transitions to your movie—you're finally ready to export your movie file. As we already know, iMovie can export either to a DV camcorder that supports DV input or to a DV-enabled video recorder; to iDVD so that the movie can be written to a DVD-R; or to a QuickTime file.

QuickTime files can be read by any Mac or PC with QuickTime enabled and then can be added to a standard data CD without requiring any special treatment. To export to a QuickTime movie file:

1.   Choose File > Export Movie; you'll be prompted with the dialog box shown in Figure 17.9.

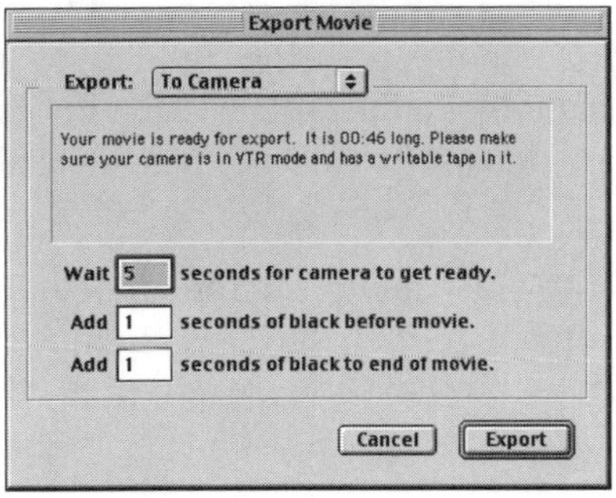

Figure 17.9
Exporting a movie
from iMovie.

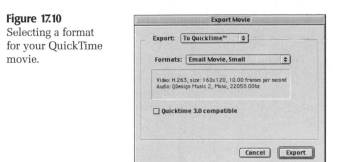

2.   Select To QuickTime from the popup menu; you'll be prompted with the dialog box shown in Figure 17.10.

Figure 17.10
Selecting a format
for your QuickTime
movie.

3.   Select the format for the exported movie. If you are exporting a movie for inclusion on a CD, there is a special CD-ROM Movie format already preset for you. The resolution is similar to that of a Video CD, albeit at a lower frame rate, and should be readable by most computers.

4.   Click the Export button. You'll be prompted to give the movie a filename and to specify a location where you wish to save the movie.

The exporting process will take some time—a thirty-seven second movie took about four minutes to export on my iBook (G3/466 MHz). The process will be quicker on a G4 machine and on most iMacs. Once the file has been created, add it to a data CD using the techniques shown in Chapter 15. If you want to see the results of the movie I created, check out the Web site for this book (**www.mcwords.com/projects/books/cdr/**), where you can download a small Web-friendly version of the movie.

VideoStudio

Ulead's VideoStudio 5.0 is one of the first products for Windows that supports the direct export of a video-editing project using the MPEG-2 standard at DVD quality without the need for a separate encoding card. This means that, just as with iMovie, you can take information in from a DV camcorder, manipulate it in VideoStudio, and then output the information in a form ready to be written to DVD. VideoStudio doesn't actually do the DVD writing for you—you must use a separate piece of DVD authoring software, such as the GoDVD! plugin, which integrates directly into VideoStudio.

Alternatively, you can generate DVD-quality video and place the video onto a CD. It won't be playable by all consumer DVD players, but it should be playable on your PC. The length of the video you can create is the only issue, with a limit of about twenty-five minutes of video on each CD.

For all intents and purposes, VideoStudio works in a similar fashion to iMovie. The main VideoStudio window can be seen in Figure 17.11. Like iMovie, the window is broken up into a number of areas. The panel on the left is the control area, where video clips and effects are set. The right-hand panel shows the media library, where picture, video, and audio clips are picked. The center panel is where you view the current version of the movie, and the bottom panel shows the timeline or storyboard view. In this screenshot, it's showing the timeline view.

In addition to the main window, the bar at the top shows the individual steps, in rough sequence—from starting a new project, through to video capture and adding titles, before finally exporting your movie into your desired format. We'll follow these steps to produce a sample movie, and the names used by VideoStudio are shown in parentheses within each of the following sections. As before, I'm using clips stored on the Content CD that comes with the VideoStudio package, so you can try out the same project.

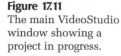

Figure 17.11
The main VideoStudio window showing a project in progress.

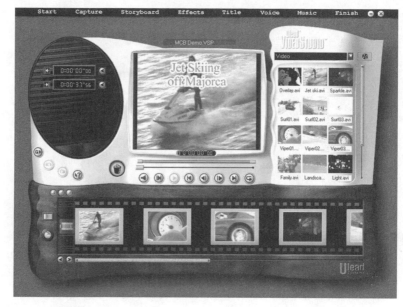

Starting a New Project (Start)

The Start step creates your movie project. This defines the file in which you store all of the information about the movie, from the clips used and their trimming details through to the technical specification of the movie you are creating. To create a new project, open VideoStudio, click on the Start button at the top of the window, then click on the New Project button—that's the top-left button in the control panel. You'll be prompted with the window shown in Figure 17.12. Give the project a name and location and pick a project template. Project templates include details about the resolution and frame rate of the movie you are creating—there are a number of predefined templates you can use that cover Video CD, DVD, and DV projects in NTSC and PAL, or you can create your own template.

TIP
Select a template that matches the video you are importing, not the video specs you want to export. This way VideoStudio can use the native format of the media captured. Always capture at the highest quality available with your device so you can export your video however you choose.

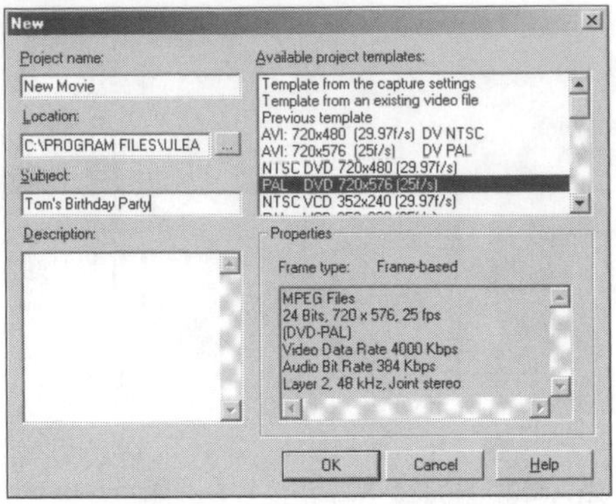

Figure 17.12
Creating a new project
in VideoStudio.

Importing Video from a DV Device (Capture)

Capturing video is straightforward. VideoStudio will take input either from an analog digitizer
card or from a DV camcorder if you have a FireWire device. We'll cover the latter method here:

1. Check to see the Capture button is set to Capture mode.

2. Turn on your camcorder and switch it to Play mode.

3. Click the Capture to Library checkbox if you want the recorded video to
   automatically be added to your video library. If you do not select this option, you
   will need to manually add the video to your library before you can use it.

4. Click the play button under the movie viewing panel within VideoStudio to tell the
   camcorder to start playing.

5. When you reach the point where you want to start recording, click the Capture video
   button (the button with the camcorder at the top-right of the control panel) shown in
   Figure 17.13.

Figure 17.13
Capturing video from
a DV Camcorder.

6. When you've finished recording, click the Capture video button again.

Laying Out Your Story (Storyboard)

Adding video clips to your storyboard or timeline is as easy as finding the video clip in your library and dragging and dropping the clip onto either the storyboard view (Figure 17.14) or the timeline view (Figure 17.15). The two modes and display characteristics identical to those demonstrated under iMovie—for more information, see "Laying out your Story" earlier in this chapter. You can switch between the two display modes using the top button next to each panel.

Figure 17.14
Storyboard view in VideoStudio.

Figure 17.15
Timeline view in VideoStudio.

To control the individual attributes of each clip, use the Control panel (top left), shown in Figure 17.16, to manipulate the duration of the clip (by setting the start and end points), the volume, and whether to fade the audio in and out during playback. Once you have made changes, remember to click the Apply button (the tick/check mark at the bottom of the control panel) to apply the changes to your project. In Timeline view, you can see each frame for frame-accurate editing and the relationships and placement of all media including video, titles, transitions, and music.

Figure 17.16
Controlling your video clips in VideoStudio.

Section IV CD Writing Software

Adding Effects (Effects)

You can control the transition from one video clip to another using the Effects panel. To change into Effects mode, click the Effects button in the menu bar. From the Control panel, select the type of transition effect that you want to use from the popup list that categorizes the available transitions (see Figure 17.17) or from the graphical samples (see Figure 17.18). Once you have selected the transition, drag and drop it into place between the two clips that you want to apply the transition to within the timeline or storyboard panels.

Figure 17.17
Transition effects
popup in VideoStudio.

Figure 17.18
Transition icons within
VideoStudio.

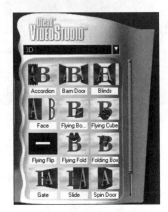

VideoStudio will handle the rest of the process, rendering the transition in order to achieve the result you want.

Adding Titles (Title)

Titles can add some useful direction about the content of a particular portion of a video. To add text to your movie, you need to follow these steps:

1. Change to Title mode using the menu bar button. The control panel will change to show the controls and options for titles—see Figure 17.19.

Figure 17.19
Adding titles to your
movie in VideoStudio.

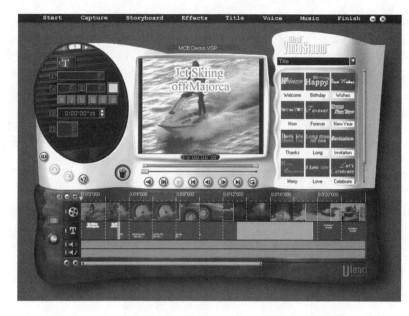

2. Move to the area within the movie where you want to add the title.

3. Click the Create or Edit title clip button (top left of the control panel). The video preview window will show a feint line and flashing cursor where you can type in your title.

4. Highlight the text and use the popups and buttons within the control panel to control the text's font, size, alignment, and other attributes. If you want to control the motion or animation of the text, use the last button within the panel to set the option. From here, you can move the text around the window or have it fade in and out.

5. If you change to page two (using the page controls), you can adjust the border width and color and change the transparency of the text. Page three allows you to add a shadow and soft edges to the text.

6. Click the Add to timeline button (bottom right of the control panel) to add the text to the timeline—you should notice a new entry within the timeline track.

Adding Music/Voiceovers (Voice/Music)

Most movies would be pretty boring without some form of background music—some soundtracks can even be as important as the movie itself. VideoStudio provides two separate tracks, one for adding music and the other for adding a voiceover track. If you already have an existing track or want to use one of the tracks supplied on the Content CD with VideoStudio, you can drag and drop sound sequences from the library panel. VideoStudio comes with some sounds, and you can add your own short sound effects and music to the library to add to your video projects. In addition, you can add narration to a project "live" while viewing the movie. Personally, I've found it easier to record the audio in another application and then add it to a project, rather than to record it live.

Creating a File for Video CD or DVD (Finish)

Once you've finished preparing all of the individual elements of your movie, it's time to export the movie from your machine into a format suitable for use on a Video CD or DVD. This is the final step of the VideoStudio process, so click on the Finish button within the menu bar.

From within the control panel, click the Make a movie button at the top left of the panel. You'll be prompted with a popup list similar to the one shown in Figure 17.20. Choose the export format, using one of the VCD templates for Video CD (MPEG-1) and the DVD and DV formats for export to an MPEG-2 file or back to a DV camcorder or video recorder, respectively.

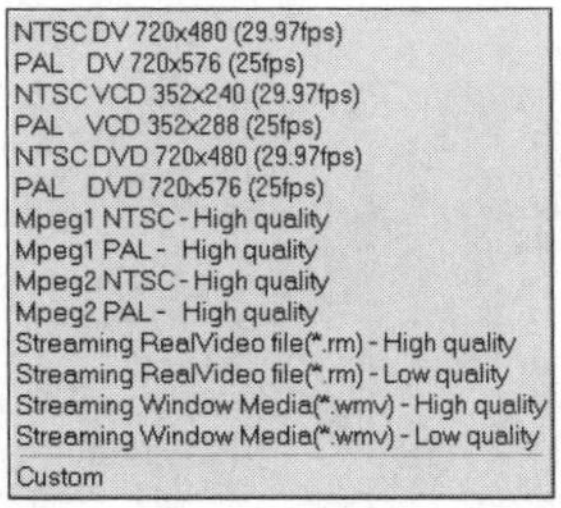
NTSC DV 720x480 (29.97fps)
PAL DV 720x576 (25fps)
NTSC VCD 352x240 (29.97fps)
PAL VCD 352x288 (25fps)
NTSC DVD 720x480 (29.97fps)
PAL DVD 720x576 (25fps)
Mpeg1 NTSC - High quality
Mpeg1 PAL - High quality
Mpeg2 NTSC - High quality
Mpeg2 PAL - High quality
Streaming RealVideo file(*.rm) - High quality
Streaming RealVideo file(*.rm) - Low quality
Streaming Window Media(*.wmv) - High quality
Streaming Window Media(*.wmv) - Low quality
Custom

Figure 17.20
Choosing an export format for your movie from VideoStudio.

If you have chosen the Video CD or DVD options, you will be prompted with the window shown in Figure 17.21. Give the file a name and choose a location. Remember that you will need a lot of space to record a large movie. Video CD runs at about 256 KB per second and DVD at 768 KB per second, or about 100 MB and 300 MB, respectively, for a ten-minute movie.

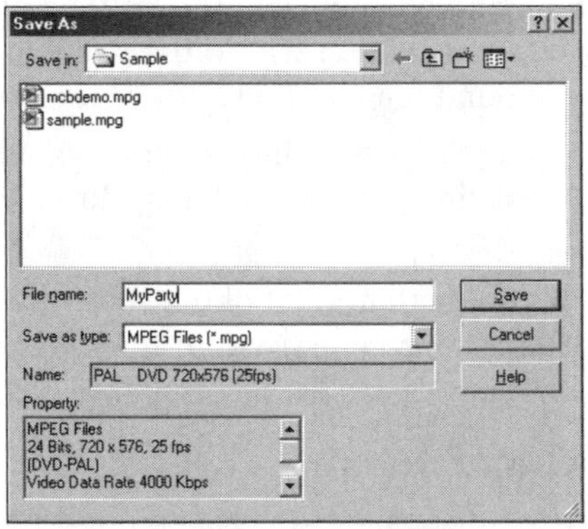
Save As
Save in: Sample
mcbdemo.mpg
sample.mpg
File name: MyParty
Save as type: MPEG Files (*.mpg)
Name: PAL DVD 720x576 (25fps)
Property:
MPEG Files
24 Bits, 720 x 576, 25 fps
(DVD-PAL)
Video Data Rate 4000 Kbps
Save
Cancel
Help

Figure 17.21
Choosing a destination for your movie file.

If you've created a Video CD movie file, you can record it onto a proper Video CD using Roxio's Easy CD Creator. Use the Project Selector to select Make a Video CD. A Wizard should automatically be started, which will take you through the process. All you need is the file that you just created.

If you've used VideoStudio so far, you can use the Ulead GoDVD! plug-in to create and burn your movie onto your CD media.

Authoring a DVD, VCD, or SVCD

Using the GoDVD! plug-in for VideoStudio 5.0, you can write your movie and the necessary menus and other information required for a DVD, Video CD, or the special SVCD format (which allows DVD quality on a normal CD) straight to a suitable disk.

> **NOTE**
>
> Your selection of a VCD, SVCD, or DVD format on CD-R/CD-RW will depend on the length of your video and the quality you desire. The VCD format is the best for long projects—holding approximately 74 minutes of video per CD—and can be played on many consumer DVD players available in the market today. The SVCD format will hold around 35 minutes of video per CD. SVCD is closer to DVD quality but can only be played on a handful of the consumer DVD players out there in the market. The final format is DVD files on CD media. This option is the best quality that you can output. Unfortunately, there are only a few DVD players available right now that will play a DVD format burned on CD media. Computer-based DVD players will play all three of these formats with no problem.

You can check the technical specifications of your DVD player to see which formats it can properly play using the GoDVD! plug-in. To start the process, you will need to save your movie in the desired format as outlined above. If you are exporting to GoDVD! right after you have encoded your video in the proper format, you will find that your video is already highlighted in the VideoStudio Library. Click on the Export button (the popup immediately below the save button in the Finish window, where we saved the final movie) and choose the Ulead GoDVD! plug-in option. You'll be prompted with a screen similar to that shown in Figure 17.22. This window shows the format, size, and other information about the video. There is only one choice to be made on this screen—whether or not to make a scene menu for your authoring project.

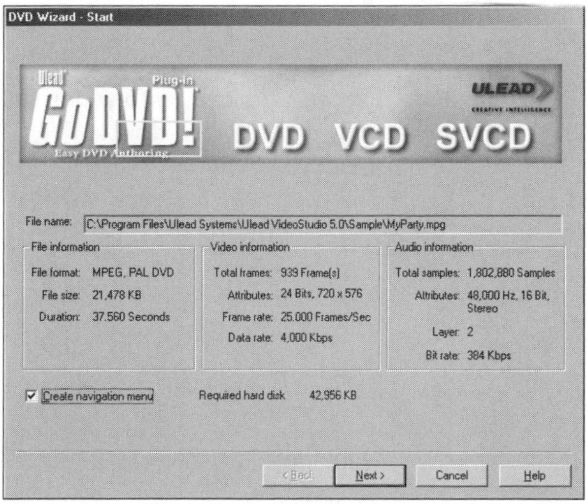

Figure 17.22
Writing your movie to DVD, VCD, or SVCD.

The next step in GoDVD! is to choose the places in your video where you wish your scene menu to jump to. As you scroll through your video, find a frame that begins a new section in your video that you wish to highlight and then click the Add Scene button. Repeat this process until you have chosen all the scenes you like. They will dump automatically into a menu on the right that you can scroll through to review. One option within this window is to select whether you wish to designate an introductory video file before your menu appears. This is another video file that must be encoded into the same format as your main video. It could be your special intro, an advertisement, a disclaimer, and so on. When someone views your project, they will first see this video clip before they can see the main scene menu that you create.

The next step designs a menu environment to display your scenes. There are many available templates to choose from and more offered by Ulead on its Web site (**www.ulead.com**) on a fairly regular basis. Once you have found a template that is suitable for your purposes, you can add text under each scene to annotate it. If there are more scenes that the template will hold, then another page to your menu will be automatically generated.

TIP

You can customize each template by replacing the background image with your own—perhaps a still scene from the video you are creating. Keep in mind that images that have less contrast or "business" will show your text better in the menu.

Once your menu has been created, it is time to test its functionality. Using a simulated remote control, you can make sure your authoring project functions the way you intended. After your testing is complete, it is time to choose a place in your computer where you wish your authored project to be stored with all its parts. This is called a program layer and is the first step in preparing to burn your Video CD. It includes all the files that will be made to make your project look and act like a DVD. These files are made up of your raw video as well as small programs that tell the video how to react to your menu commands. You'll need ample disk space to build your program layer.

Finally, the last step is to actually burn that program layer onto your CD. Press the Create button and GoDVD! will automatically find your CD-R/CD-RW hardware. The rest is done for you. It's now time to send that CD to your friends, family, or clients or take it to your own living room to view on the DVD player.

18

Backup and Archiving Software

Backing up and archiving systems should be a daily part of your computer regime. There is nothing worse than working on a project for a number of days, weeks, or even months and then losing the information either due to a computer failure or by pressing the wrong button on your machine at some point.

Although it's tempting just to copy your files onto a CD, which is better than nothing, a much better solution is to use a piece of software which can automatically back up the files on your machine. Good software will also allow you to append further changes, automatically adding the files that have been updated since the last backup.

There is lots of different backup software out there, but the best in my experience, and the only one I know of which handles CD-R and CD-RW drives, is Retrospect. Retrospect is both Mac- and Windows-compatible and offers manual and automatic backups. Under Windows, as part of Easy CD Creator, you get Take Two. Take Two is not backup software in the same sense as Retrospect; instead, it backs up your entire machine to CD so that you can recover the machine, and all its files, in the event of a failure.

If you are archiving only information, then you can use the standard CD writing tools we've already covered in chapters 14, 15, and 16. Once the information is archived, though, you need a way of finding a particular file—at the end of this chapter we look at some of the tools and tricks available for creating a catalog of the files on individual CDs.

Retrospect

Retrospect is far and away my favorite piece of software—not because it allows me to back up my machine, which is always an important step, but because it does exactly what it says it does, and does it well. Originally, Retrospect grew out of a need to back up the Macintosh using floppy disks. As tape drives became available, Retrospect started to support tape as the backup medium of choice. Now, with the explosion of CD-R/RW drives, Retrospect also supports backups on CD media.

Retrospect is supported on both Windows and Mac platforms and supports a huge variety of tape, removable, and CD-R/RW drives. Retrospect comes in a number of different versions. The basic version, Retrospect Express, supports all types of removable media, including floppy, Jaz, Zip, and, of course CD-R/RW. The full version, Retrospect Desktop, also supports a full range of tape drives. Beyond the desktop products, there are also Workgroup and Server products for backing up multiple machines across a network.

NOTE

If you want to try Retrospect for yourself, you can download a limited trial version from the Dantz site, **www.dantz.com**.

Whatever version you choose, the interface is consistent across both Windows and Mac platforms—the main window is shown in Figure 18.1.

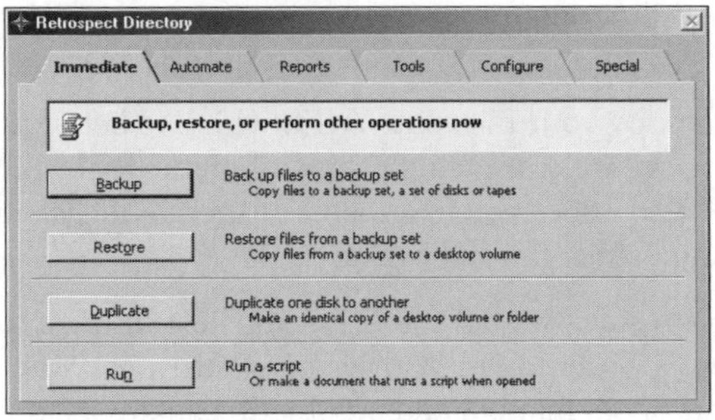

Figure 18.1
The main
Retrospect window.

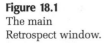

Retrospect looks like a very complicated piece of software—and if you want to make use of all the different features, from progressive backups, selective file backup, multiple catalog,s and networked backup procedures, it is indeed a complex piece of software. But for the simple purposes of performing a backup, Retrospect is quite straightforward.

Backing Up Files with Retrospect

For the moment, we can ignore complexities such as backup strategies and instead concentrate on the basic process of creating a backup to CD. Retrospect makes this process very easy—all you need to do is specify the source and destination, then start the backup running. The source is, of course, your hard disk partitions. The destination is a CD-R/RW disc in a packet-writing capable drive.

Backups with Retrospect can span multiple discs, and to aid in the process, a catalog of the information stored on the disc is kept on your hard drive. Backup discs are also members of a particular "Backup Set"—this allows you to have a number of different sets, either for holding different backup files or for supporting one of the backup methodologies we saw in Chapter 9.

To do an immediate backup:

1. Open Retrospect through the Start menu or, if starting on a Mac, find the Retrospect folder on your hard drive and double-click on the Retrospect backup.

2. Click on the Backup button in the main window.

3. You will immediately be prompted for a source volume or volumes to back up, as shown by the dialog box in Figure 18.2. If you want only to backup a folder with a volume, click on the Subvolume button—you'll be prompted with a modified file dialog box (shown in Figure 18.3), where you can find the folder you want to back up. Once you've found the folder you want to back up, click on the Define button. Retrospect will remember your decision, so you can choose the subvolume from the volumes listed in the main window. Once you've select the volumes, including any subvolumes that you want to back up, click on the OK button.

Figure 18.2
Choosing source
volumes for backup.

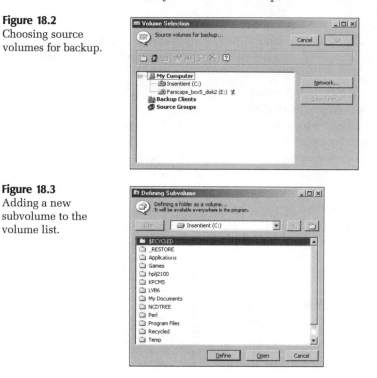

Figure 18.3
Adding a new
subvolume to the
volume list.

4. You will then be asked to specify the backup set to use. If you have not already created a backup set, or you want to create a new backup set, click on the Create New button to get the dialog box shown in Figure 18.4. From the Storage type drop-down list, choose CD-R. If you want to encrypt your backup so that it needs a valid password before the information can be restored, click on the Security button and enter a password. Finally, give the backup set a name. Note that individual CDs within the backup set will be named "#-name" where # is the CD number within the set. The name you enter refers to the entire backup set, not the first CD within the set. Click New and then click OK to use the backup set you just created.

Section IV CD Writing Software

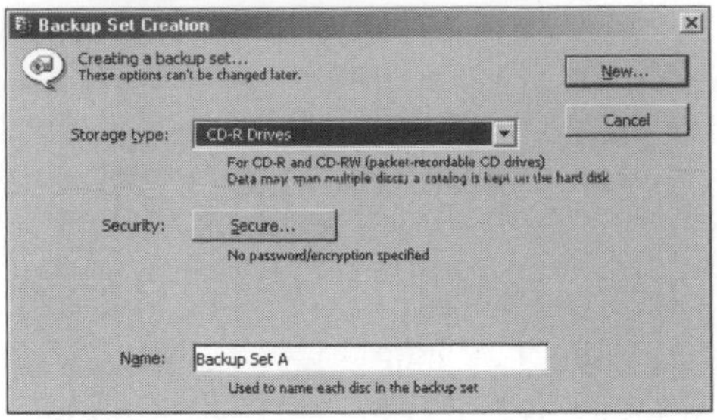

Figure 18.4
Creating a new
backup set.

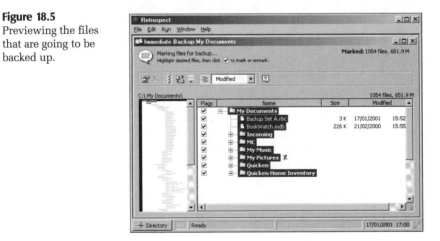

5.   You're now in a position to actually perform the backup—there's nothing left for you to do. However, if you want to control how the backup proceeds, including how to reduce the number of files added to the backup, you will need to configure further options.

6.   The Selecting button allows you to select one of the "selectors"—this is an advanced filtering system that allows you to explicitly include or exclude files or folders with specific names, extensions, or even according to dates. On a Mac, you can also filter by the file and type creator codes, system labels, and other factors. The default All Files selector just backs up everything; other selectors include Documents, which ignores all applications, libraries, extensions, and system files; and All Files Except Cache Files, which backs up everything except the files that make up your Netscape or Internet Explorer cache.

7.   The Preview button gives you the window you see in Figure 18.5—from here, you can see exactly which files are going to be backed up by Retrospect, according to the volumes you have selected, and the current selector that is in force. You can also explicitly remove files and folders from the list that is about to be backed up.

Figure 18.5
Previewing the files
that are going to be
backed up.

8. The last button, Options, allows you to control the options for the current backup. You can see the main Options window in Figure 18.6. The most important options are Verification, which, if switched on, will compare the files on the hard disk with those just written to CD; Data compression, which enables Retrospect's compression system to save spacing; and the "matching" configuration. The matching system (accessible by clicking on the More Choices button) determines how files that have the same name, file size, and modification and creation times are backed up. The default is to back up only files that match these criteria once—that is, if you have a file called README.TXT and another file on the system has the same name and other criteria, only the first will be backed up. I recommend instead that you select the Match only same location option to guarantee that all files will be backed up.

Figure 18.6
Changing the
backup options.

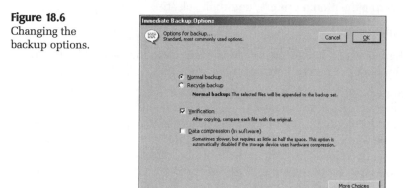

9. Once you've configured everything, click on the Backup button and let the process commence. Retrospect will start the backup process and give you a progress meter, showing the amount of time taken and remaining, seen in Figure 18.7.

Figure 18.7
Monitoring the
backup process
in Retrospect.

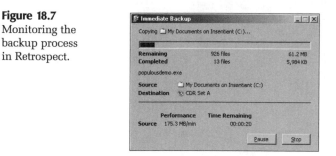

Obviously, depending on how much information you need to back up, you may need additional CDs. Retrospect will prompt you when it needs one.

Adding/Updating Files to an Existing Backup

Because Retrospect is a proper backup program, we can back up the same source again to the same backup set. Retrospect will only back up the files that have changed since the last backup, which it determines by comparing the modification dates and times stored in the catalog. To back up to an existing backup set, follow the instructions above, but select the existing backup set, instead of creating a new one. Retrospect will do the rest.

Restoring Files from a Previous Backup

If you mistakenly deleted a file that you wanted to keep, you will need to recover the file from a backup. The restoration process is just a case of selecting the backup set (or sets) that you want to search for information, entering the search criteria, and then selecting the files you want.

To restore a file or folder from a backup:

1. Choose Start > Retrospect or, if starting on a Mac, find the Retrospect folder on your hard drive and double-click on the Retrospect backup.

2. Click on the Restore button—you'll be prompted to select the type of restore you want, as shown in Figure 18.8. If you choose to Restore an entire disk, you will be able to restore all of the contents of a disk when it was backed up—this is the best method to use if you are restoring after a crash or machine failure. Restore files from a backup allows you to choose files from a backup to restore. Search and Retrieve files allows you to search for files from backup sets by their name, the name of their enclosing directory, or other criteria—we'll use this option as it's the most practical for finding most files.

Figure 18.8
Choosing the right restore method.

3. You'll be prompted, as shown in Figure 18.9, to select the backup sets that you want to search. Use Control to select multiple backup sets and then click OK to continue.

Figure 18.9
Selecting the backup sets to search.

4. Now, you need to choose a location into which you can retrieve the files. Again, you get a number of options, including the ability to completely replace an existing disk (useful for recovery purposes), but we'll choose Retrieve Files & Folders, which will restore the files into a new directory, with the same name as the backup set from which they were retrieved. You'll need to choose the location using the modified file dialog box, as shown in Figure 18.10.

Figure 18.10
Choosing a
location to save the
restored files.

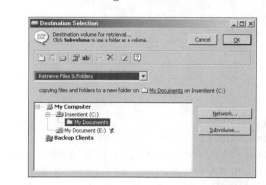

5. Now, you get the search screen, as shown in Figure 18.11. You can search for files or folders with a given name, date, or other criteria using the popup boxes. If you want to be more specific, click on the More Choices button, where you can then enter additional criteria to narrow the search. You can see here that I've decided to look for Word documents by looking for the .DOC extension.

Figure 18.11
Entering the
search criteria for
finding your files.

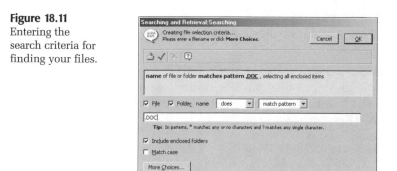

6. The final windows show the backup sets that match the search criteria you entered, as shown in Figure 18.12. Click on the Files Chosen button to select any more specific files that you are looking to restore, or just press the Retrieve button to start the restore process. You'll be asked to insert each CD as it's required, until all the files you requested have been restored.

Figure 18.12
The found files
report and dialog.

Automating the Backup Process

Doing a manual backup each time is not a suitable way of doing backups, mostly because it relies on your memory to do the backup—if you don't back up regularly, a backup become useless very quickly, especially if you update files on a daily basis. Retrospect supports a system of scripts which allows you at the simple level to record the backup settings that we've already seen and, at a more complex level, to automatically run a backup at a particular time.

To create a new script:

1. Choose Start > Retrospect or, if starting on a Mac, find the Retrospect folder on your hard drive and double-click on the Retrospect backup.

2. Click on the Automate panel.

3. Click on the Scripts button—you should get a window showing the list of scripts currently configured.

4. Click the the New button to create a new script. You'll get the option to use EasyScript, which will ask you a series of easy questions about how you want to back up your machine. Click Yes to go through the EasyScript wizard. You'll be prompted with the first EasyScript window, seen in Figure 18.13.

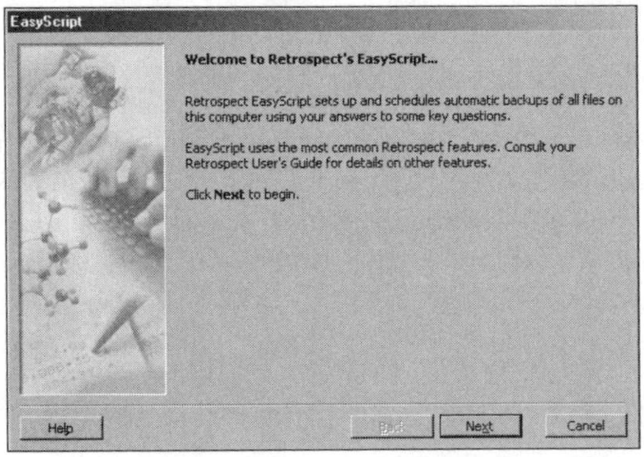

Figure 18.13
Creating a new script
with EasyScript.

5. Figure 18.14 shows that you'll first be asked to choose whether you are doing a
    network backup—this option will be displayed only if you have a Desktop or
    Workgroup version of Retrospect. Click No > Next.

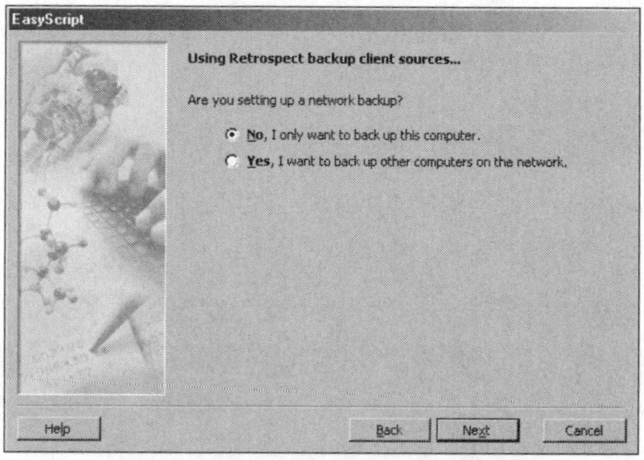

Figure 18.14
Selecting the type of
backup to perform.

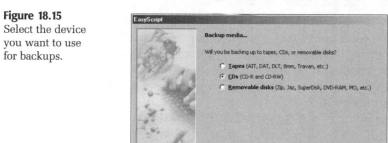

6. Select the type of device that you want to back up to—in this case, CDs. The other
    options are shown in Figure 18.15.

Figure 18.15
Select the device
you want to use
for backups.

7. Select the desired frequency of your backup. If you use only your machine on
    weekends, a weekly backup should be fine. If you use it more regularly, however,
    select Every day from the radio buttons shown in Figure 18.16.

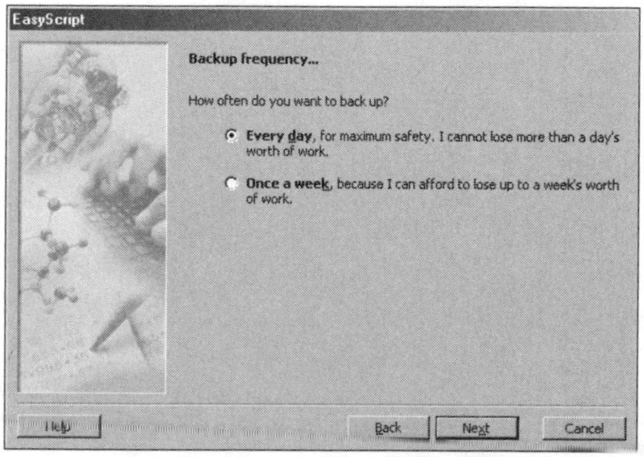

Figure 18.16
Choosing the
frequency of
the backup.

8. Choose how frequently you want to rotate the media (see Chapter 8). Choose No rotation if you back up only a home machine. Choose Weekly if you want to change backup sets each week, a good idea in a low volume company, as you can keep one version of the CDs off site. Alternatively, choose Daily if you want to have a different CD for each day of the week. You can see the window displayed at this point in Figure 18.17.

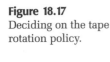

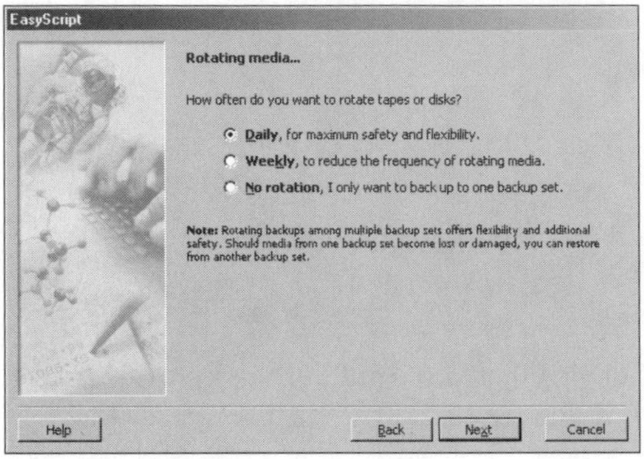

Figure 18.17
Deciding on the tape rotation policy.

9. The last stage is to choose the time when you want the backup to take place. I recommend you choose a period that is either not during normal working hours, so you can leave the machine and backup running overnight, or a time during working hours so you can move the CD immediately to a secure location when the backup has finished. At all times, remember that you need to protect the files you worked on during the day, so it's best to choose an evening rather than morning schedule. The default, shown in Figure 18.18, is 10 p.m. Click the Create button to finally create the script.

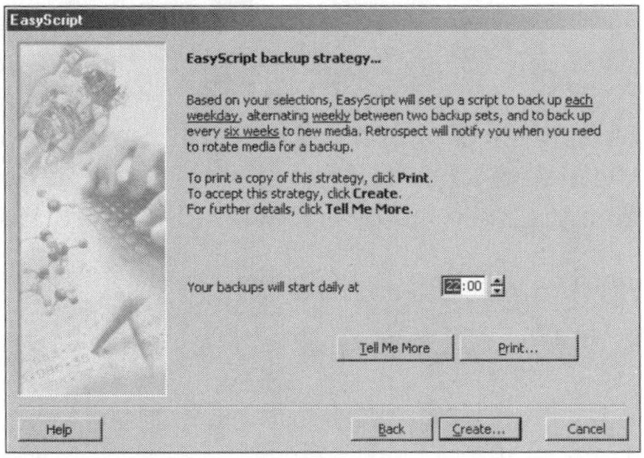

Figure 18.18
Choosing the time for the backup to take place.

10. You will be asked to name the backup sets required to support your backup strategy. Retrospect will go through the final motions to create the script. Once it's completed, you'll be back at the Scripts window—double-click the EasyScript Backup script to display the information about what EasyScript has done. You can see a sample in Figure 18.19. You'll notice that the schedule and other information have already been filled in, along with other information settings about the backup process.

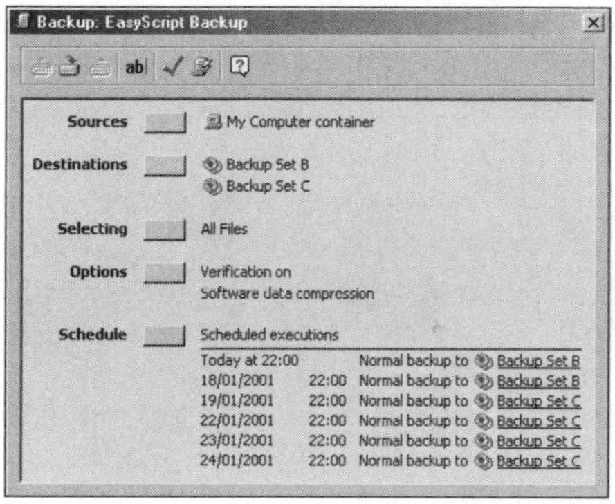

Figure 18.19
The final Retrospect script for automatic backup.

Take Two

Take Two, which is part of the Easy CD Creator package for Windows, is a very simple, but also practical, tool for backing up your machine to CD media. What it actually does is create an image (a direct copy) of your hard disk onto CD using directCD (see Chapter 15). Once the image has been created, you need to create a bootable floppy disk that you can then use to boot and restore your machine in the event of failure. However, this is the limit of its abilities—you cannot selectively back up and restore individual files to and from CD, as you can with Retrospect.

One of the problems with using CD as a backup medium is the difference in size between a hard disk and a CD. A typical hard disk is 20 GB in size, but a CD holds only 650 MB—you'd need thirty-one CDs to create a byte-for-byte backup. As with Retrospect, you can compress the contents to save space on the CD, but unlike Retrospect, it's not possible to selectively ignore files and directories that you don't want or need to backup.

Backing Up with Take Two

Take Two uses a very simple three-step process—you first select the source drive, then the destination drive, and then start the process.

There are a couple things you need to do before you begin creating a backup. First, you need to reduce the number of applications running on your machine—this will stop your PC from writing changes to the disk, which may upset the backup process. As a general rule, quit all "user" applications (Microsoft Word, Excel, Outlook etc.) and then also stop any "background" processes that you may have enabled, included fax-receiving software or "distributed" applications such as SETI, Parabon, or distributed.net.

Now you're ready to back up. The process for creating a backup onto CD using Take Two is as follows:

1. Open Take Two using the Create CD Wizard. You'll need to click Data CD > System Backup CD. Alternatively, right-click on the Easy CD Creator icon in the system tray and select System Backup CD from the Data CD submenu. You'll be prompted with the window in Figure 18.20.

Figure 18.20
The main Take Two window.

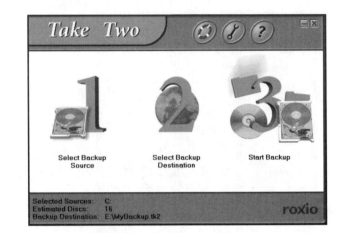

2. First, click on Step #1 to get to the screen shown in Figure 18.21. Select the drive that you want to back up—it will probably be your C drive. Once you've selected the drive, click on the 123 button to get back to the main window or click the arrow button to move on to Step #2.

Figure 18.21
The first step— choosing a source drive.

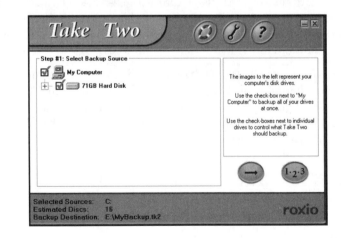

3. Second, click on Step #2 to select the CD-R/RW drive to use—see Figure 18.22. Once you have selected the drive you want to use, click on the 123 button to get back to the main window or click the arrow button to move on to Step #3 and start the backup.

Figure 18.22
Step two—selecting the CD-R/RW drive to use.

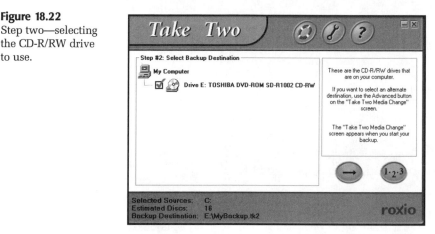

4. Click on the Options tab shown in Figure 18.23. Check the Compression box if you want to compress the data as it is being written to disc. I recommend this, as it will reduce the number of CDs required to back up your machine without affecting the quality of the backup.

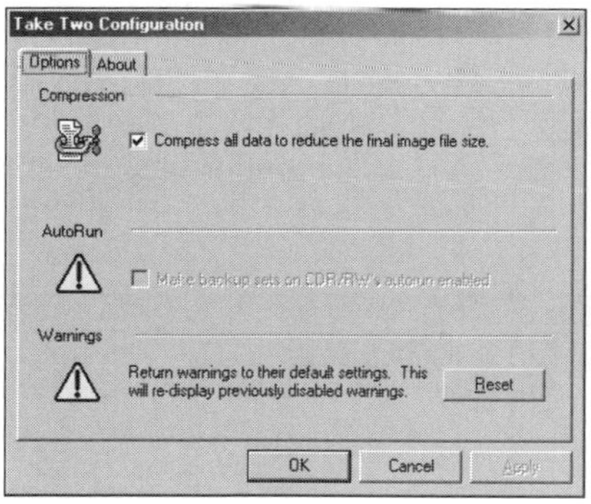

Figure 18.23
Choosing compression for your backup.

5. Click on Step #3 to actually start the writing process. You'll be asked to confirm the operation and to keep changes on your machine to a minimum. Once you are happy, click the Yes button.

6.   You'll be prompted to insert a blank disc (see Figure 18.24).

Figure 18.24
Inserting the first disc.

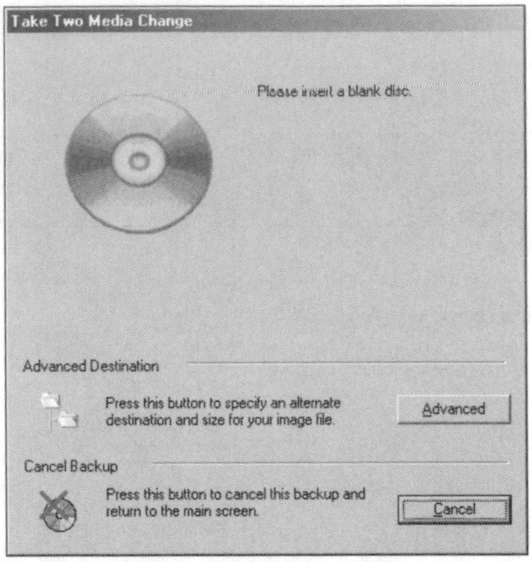

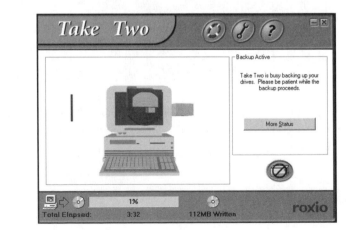

TIP

You can, at this point, click on the Advanced button (shown in Figure 18.25) and change the destination to something other than a CD-R/RW drive. You could use Take Two to back up onto removable media, such as Zip or Jaz, or, if you are on a network, to a networked hard drive.

7.   As the backup progresses, you will need more media, so be prepared to return to your machine periodically to insert another CD. As you remove each CD, make sure you label the CD clearly. You'll get a window like the one shown in Figure 18.25 showing the progress of the backup. Click on the More Status button for more detailed information about the progress of the backup, including an estimation of the time remaining.

Figure 18.25
Monitoring the
backup process.

Be warned that my machine, which uses about 15 GB of a 75 GB drive, took almost seven hours to produce a backup!

Creating a Bootable Floppy

Once the backup has been completed, you will need to create a bootable floppy disk for Take Two that you can use to boot the machine and restore the information from CD. The floppy that is created is based on an existing bootable floppy, such as the "rescue" floppy created by Windows. To create a floppy with these files, go into Control Panels > Add/Remove Programs, select the Startup Disk option, and follow the on screen prompts. You will need a blank floppy that Windows will format and then install the system files.

To create a bootable floppy for starting Take Two:

1. Open Take Two using the Create CD Wizard. You'll need to click Data CD > System Backup CD. Alternatively, right-click on the Easy CD Creator icon in the system tray and select System Backup CD from the Data CD submenu.

2. Click on the lifebelt button at the top of the window. You'll be prompted by the window shown in Figure 18.26. Insert the bootable floppy you have already created into your floppy drive and click Next. Take Two will copy the files off of your boot floppy, in preparation for creating a new floppy. Once the files have been copied, click OK to continue the process.

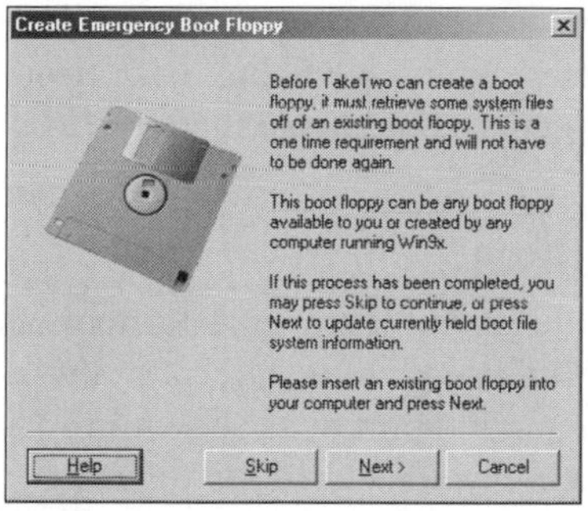

Figure 18.26
Creating a boot disk for use with Take Two.

3. You'll be prompted with the standard floppy disk formatting window. Insert a new blank disk and then click Start to format the disk.

4. Once the formatting has been completed, click Close to close the formatting window.

5. Take Two will now start to copy and install the system files required to create a bootable CD.

6.   Once the process has been completed, the dialog box in Figure 18.27 will appear. Click OK to complete the process.

Figure 18.27
The final stage
to creating your
boot floppy.

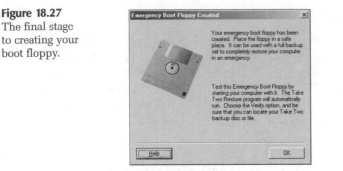

You should now try booting from the floppy you just created—the Take Two application should automatically start and allow you to verify the CD-based backup that you have just created.

Creating a Disc Catalog

If you are archiving information rather than backing it up, your most important consideration is how to find the information that you've archived. The obvious solution is to create a catalog of the information using some software that you can search, without requiring the CDs themselves. There are special products for image archives, which have their own needs beyond simple filename searches (see Chapter 8), but for file-based archives there are less complex solutions.

Creating a Catalog under Windows

There is no "standard" software under Windows, but there are a number of different packages if you go looking for them. The Advanced Disk Catalog software, which I've downloaded from Tucows (**www.tucows.com**) fits the bill. The main window is shown in Figure 18.28. All you need to do is choose Edit > Add volume to select a new disc to add to the catalog. You can search for a given file across the catalog by clicking on the magnifying glass, or by choosing Tools > Search.

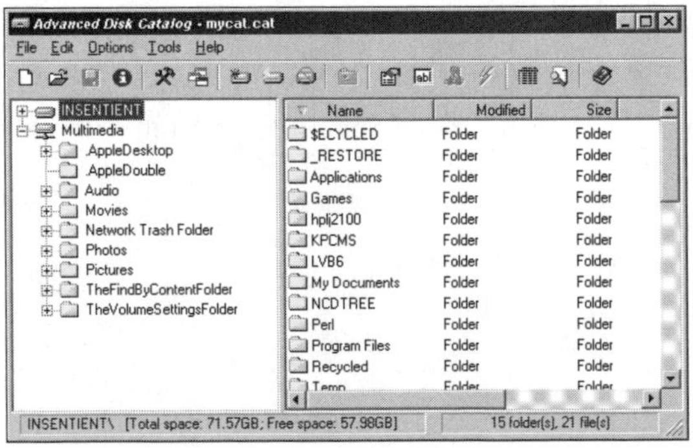

Figure 18.28
The Advanced
Disk Catalog software
under Windows.

Creating a Catalog under Mac OS

As with Windows, there is no standard disk cataloging system under Mac OS and, surprisingly, none is supplied with the Toast CD writing software. However, a simple search for disk cataloging programs on **www.macupdate.com** will list about seven different packages. Although there are no clear winners, I've been using AutoCat on and off for years. The benefit of AutoCat is that it creates a directory of aliases to the original source rather than a simple catalog.

This means that you can search for files that you have archived and added to the catalog within Sherlock. When you find the file you are looking for, double-clicking on the alias that Sherlock found will prompt you for the CD that you need which contains the original file. When you start AutoCat, you are prompted with a simple window, shown in Figure 18.29, onto which you need to drag and drop the icon for the CD (or other volume or folder) that you want to catalog.

Figure 18.29
The AutoCat drag-and-drop cataloging window.

This creates a folder with aliases to the files using the original structure. To search the catalog, open Sherlock and then drag and drop the folder (which is by default created on the desktop) onto the Sherlock window. You'll see it appear as another volume in the main Sherlock volume list, as shown in Figure 18.30.

Figure 18.30
Searching your catalog using Sherlock.

Now you can search within Sherlock as you would any other file or folder.

Creating a Catalog under Unix

Probably the best way to create a catalog under Unix is to mount the disk and then use the **find** command to create a text file of all the files on the CD, which we can later search with **grep**. For example:

```
$ cd /cdrom
$ find . -print >/usr/local/catalogs/archive.001
```

The catalog name should match the name of the archive CD that you have just created, so that when you search the catalog with **grep**, the filename, and therefore CD name, is the first element listed:

```
$ cd /usr/local/catalogs
$ grep '.doc' *
archive.001:Projects/CDR/Chapters/Chapter01/CDR01.doc
archive.001:Projects/CDR/Chapters/Chapter02/CDR02.doc
archive.001:Projects/CDR/Chapters/Chapter03/CDR03.doc
archive.001:Projects/CDR/Chapters/Chapter04/CDR04.doc
archive.001:Projects/CDR/Chapters/Chapter05/CDR05.doc
archive.001:Projects/CDR/Chapters/Chapter06/CDR06.doc
...
archive.003:Projects/PyTCR/Chapters/Chapter01/PyTCR01.doc
archive.003:Projects/PyTCR/Chapters/Chapter02/PyTCR02b.doc
archive.003:Projects/PyTCR/Chapters/Chapter03/PyTCR03a.doc
archive.003:Projects/PyTCR/Chapters/Chapter04/PyTCR04.doc
```

Now, when I've found the document I was looking for, I know which CD to find it on!

19
Labeling Software

You've finished recording your CD, you've verified that it's operating correctly, and you are ready to put the CD into circulation or pop it onto your shelf for later retrieval. However, the disc is useful only if you know where to find it again, and for that, you need some way of labeling the disc for easy retrieval. You can get by using a felt tip pen and a ballpoint pen to write on the label surface of the CD and the jewel case inserts respectively, but this doesn't look very professional, and the pen can be easily rubbed off. A much better alternative is to produce your own custom label and insert on your printer.

There are, of course, different types of CDs and, therefore, different types of information that you will want to store on the cover. In the case of an archive CD, you probably just want to give it a name and number and perhaps a date. Similarly, an image archive probably will be given only a simple number and reference. For an audio CD, however, you will probably want to include a list of the tracks and artists on the CD—remember that your stereo system won't display this information for you!

There are a number of ways you can accomplish the labeling. Some CD writing software comes with special software, such as CD Label Creator, for creating the labels. It uses media from people like Avery and Neato that is precut and, in the case of the CD label, already gummed, so all you have to do is print it out and insert the components into the jewel case and attach the label to the CD top (not bottom!). Alternatively, you can use any one of the myriad shareware tools available on the Internet specifically for this purpose. Finally, you can just use simple templates—even Microsoft Word 2000 comes with templates for CD inserts and labels.

Printing is only part of the process—you'll also need to attach the label to the CD. Attaching it by hand is not recommended, as getting the location wrong can render the CD useless. Putting the label in the wrong place can unbalance a CD, with serious consequences. Most labels are also designed to be fitted once—you can't remove them. It's therefore worth working with a labeling device to apply the label to the disc.

CD Label Creator

CD Label Creator (formerly Jewel Case Creator) comes as part of the Easy CD Creator 5.0 Platinum package. It uses a number of pre-configured themes using images, colors, and fonts so that all you have to do is choose the theme you want, add the CD contents, and print the CD labels and jewel case inserts. If you're using it for recording music CDs, it'll even update the text according to the CD you are recording using CDDB (see Chapter 9).

CD Label Creator will print out labels for the CD (using suitable CD label sheets), a foldable insert for the inside and outside of the hinged portion of the jewel case, and a printed section including end pieces for the section behind the CD holder. This last section is what you see when you put the CD upright like a book on the shelf, and on the back. Although it's designed to work with various CD label media, it can print on standard paper with suitable crop and fold marks so that you can cut out the labels and inserts ready for insertion into the jewel case.

Figure 19.1 shows the main window, displaying the contents of a Salt 'n Pepa "Best Of" album. This shows both the front cover and the inside cover (on the fold over); the contents of the back cover and spine can be seen in Figure 19.2.

Figure 19.1
Creating a label with
CD Label Creator.

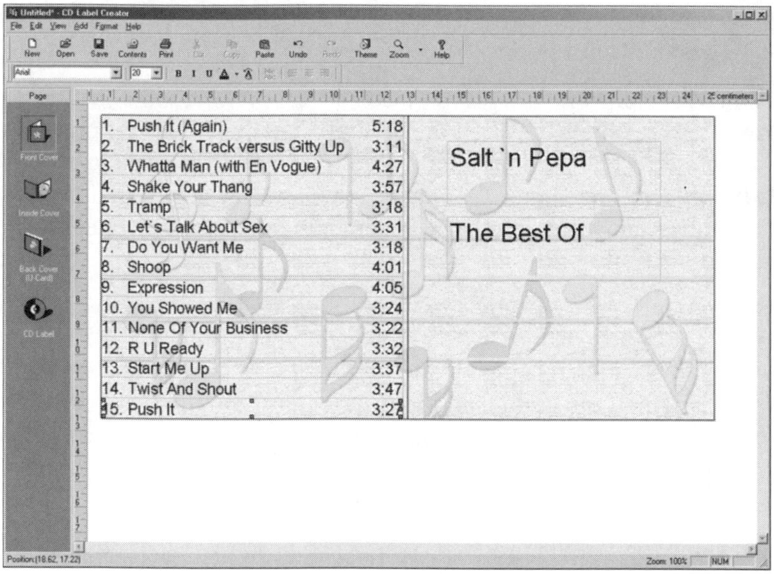

Figure 19.2
The back cover/spine
insert layout.

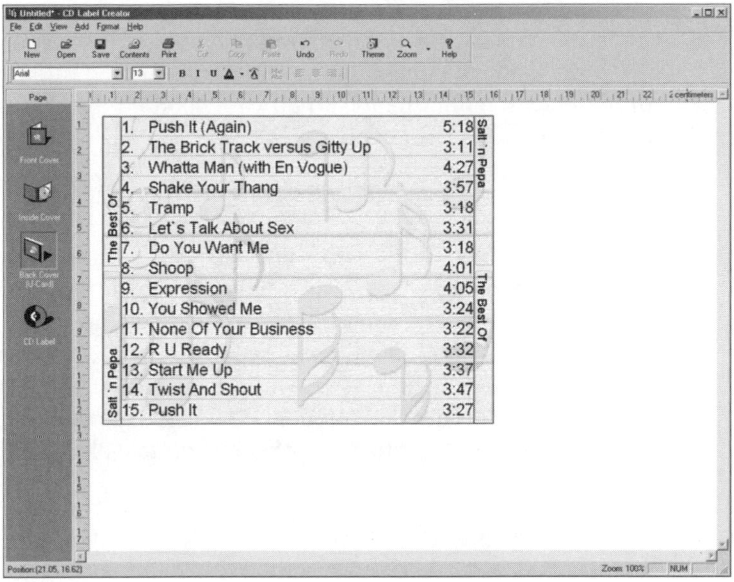

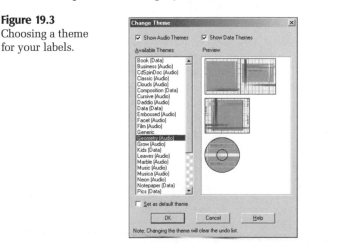

The basic method for creating a label using CD Label Creator is:

1. Open the CD Label Creator program from the Start menu or click on the CD Label Creator icon in the Project Selector window. Your screen should look similar to what you see in Figure 19.1.

2. Choose a new theme for your label by selecting Format > Change Theme or clicking on the Themes button in the tool bar. This will bring up the window shown in Figure 19.3. There are about twenty standard themes available. Most are designed for audio CDs, but a few (Book, Composition, Datafiles, Notepaper, and Pics) have been developed for data discs. The default is Generic, but you can choose any theme you like. Roxio occasionally adds new themes as a free download. Click web-check-up on the main project selector window to see what's available.

Figure 19.3
Choosing a theme
for your labels.

3. For an audio CD, put the CD you recorded into your drive and then choose Add > CD Contents—this will read the information about the track titles from the CD you have recorded and automatically insert the information into the template for you. If you didn't enter the information when you recorded the CD, there are two ways of getting the information onto your label:

    — **Using CDDB**—If you've duplicated an existing CD, CD Label Creator can download the track information from the Internet CD database and insert it directly into your template.

    — **Using your keyboard**—If you can't determine the information automatically using one of the tricks above—probably because it's a compilation CD—then you can always type in the information manually. To do this, select Add > Track; you'll get the Insert New Track window shown in Figure 19.4. You'll need to type in the track number, title, and the duration of the track. To change the information on the CD and case for the CD title and artist, just double-click on the text and start typing to change it.

Figure 19.4
Adding track
information by hand.

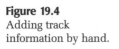

4. For a data CD, you'll need to double-click on each of the elements to update the track and CD title information. Data CDs have a title, ID number, and date (see Chapter 7). You'll need to double-click on each item that you want to change—just like the audio CD, you need to change the information only once, so the ID number and date will be copied to the spine, and the title and ID number will be copied from the jewel case insert to the CD label.

5. Once you are happy with the contents, you can tweak the fonts, size, and orientation of the text on the label and inserts using the toolbar. You can also adjust the background images used on the different label components by choosing Format > Change Background. You could, for example, place your company logo onto your archive CDs or perhaps a picture of your family on your CD of family photos.

6. To print your labels out, select File > Print. You'll need to click on the Page Setup button to tell CD Label Creator what sort of media you are using. You can see a sample in Figure 19.5, here showing the CD labels. You'll need to select the label position depending on the sheet you've selected. You, of course, need only one CD label, and most sheets allow two, and sometimes even three, labels to a single sheet, so you can reuse the sheet by selecting a different label from the layout.

Figure 19.5
Selecting the correct paper type for your labels and inserts.

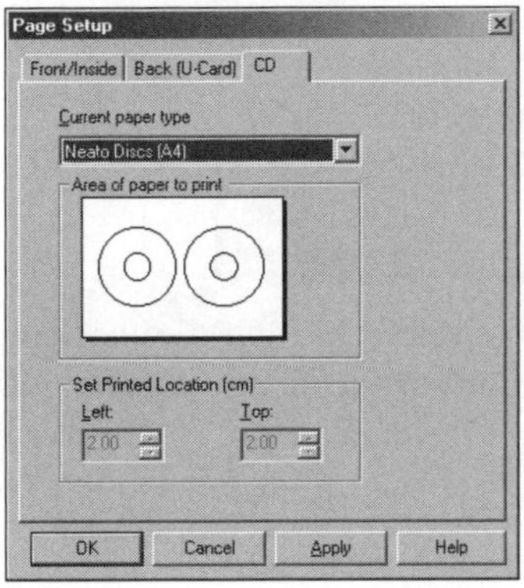

7. Load the paper into your printer. I recommend an inkjet printer for this, as it's less likely to fold and curl the paper, which can cause problems when you try to attach the label to your CD. You can use a laser printer, of course, and it will probably give better results and is certainly more convenient if you are printing out a number of identical labels.

8. Click OK and let your printer do its thing.

9. Once the label has been printed, you'll need to attach the label to your CD. See the section on labeling devices later in this chapter for more information.

If you are creating a label or label format that you expect to use a number of times, you can save the CD Label Creator label you have created into a file. This saves the information you've entered and any font and picture settings. Although you can't create your own themes, you can create your own "blank" template file and then use it each time in place of selecting a theme.

Ultimate Label Printer Pro

Aside from Magic Mouse Discus, which is included in Toast 5.0 Titanium, you can use one of the many shareware programs available for CD labeling. Although there are a few possibilities, my own personal favorite is Ultimate Label Printer Pro (Ultimate LPP). Ultimate LPP has the advantage of being able to create labels for a number of different formats, from the humble floppy through to Zip, Jaz, and, of course, CD-ROM. Its only failing is that it handles only the insert and back cover/spine for a jewel case—it doesn't handle the actual CD labels.

To create a CD-ROM label with Ultimate LPP, start the program by double-clicking on it—you should get a dialog box like the one in Figure 19.6. This lets let you select the type of label that you want to produce.

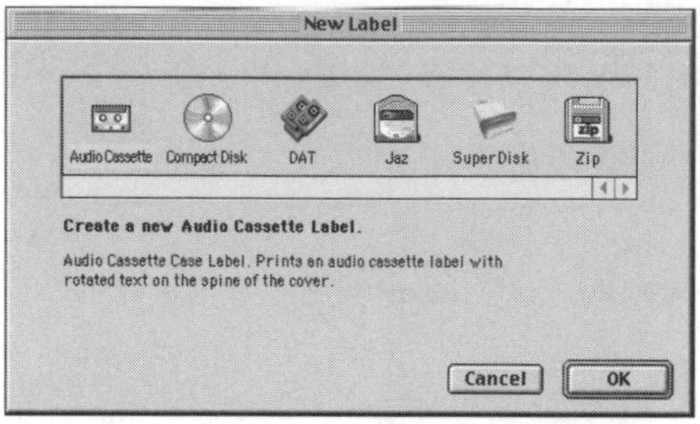

Figure 19.6
Choosing a label
style in Ultimate
Label Printer Pro.

Once you've selected your label, your screen will look similar to what you see in Figure 19.7. The figure shows the layout for the jewel case insert—you can use the tabs at the bottom of the window to change to the back cover and spine insert. You can see in this example that I've designed a nice front cover using suitable fonts for *Carmina Burana* (a classical work), and the insert has a list of the tracks.

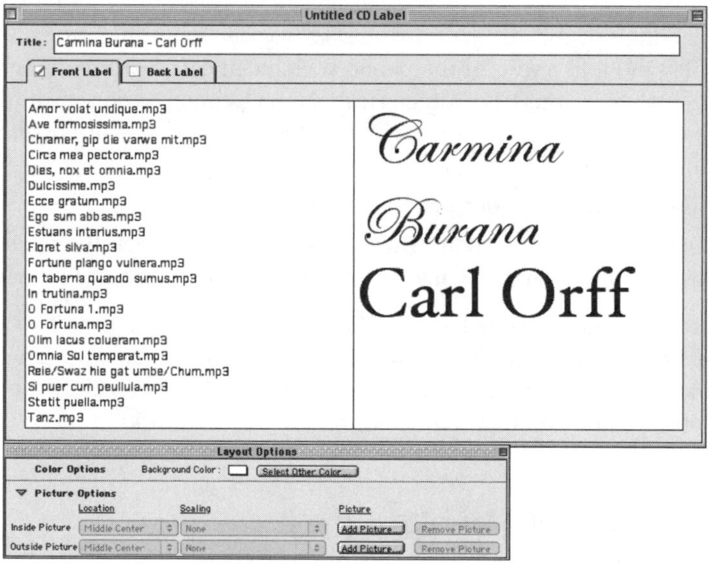

Figure 19.7
Filling in the blanks
in Ultimate LPP.

TIP

If you have a list of files that you are recording onto a CD—in this case, they are MP3s that I'd created from my original *Carmina Burana* CD—you can highlight them all and then select Edit > Copy, and your Mac will copy the filenames onto the clipboard. Now, you can go back to your CD insert layout and paste the filenames in. Sure saves a lot of typing!

Alternatively, you can get Ultimate LPP to scan a folder for you to produce a list of files. This is useful for archive CDs, although remember that a large folder with hundreds of files won't fit onto the inserts! To use this feature, choose File > Scan Volume/Folder option—you'll be presented with a standard file dialog box where you can select the folder that contains your CD source.

To change the font, size, or style of any text on the inserts, use the corresponding menus. You can also add pictures using the toolbar at the bottom of the insert window—you can scale and align the picture to the different areas of the CD to make up the final layout. You can see an example, supplied with Ultimate LPP, in Figure 19.8.

Figure 19.8
Using pictures in
your inserts with
Ultimate LPP.

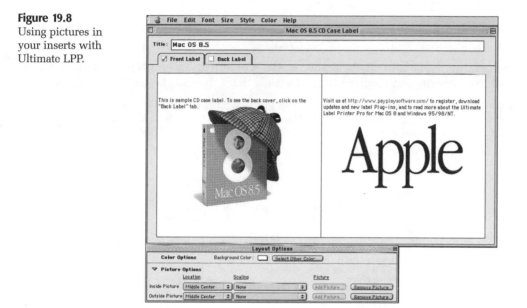

Once you're ready, all you've got to do is print them out, trim them, and put them into your jewel case. You'll need to write the label by hand or, if you have AppleWorks, QuarkXpress or Macromedia Freehand, use one of the templates supplied with Toast.

Using cdlabelgen

The cdlabelgen application from B.W. Fitzpatrick can be download from Freshmeat (**www.freshmeat.net**). The application is made up of a Perl script and a series of Postscript templates—the Perl script merges the information about the CD tracks and contents and the Postscript files together in order to produce the final label. The only downside to this approach is that you will need either a Postscript printer attached to your Unix/Linux box, or have installed the Ghostscript package (available from **www.cs.wisc.edu/~ghost/**) to translate the Postscript into an inkjet or deskjet compatible format.

Once you've downloaded cdlabelgen, you can either install it by running:

> $ make install

…or use it straight from the archive directory. To create a label, you need to use the **-c**, **-s**, and **-i** options to specify the category (or artist), subcategory (or album title) and individual items (or tracks) on the CD. For example, to create a simple label for our Salt 'n Pepa album we might use:

> $ cdlabelgen -c "Salt 'n' Pepa" -s "Best of"

The resultant Postscript file will be sent to the standard output, so you'll either need to pipe the output to a printer, for example:

> $ cdlabelgen -c "Salt 'n' Pepa" -s "Best of" | lp

Or you can send the output to a file:

> $ cdlabelgen -c "Salt 'n' Pepa" -s "Best of" >snpbestof.ps

To specify the individual tracks on an album, use the **-i** option and then list each track in one quoted block. You can separate individual tracks using the % (percent) sign. For example:

> $ cdlabelgen -c "Salt 'n' Pepa" -s "Best of" -i "Push It(Again)%The Brick Track versus Gitty Up%Whatta Man%Shake Your Thang%Tramp%Lets Talk About Sex%Do You Want Me%Shoop%Expression%You Showed Me%None of your Business%R U Ready%Start Me Up%Twist and Shout%Push It"

You can see a sample of the back cover label created using the above command in Figure 19.9.

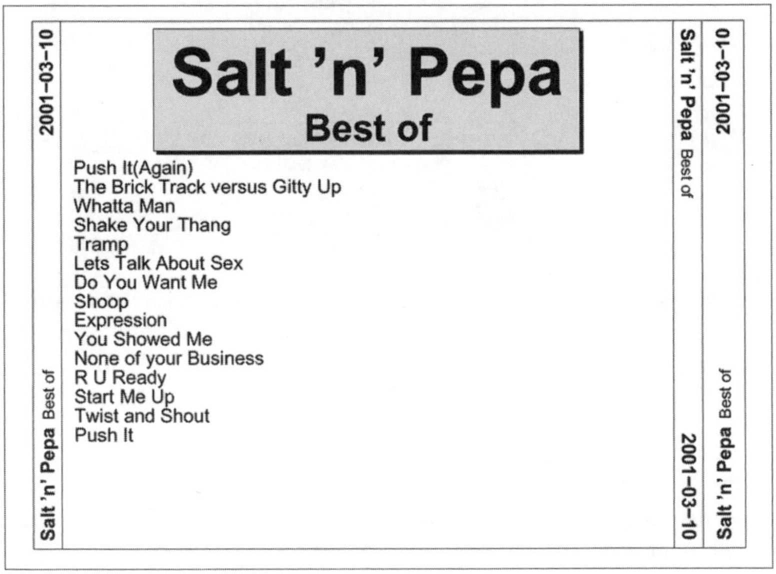

Figure 19.9
A Postscript label generated by cdlabelgen.

Using Templates

Under Toast, instead of providing a separate application for labeling, the software provides a set of templates for use under Freehand, QuarkXpress, and AppleWorks. Since AppleWorks is provided with many Apple machines, this is the one you'll most likely use. For example, the *Carmina Burana* CD label in AppleWorks is shown in Figure 19.10.

Figure 19.10
Using the AppleWorks template for your CD label.

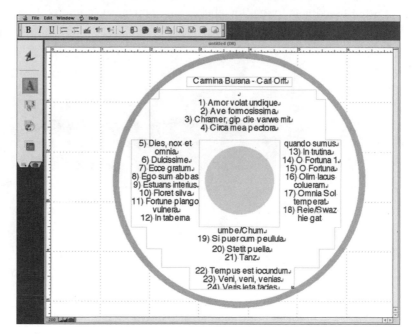

Obviously, because these are templates, you need to open them within the corresponding application and then fill in the information for yourself. The big benefit, however, is that you can do whatever you like within the confines of those templates. For example, I've designed templates in Quark that use a complex background and text runaround to fit on a CD label for a client.

Alternatively, all the templates are supplied with an AppleScript that will work in conjunction with Toast to automatically fill in the information for you. To use the AppleScript, open Toast and create your CD as normal. However, don't quit Toast at the end of the process. Instead, open one of the templates from the Template folder in the main Toast folder and then double-click on the AppleScript. The AppleScript should execute, asking Toast for a list of tracks and then pasting the track list into AppleWorks, Quark or Freehand—depending on which AppleScript you have selected.

Remember, even with templates you are still going to need special media to actually print out the labels suitable for attaching to your CD.

Labeling Devices

One of the problems with CD labels is that they are incredibly difficult to fit. Because they are circular, and because they have to be fitted so precisely, doing it by hand is virtually impossible. In fact, I wouldn't even recommend that you try it.

However, help is at hand. Most labeling systems have a device that allows you to apply a label to a CD without having to touch the label at all. You can see a photo of the HP CD-Labeler II in Figure 19.11.

Figure 19.11
Using the HP
CD-Labeler II for
applying labels.

The way it works is that you put the label, face down (that is, the label side), onto the base of the unit and peel off the backing. Then, you put the CD, again face down, and push the two together. Because they are both aligned on a central spindle, the two—label and CD—should marry perfectly, and, presto!—your label is attached to your CD without you getting your fingers dirty!

Index

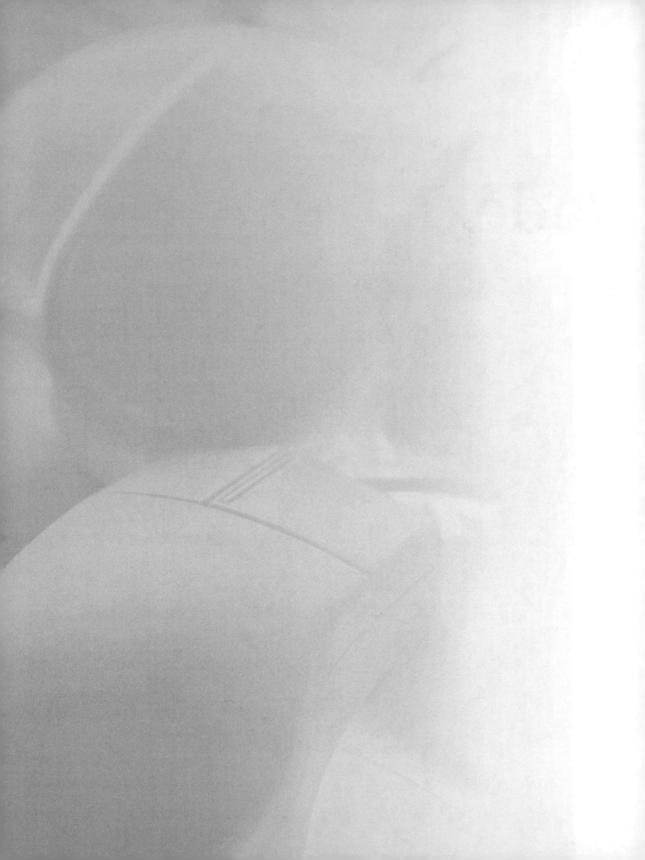

Index

Index

B

C

Index

E

Index

Index

V

Index

Order Form

Postal Orders:
Muska & Lipman Publishing
P.O. Box 8225
Cincinnati, Ohio 45208

Online Orders or more information:
http://www.muskalipman.com
Fax Orders:
(513) 924-9333

Title/ISBN	Price/Cost
Cakewalk Power!	
1-929685-02-5	
Quantity _____	
	× $29.95
Total Cost _____	
Digital Camera Solutions	
0-9662889-6-3	
Quantity _____	
	× $29.95
Total Cost _____	
Online Broadcasting Power!	
0-9662889-8-X	
Quantity _____	
	× $29.95
Total Cost _____	

Title/ISBN	Price/Cost
MP3/FYI	
1-929685-05-X	
Quantity _____	
	× $14.95
Total Cost _____	
Subtotal _____	
Sales Tax _____	
(please add 6% for books shipped to Ohio addresses)	
Shipping _____	
($6.00 for US and Canada $12.00 other countries)	
TOTAL PAYMENT ENCLOSED _____	

Ship to:

Company _____

Name _____

Address _____

City _____ State _____ Zip _____ Country _____

E-mail _____

Educational facilities, companies, and organizations interested in multiple copies of these books should contact the publisher for quantity discount information. Training manuals, CD-ROMs, electronic versions, and portions of these books are also available individually or can be tailored for specific needs.

Thank you for your order.